THE
MYTH
OF
MORAL
JUSTICE

—THE—
MYTH
—OF—
MORAL
JUSTICE

*Why Our Legal System
Fails to Do What's Right*

THANE ROSENBAUM

HarperCollins*Publishers*

HarperCollins books may be purchased for educational, business, or sales promotional use. For information, please write: Special Markets Department, Harper-Collins Publishers Inc., 10 East 53rd Street, New York, NY 10022.

FIRST EDITION
Designed by Joseph Rutt

Credits and permissions appear on page 353.

Library of Congress Cataloging-in-Publication Data
Rosenbaum, Thane.
The myth of moral justice ; why our legal system fails to do what's right /
Thane Rosenbaum.—1st ed.
p.   cm.
Includes bibliographical references and index.
ISBN 0-06-018816-2
1. Justice, Administration of—United States.   2. Justice, Administration of,
in literature.   3. Justice, Administration of, in motion pictures.
4. Courts—United States.   5. Law—United States.   6. Law and ethics.
I. Title.

KF8700.R658 2004
340'.11—dc22   2003056989

04 05 06 07 08 NMSG/RRD 10 9 8 7 6 5 4 3 2 1

For Carol and Seymour, Tom, Ellen, Sam, and Basia Tess

CONTENTS

Contents

[I]t never occurred to the lawyers that they should suggest or insist on any improvements in the system.

—Franz Kafka,
The Trial

INTRODUCTION

L ike most people, I have mixed feelings about the law, and the judges and lawyers who serve it. Of course I'm relieved to know that we have laws, yet I would prefer that the legal system shine its light elsewhere, anywhere but in my direction. I'm interested in legal trials, but really only from a distance. I don't want to be a party to any action, and yet I would like to know that the courtroom is available to me should I ever have a grievance that can't be resolved any other way. Like an unloaded gun, the law can both offer peace of mind and serve as a weapon of destruction—to both body and soul. It is reassuring and forbidding, alluring and dangerous, restorative and crushing, all at the same time.

I had once been a Wall Street lawyer myself, as well as a law clerk to a federal judge, and the editor in chief of my law review back when I was in law school. On a few occasions, I have also had to be a litigant. I have a solid, if in some ways ambivalent, legal background. I am not impartial to the courthouse, or dispassionate about what happens there. Justice isn't truly blind, and neither am I.

Today, I'm not really a lawyer at all. I don't admit to even

being one; in fact, I qualify and marginalize my legal associations to the point where my law degree seems trivial to my existence. I act as though I am ashamed of the pedigree, stigmatized
by the scarlet letters that form "Esq." Maybe I'm simply a recovering attorney, someone who has had to modify his behavior
so that his days are less morally compromising, and make more
sense. A professional trained in the art of arguing, hair-splitting,
and loophole-seeking, I am now simply trying to make amends.

I regard myself primarily as a novelist and cultural essayist,
yet I also teach courses in human rights, legal humanities, and
law and literature. Perhaps the part of me that writes serious fiction feels antagonism toward the moonlighting law professor. I
am in the middle of my own internal rivalry, two mindsets—one
for the novelist, a different one for the lawyer—at war with
themselves. The lawyer's perspective is one I can and prefer to
live without, while I am overly protective and proud of what I
consider to be my more soulful side, which I associate with the
artist in me. For this reason, I feel as though I am stuck in two
seemingly irreconcilable worlds—the storyteller who depends on
the imagination, emotion, nuance, and the uncertainty of direction; and the lawyer, whose world is increasingly narrowed, iso-
lated, cut off from the human experience and focused far too
much on achieving prescribed, predictable results.

I surely understand why people are cynical about lawyers
and the law. Novelists and artists in particular have had a long
history of looking critically at what the law can do to individuals
hapless enough to be caught within its slow-moving, soul-
murdering gears. Yet, as a lawyer, I am also an insider, someone
with working knowledge of its best and worst values, and the
considerable benefits the law can bring to any society. I know all
the secret handshakes, the smoke signals, the shorthand that is
attached to the long arm of the law. I have insight into why the
law does what it does when it does it—its self-justifying ratio-
nale, its self-references and organizing principles—and for this

reason, I am unsurprised by, although keenly sympathetic to, situations in which the law comes across as unjust and quixotic, when its results don't feel right emotionally to those who are neither its insiders nor cast members.

We are all in some ways resigned to having conflicting emotions about the legal system. It is our burden, the consequences of submitting ourselves to an institution that promises order in return for some measure of sacrificed freedom. As human beings, we draw comfort from knowing that we are all bound by rules, that our external conduct is not limitless, that the daily collisions and accidental encounters of life are not without boundaries. Rules are supposed to make us feel safer. We are better off knowing that some lines can't be crossed, and that certain kinds of behavior won't be tolerated by a civilized society. There are promises and duties that must be honored. For those who test the contours of these restrictions, there are punishments and liabilities, jail sentences and damages awarded against them. Boundaries, by design, manage to keep most people in line. This is good for everyone, because without the law, nothing could prevent lawlessness, frontier justice, self-help remedies, disputes resolved only by way of bullies, bullets, and blood. And who would want to live in a world like that?

There is almost a primal sense, or perhaps it is simply an unconscious shared wish, that the law be a steadying force in our lives. We want our justice to be just, and that it be totally blind to bias and prejudice. The law should offer moral lessons that make sense. We want our judges to be wise and our lawyers honorable. Travesties cause people to enter the courthouse in search of justice. A travesty is not what they should find when they get there.

We need to know that some higher authority—one that is not divine, celestial, or mystical, but rather concrete, temporal, and just—is empowered to sift through the maze of human interactions gone wrong, punish those who went too far, compensate others for their material losses, and find some measure of rough justice for the rest. We ask that our courts provide forums so that we can speak about the harms done to us, the property taken away, the promises broken, the duties and obligations ignored, the responsibilities placed in the hands of the irresponsible. Most of all, we need to know that some empowered entity will be there after the accidents, not to gawk but to provide remedies, to set things right again, or as right as they'll ever be. We can all breathe easier knowing that we are protected from the violators among us, and from our own rash desires for vengeance.

But sometimes our interest in the law is not merely personal. At times the law serves a communal function. The moral foundations of civilization are more grounded and stable when truths are acknowledged, stories are told, and lies exposed—all out in the open. What makes trials different from star-chambers and confessional booths is the moral necessity of having the public witness the outcome. We are somehow better off by having participated in the experience of watching a conflict resolve itself, a punishment handed down, a judgment rendered and received. In the best of these circumstances, we all—not just the parties to the action—learn a lesson.

Yet aside from the gains made on moral capital, there is also the lurid fascination that so many share in the freak and peep show of the courthouse. There is endless, often mindless, cultural obsession with the law, and the intensity of these feelings invariably transcends abstract notions of the law as a provider of freedom and security. This kind of infatuation falls not within the province of legal philosophy, but rather human curiosity, the vicarious thrill that people receive from witnessing the law. It is the joining of the emotions and the imagination, all in the hope of making sense of the human experience.

Sadly, this is an unreciprocated, one-sided enterprise, because judges and lawyers are not driven by the same human impulses.

The law and its practitioners simply wish to streamline the system in search of the bottom line, to move cases along, to create a process that allows rules to develop and precedents to evolve, and, most important of all, to achieve the correct legal result. Legal, and not moral, outcomes occupy the legal mind. But the public cares little about the efficiency of court administrations and the evolution of legal rules. People look to the law to provide remedies for their grievances and relief from their hurts, to receive moral lessons about life, to better themselves and their communities. What most people don't realize is that judges and lawyers are motivated by entirely different agendas and mindsets.

Trials are where the human drama unfolds in a public spectacle of infinite variety and amusement. The dress code is formal, even though the secrets and lies are laid bare. It is an atmosphere that looms with solemnity and ceremony, yet the disclosures that arise from such proceedings are often indiscreet and out of order. The characters are believable precisely because they are real. There is no need for central casting in a courthouse. The roles are already taken by people who don't know their lines. The stories are their own; the emotions raw and yet, at the same time, overcooked. It is in a courtroom where the presumptions of justice, innocence, and guilt must contend with the more primal, less predictable stuff of life—the dashed hopes and false dreams, the longings that have gone on far too long, the resentments that linger, and the grievances that never found time, or the proper place, to grieve. The courthouse turns each of us into witnesses. The confessions and admissions, the shame and the stain, the broken silences and invoked privileges, the surprise turns and numbing tedium, all catch our attention and hold us willing prisoners. Pure entertainment under the cover and pretense of a legal system at work.

We live in a culture that worships the law, not because we are more lawful, but because our preoccupation with the legal system is insatiable. There are numerous afternoon television programs featuring live litigants who settle their scores right in front of a national audience, with all the dignity and emotional closure of a game show. Prime time is dominated by network and syndicated-cable dramas where earnest lawyers are both lead characters and flawed people. Moral issues masking as legal problems provide the necessary plot tension to fill the entire hour, even though such moral concerns rarely make it onto the time sheets of actual, practicing attorneys. Talk shows host lawyers who expound on the legal events of the day. There are courtroom thrillers written by former lawyers, and books about sensational court cases written by those who wish they were lawyers. Many feature films end with climactic moments that take place during confessional courtroom scenes.

And there are the more serious literary efforts, with writers as prominent and varied as Sophocles, Shakespeare, Melville, Dickens, Dostoevsky, Kafka, and Camus. In their novels and plays, the law is often depicted as a venue for crushed sprits. Courts are exposed for what they are incapable or unwilling to subject to cross-examination: the interior world of the emotions, with all its mitigating complexity, and the extenuation of backstory. The intangible hurts that accompany people to the courthouse are undetectable by the eyewitness yet perhaps explain more about what ails society than what is written in a formal, legal complaint.

Finally, if you take as a measure the increasing number of people in the past few decades who have chosen to become lawyers, or the way in which so many citizens organize their lives around the law and what lawyers tell them to do, the fact is, society can't seem to get enough of a profession that it otherwise despises. We watch fictional lawyers on television, and read about them in pulp-fiction novels while flying on airplanes, but in our hearts, most people who are neither lawyers nor their relatives wouldn't disagree with Dick the Butcher in *King Henry VI, Part II*, when he said: "The first thing we do, let's kill all the lawyers." There is indeed a paradox with this cultural obsession, because amidst all the widespread and alluring appeal, there is an equally passionate and seemingly natural disgust with the law.

How can this be the case? Perhaps the public is as ambivalent about its legal system as I am about the profession I had once abandoned. Like the lapsed lawyer in me, those who stand outside the courthouse may be equally caught in an existential crisis about how the law affects individuals and society. On the one hand, the law fulfills certain basic needs of certainty and security, and yet on the whole it produces mistrust, resentment, and unfulfilled longing.

I spend my days writing fiction, but I also teach American law students how to enter their chosen profession with a deeper spiritual and moral awareness of what the law lacks. It is the novelist in me that intuitively understands this common lament about the law, because the interior, emotional world of the novel is precisely what gets left out of judicial opinions, and what never enters into a conversation about law. For the novelist, what's important is the world that exists outside the courthouse, and not what simply reveals itself inside the witness box, even when the novel is focused on the law. It is the backstory that drives the novel forward, the emotional history of hurts, grievances, and motives that explains how citizens come to, or are brought to, the law in the first place. But the law itself, focused on the external world of observable human conduct rather than on the labyrinths of interior pain, knows of no such backstory. All that matters is what evolves in front of the judge on a given day, the performance and spectacle of human vulnerability, absent the raw emotions of past history that made it so.

This is why throughout this book I will often be referring to depictions of the law and the legal system in novels, films, plays, and TV dramas to illustrate just how immoral justice can be. These works speak to the moral deficiencies of the law in ways that actual cases never do. The artist illuminates the very moral bleakness that the law, on its own, always manages to keep in the dark. Indeed, artists—principally novelists, filmmakers, and television dramatists—are very much aware of the moral dimension that is absent in the law, the fragility of the human spirit within this absence, and the absurdity of having faith in such a legal system.

The beauty of art is that it can reveal vistas of human complexity that are often ignored in the muted dramas of the courthouse. Artists have long been fascinated with trials and the legal process, and have used the law as inspiration to address large moral and redemptive themes. Humanity is not only judged by the law; it is also sacrificed when it surrenders to it. But the real life of the law is a drama without emotional texture. It's difficult to learn a moral lesson from watching an actual case, because so few either present a moral dilemma or frame the case in moral terms. Most suffer from the staidness of ritual and routine, and the predictability of precedent. But art and literature that focus on legal themes, which are so abundant in our culture, provide easy reference points that make the moral themes of this book more universally understood. Indeed, the literature that invokes law as a plot device is nearly always steeped in moral and spiritual concerns. We may all know the story of *The Merchant of Venice*, but what we may not know is its moral critique on the rigidity of law and its failure as a facilitator of either revenge or repair. The artist continually reminds lawyers of what the law often fails to do in the name of justice.

This cynicism about the legal profession is not so much about lawyers being perceived as dishonest, or only in it for the money, or that the law is often unjust. Some of those perceptions are either true or have become clichés about the legal system. But they are not the main sources of collective mistrust. There is yet another flaw, one that is unnamed but widely felt, which better underscores the public's ambivalence about the law.

What is unforgivable, and what is rarely acknowledged, is that the law lacks soul, that it is without tenderness. It has no tolerance for the emotional complexity of those who muster the courage to enter a courtroom, with all of their consolidated ambitions and repressed rage, wounded egos, petty jealousies and perennial rivalries, competitive fires and thwarted dreams. The law places too much faith in its own ability to know the facts, to know with certainty what happened and what did not. It focuses too ferociously on what is utterly unreliable: the search for the concrete, literal truth. But that is such an illusory and elusive quest. Some truths the court will never discover. And some discoverable facts have no relation to actual truths. And yet in looking for hard evidence, it will ignore all those soft but clashing emotional truths that are spoken before the bench and inside the witness box—and lurk outside the courthouse—each day. Facts are never cold, but are forever heated. The law assumes an objectivity that has no place in life, because life is populated with the subjective judgments of irrational men and women, which is precisely the pool from which empaneled jurors and sworn witnesses wade in and from which they are selected.

With its obsessive insularity and narrowness, its pretense that all that matters is what takes place under oath, the law misses the emotional backstory, the suppressed part of every lawsuit. The real drama of the human experience gets played out not in a courtroom, but on the streets, inside offices and homes. Human trial and error precedes the legal trial and supersedes it in importance. Beyond the solemn corridors of the courtroom, life is dynamic, animated, volatile. This is where paths are totally unprescribed, where nuance and ambiguity live amidst messy irresolution. Justice deludes itself into believing that final judgments are indeed final. Legal finality provides nothing but a false closure. Even the victors don't leave courthouses believing that emotionally the case is all over and the issues are all settled. And this moral critique against the legal system applies to both the criminal and civil areas of the law.

The law perceives itself as blind to prejudgment, yet it is as biased as any other institution. It ignores the opportunities that are offered by way of a simple apology, and it fails to appreciate

the healing power of acknowledgment, forgiveness, the acceptance of responsibility, and shame. It shuns the interior world
where spirits get broken and hurt feelings fester. The law only
looks to what is visible, external, and obvious on its face, rather
than what resides inside those who come before the law. It
smugly prides itself on the wisdom in its head rather than on the
compassion of its heart. It relies too much on logic and not
enough on love.

DOING THE RIGHT THING:
THE SPLIT BETWEEN THE
MORAL AND THE LEGAL

In the motion picture *The Verdict* (1982), directed by Sidney
Lumet from a screenplay written by David Mamet, Paul
Newman, playing the role of Frank Galvin, a washed-up,
ambulance-chasing, alcoholic attorney desperate for a second
chance, sums up his case to the jury by imploring, and empower-
ing them, to simply do the right thing.

Throughout the film the jurors become witnesses to an
avalanche of moral corruption and cynicism—all courtesy of the
legal system. They see the artifice that shadows the spectacle of a
trial, the breaches of professional duty and lapses in human
character, the way the courtroom, despite its sturdy, marbled appearance, can serve as an unbalanced playing field for those out-
matched by resources and foiled by foul play. And there are so
many instances of tampering, not with the jury, but with what
the jury is exposed to: manipulated procedural and evidentiary
rules, and the ways in which money is used to silence the truth.
Having faith that the jury will be able to judge what is real,
honest, and human from the staged facades and deceit that dominated the courtroom, Paul Newman ultimately summed up what
most people expect and wish the law to be:

So much of the time we're just lost. We say, please God, tell us what is right, tell us what is true. When there is no justice, the rich win, the poor are powerless. We become tired of hearing people lie. And after a time we become dead. We think of ourselves as victims, and we become victims. . . . We doubt ourselves, we doubt our beliefs, we doubt our institutions. We doubt the law. But today you are the law. Not some book. Not some lawyer. . . . These are just symbols of our desire to be just. They are in fact a prayer, a fervent and frightened prayer. . . . In my religion we say, "Act as if thee had faith." Faith will be given to you. If we are to have faith in justice we are only to believe in ourselves and act with justice.

Law and religion. Judges and clergy. Verdicts and absolutions. Blind faith and blind justice.

For most people, there is a belief that the values and teachings that are embodied in both law and religion—the consciousness and ideals that are invoked in cathedrals and courthouses—are basically the same, that they go hand in hand. In practice, however, they are connected by left feet. Law and religion are, in fact, largely and unfortunately not inspired by the same values, although most of us wish to believe otherwise.

We assume that an exalted sense of rightness, and knowing the proper standards for engaging in the world and dealing with our fellow human beings, is what clergy and judges have in common. But men of the cloth and men who sit on judicial benches see the world quite differently from one another. And it's not merely their elevated pedestals that make it so. Let us not be fooled by the robes: priests, rabbis, ministers, imams, and jurists may dress the same, but they are not the same. Uniforms can be deceiving; the mirage of uniformity—despite the fact that judges wear black robes and clergy are sometimes dressed in white—may be more of a caveat than sartorial coincidence. And yes, courts and churches are decorated with similar props and vestments. But, once more, the similarity here is only one of interior design. The decor is intended to elicit a particular emotion, an aura that isn't always deserved, but does command respect.

Despite *The Verdict*'s spirited call to faith, the faith that animates religion does not exist in the law. In the film, the jury exercises faith in its own judgment, ultimately rejecting what it sees as the immoral shenanigans of a system that plays by its own blighted rules. But, of course, *The Verdict* is a movie, and the jurors are only actors. Most actual juries don't have the kind of moral courage to flagrantly ignore the instructions of the judge, and even if they did, the judge would ultimately nullify their verdict.

In another Sidney Lumet movie, in fact, his first feature film, *12 Angry Men* (1957), the jury once more commands center stage—not in the jury box, but in the jury room itself. It is a film that deals with the conflicts and deliberations that precede the actual verdict. It is a fictional, inside glance of what the law looks like as it arrives at its judgments. But unlike the jury in *The Verdict*, the one in *12 Angry Men* prevailed over its own human failings and redeemed itself by exposing emotional truths that the trial would never have uncovered. For reasons of prejudice and expediency, the jurors, at the outset of their deliberations, presume that the defendant is guilty, even though, in a criminal trial, innocence is always presumed until proven otherwise. The deliberations in *12 Angry Men* transform the jury from one that shares a nonchalant certainty about guilt to one that eventually sees more complexity in the story of this defendant, which lead them to find him innocent. One juror, played by Henry Fonda, calls attention to other values, motives, and events that his colleagues had been willing to overlook. Ultimately they arrive at a verdict that is both legally and morally correct.

In *The Verdict* and *12 Angry Men*, Lumet provides two portraits of juries, each overcoming either the perversions of the system or their own prejudices, and, in the end, doing what's right. But since the law sets such a bad example in guiding their conscience, the jury must have faith in each other to impose justice on a system that is equally disposed to injustice.

Yet this faith in a moral universe that can reveal itself in law, and the similar faith that inspires common men and women of the jury to courageously stand up and do the right thing, is really a cry of longing, made by artists, not lawyers. It is also a figment of the artist's imagination. Faith has no counterpart in the legal system itself. Once a witness swears to tell the truth with his hand over the Bible and his fingers crossed behind his back, the spiritual world of God and faith ceases to be part of the proceedings.

It shouldn't be all that surprising that *The Verdict* brings law and religion into the same film only to show how irreconcilably needy of salvation, and empty of faith, both institutions actually are. Paul Newman's stirring summation to the jury addresses this natural desire—almost a religious longing—to think of judgment and faith in the same vein. Indeed, he even calls this impulse a "prayer." But as a prayer, it is very much an unanswered one.

Now, I've referred to the imperative of doing the right thing several times. And perhaps it's a good idea to explain what I mean by the phrase, because in an age where we are naturally suspicious of moral absolutes, and where moral relativism reigns supreme, some people are made uncomfortable by any notion that there is a universally shared standard of morality, or that there even is such a thing as doing the right thing. But what's right and what's moral doesn't have to conform to a particular religious ethos. In our fear of religious intolerance, we shouldn't ignore that morality and conscience can and should guide private lives.

Sometimes what's right is simply obvious, because its opposite is so clearly wrong—like failing to apologize or acknowledge someone else's pain. We were taught these basic moral lessons as children, and we have conveniently forgotten them as adults. The very things that we were properly warned not to do as children, like lying, blaming others, and failing to take personal responsibility for our actions, underlie the lawsuits that crowd our dockets and choke the decency out of our morally challenged legal system.

The presumption that law and religion are, in many ways, motivated by the same values is an understandable one. After all, there is a widespread belief that the law is primarily in the business of seeking out truths and revealing the just path. Its task is to do what's fair and what's right. Judges hand down judgments. They judge. They make hard decisions. But these decisions should make sense, they should feel right emotionally and morally to those not only on the receiving end of these judgments, but to the rest of us, the outside witnesses to these private proceedings. This expectation of fairness, wisdom, and justice is precisely what draws people to the law in the first place—the desire for a just resolution to a conflict that simply can't be mediated elsewhere.

As for religion, most people attend churches, synagogues, and mosques in search of moral and spiritual guidance, among other things. They want to expand their moral vision and consciousness, wishing to anchor themselves temporally to this world while at the same time aspiring to a more transcendent existence. We all want to know the recipe for virtue, the secret formula for becoming a better person. Is there a way to live righteously when our daily endeavors are marked by so much personal failure? As Paul Newman explains to the jury, most people want to know "what is right, what is true."

Unfortunately, the law is not the place to find those answers. Justice may be about many things, but the moral complexity of distinguishing between right and wrong, or arriving at the truth of a given situation, is neither its strength nor its ostensible mission. Courts of law are there to administer justice, to efficiently streamline cases, to ensure the availability of a forum that offers the chance at some relief. It's the possibility of justice that it guarantees, not the quality of that justice, nor the certainty that, in the end, justice will make sense, feel right, and resolve matters in a way that leaves the parties better off and reconciled to move on with their lives. The institution of law defines itself as an arbiter of legal disputes, and not as a dispenser of moral lessons or seeker of truths. It thrives on an adversarial process that only takes prisoners and leaves little room for peace.

Truth has a way of seeming incidental to the law, an accidental by-product of a stated goal that generally gets short shrift. The legal system justifies its role in society by imposing discipline on the lawless and resolving conflicts—often inadequately—among the rest. These are its fundamentally narrow objectives. As long as caseloads progress, justice is done. That's what servants of the law mean when they proclaim, unapologetically, even after an unjust verdict, that "the law has spoken." But when the results are immoral, what can be said about the words that were used to justify the law's spoken decree? When the application of the law is perceived as senseless, it has a shattering effect on the capacity of the parties and the community to reconcile and move on.

The legal system always seems to ignore that the public has inherent expectations about the law, which conflict with the more circumscribed vision of what the law has in mind for itself. Truth is one example of this broken trust. The legal system functions quite well knowing that most cases don't end up achieving any measure of truth. In fact, trials, legal settlements, and plea bargains generally result in either silencing the truth or bastardizing it. The legal system, for its part, is satisfied with learning facts. If the facts also turn out to be true, that's a fortuity of the legal system, not an aspiration. But facts and truths are two different concepts entirely. Facts don't have to be true. They just need to be found and applied to the law. Facts are artifacts of the justice system, while truths are trademarks of the moral universe. Fact is a legal term; truth is a moral one. The legal system's notion of justice is served by merely finding legal facts without also incorporating the moral dimensions of emotional and literal truth.

The law is inured to these practical realities of providing justice. The public, however, finds this situation intolerable, and it contributes to a kind of moral revulsion toward the legal system for its complacency about discovering truth. Two parties come before the law, each telling a different story. Which story is true, or is there yet another story that approximates the truth more accurately? The public needs to believe that the law can reveal the truth—that it even cares about the truth—as much as it needs to believe that the law can punish offenders and resolve conflicts. But on this treadmill toward resolution, the truth loses traction—the zeal for finality overrides the truth behind the story.

This failure to distinguish facts from truths—what many believe ought to be the law's central aim—is one source of hostility that artists have long directed at the legal system. How can the law be about anything if it's not about establishing the truth? And why should the public have faith in an institution that professes to be about truth but then delivers a brand of justice that ends up undermining and subverting the truth?

In the film *A Civil Action* (1998), directed and written by Steven Zaillian, based on a true story written by Jonathan Harr, a high-powered, cynically seasoned defense attorney played by Robert Duvall acknowledges to his adversary that courtrooms are not places of truth, and that the law has very little to do with finding truth.

There is a difference between justice and doing what's just. Justice is a legal term. It involves the administration and maintenance of the legal system, the manner in which it is institutionally organized, the way it presents itself to the outside world. Justice lives according to its own set of internal rules. It is governed by its own proprietary rituals and formalities. It exists within a vast labyrinthine maze of bureaucratic and technical procedures, fed by an inexhaustible supply of lifeless statutes and precedent-affirming cases, choked by all those court records, docket numbers, and written forms.

Justice, in many ways, has far more in common with the soulless, airless atmosphere that Franz Kafka concocted for his character, Joseph K., in his novel *The Trial*, than anything that approximates just treatment or a just result at the end of a long trial. Paradoxically, there is no actual, legal trial in *The Trial*—only one that is spiritually imprisoning. Joseph K. never gets that far. He's too busy living under the gaze of accusation and suspicion, preparing for a trial that never comes, yet a death sentence arrives anyway. Kafka's portrayal of justice is horrific, but perhaps all too accurate. The legal system's path to justice has a consumptive, machine-like quality to it, with all its grinding wheels and soul-crushing, dehumanizing dimensions. The corridors of justice in *The Trial* are only attic-size, providing nothing but suffocation and despair.

Similarly, nearly three quarters of a century earlier, not in Prague but in London, Charles Dickens, in his Victorian masterpiece *Bleak House*, imagined the dense fog of endless legal confusion surrounding the estate matter of *Jarndyce v. Jarndyce*. And throughout the more than eight hundred pages, there is no resolution, just black-hole anguish and ruination. This was Dickens's vision of what the Court of Chancery offered citizens who came before it each day like addicted beggars, seeking relief and justice but receiving nothing in return other than wasted time and arrested lives.

The word "just," however, quite separate from the word "justice," implies a moral dimension. It speaks entirely to the moral realm of our humanity. Doing what's just is the experience of providing, and ultimately receiving, true relief. To be just is not a legal aspiration but a moral one. When someone is acting justly, the outcome makes sense not just to the mind, but also in the heart and soul.

Of course, soul and morality are hardly ever mentioned in law school. This, among other reasons, is what sets legal trade schools apart from divinity schools. These words constitute the language of the spiritual sphere, the interior world of human beings and the vocabulary of priests, rabbis, ministers, and mullahs—and not judges. Morality does not appear in a law-school syllabus. Nor is it a word that lawyers think about when performing their jobs. Law school does not teach moral education, which explains why the practice of law is never framed in moral terms, only in legal ones.

And that's why there is a tremendous difference between legal ethics, which is taken very seriously by the profession, and private morality, which usually plays no role in the performance of a lawyer's job. One has to do with the way lawyers police themselves in their dealings with clients and each other; the other concerns a lawyer's moral duty to the world at large, beyond the attorney-client relationship, beyond the rules of court, beyond anything other than their own humanity and private conscience. An individual can fastidiously maintain all the ethical requirements of his or her profession and still spend the workday engaged in morally questionable practices. And all this fidelity to legal ethics seems to have no connection to producing morally just results. Justice is merely what the law provides as an answer to your injury, even if it is otherwise unjust. All that matters is that it be legally correct.

Indeed, what passes for justice in America is often immoral justice—a resolution that makes sense legally and can be explained and justified by judges, lawyers, and law professors simply by conforming, in a very narrow formalistic sense, to precedent and procedure, but ultimately feels emotionally and morally wrong to everyone else. Justice that doesn't feel just, but instead feels like a colossal misnomer.

There is a cold bottom-line to justice. Bureaucratic efficiencies trample all other values. The human drama, with its variety of upended, disrupted lives, and backstory that never receives front-and-center attention, goes undetected and unremedied.

These discontinuities, often misunderstood by laymen and ignored by lawyers, account for much of the public's general disdain for the legal system. The fact is, many of the foundational principles of the legal system leave people with an empty feeling and a sour taste that doesn't go away anytime soon after a legal resolution. For ordinary people, what passes for justice is simply too hard to stomach.

In every legal action there is going to be a winner and a loser. That's how the combative, adversarial system is set up to work. And make no mistake about it: the system is adversarial. Even with corporate mergers and acquisitions, takeovers are usually deemed hostile. The advocacy is supposed to be zealous, which only heightens the winner-take-all dimensions of the conflict. Two parties present their cases, trying to sway, if not manipulate, the story in their direction, even as their versions may stray from the actual truth. Courts are designed to facilitate the resolution of these conflicts, to essentially pick the winners, officiating this zero-sum exchange between parties who somehow, through life and its varied transactions and mishaps, wound up as adversaries, or worse, enemies.

But in a pure winner-take-all paradigm, where the advocacy is always fierce and strategically played out, victory is not synonymous with justice, because the right party—the party that was right and should have won—may not end up victorious. Sometimes the outcome of a legal conflict is determined for reasons wholly apart from the truth or from what the morally correct result should have been. Often it's a matter of one side having superior resources over the other and exploiting them mercilessly. One lawyer—or a team of lawyers—might be simply more skilled than his adversary. Sometimes the government's prosecutorial power is insurmountable, or the political passions that exist outside the courthouse make it impossible for the defendant to receive a fair trial. In some cases, the presumptions go in the opposite direction, where the community—in the form of a representative jury—sends a message by allowing a guilty person to go free. Then there are those occasions when technical, procedural, or constitutional irregularities dictate a result that is morally wrong, but one that justice somehow demands. Such an instance occurs when the police mishandle or obtain evidence unlawfully. Had it not been for a procedural error, the defendant would have been found guilty.

The legal system reveals its own cynicism—and undermines its legitimacy as an arbiter of truth—by declaring unjust winners. Most people realize this, but that doesn't make it any more palatable. In fact, the more immoral and unconscionable the law appears, the greater the critical mass of cynicism and faithlessness that accumulates. The O. J. Simpson trial was a horrifying example of this phenomenon for the Goldman and Brown families. And when such cases occur and we become witnesses to them, it invariably reshapes and prejudices our attitudes toward the law. Powerful attorneys, and biases that had no actual bearing on the truth, produced an outcome that most people felt was wrong, although legally sanctioned and deemed correct. For many people, the *Bush v. Gore* Supreme Court decision was similarly unjust, governed by the political leanings of the justices and their partisan readings of the law, and not by what was right. But why are such travesties of justice tolerated? We accept decisions that are plainly wrong, all because legally they are completely justified.

If the community believes that the legal system is there to do what's just and to discover the truth—indeed, to provide an official record of the truth—then a sporting theory of justice, where one side is anointed the winner while the other is banished as the loser, may not achieve a legitimate sense of justness, or truth.

Winning, after all, is a contest of skill and luck, story-spinning and manipulation, and not a referendum on truth. Justice, as defined by a legal resolution, may be done, but sometimes not at all served, because the result is a gruesome miscarriage, and not just at all. The winner-take-all structure of the legal system is morally deficient because it creates a presumption that justice has been achieved when morally it has not. Sometimes the ultimate winner should not have been victorious, and the losing party, nonparty victims, and the outside community know this to be true. And often the best moral result would seek not to trounce the loser but to approximate some measure of victory in both parties—to send them both home healed rather than ambivalent or enraged. Everyone is made worse off by unjust outcomes. And the discovery of the truth has to be given the same prominence as the bottom-line, efficient disposal of cases.

The question then becomes whether, instead of limiting their role to presiding over zero-sum contests, courts can entertain broader conversations about moral outcomes that don't rely exclusively on crowning winners. Is it possible for courts to infuse and align their legal decisions with an appreciation of the moral universe? And, in doing so, can judges and lawyers find ways to humanize the law so that it does not coldly ignore the pain that resides within and around the creases of human conflict?

One of the best examples of the absence of a moral dimension to the legal system is found in the reasonable man, or person, test, which guides the application of most legal rules. As every lawyer and law student knows, many legal rules are determined according to the reasonable man test, an objective standard that can be summed up as follows: In thinking about what conduct is lawful, we ask what would most people, in a particular community, do in a given situation. The reasonable man—objective and rational, all the while mythical and hypothetical—largely determines the legal standard in American jurisprudence.

Yet, in elevating and emulating this faceless, anonymous,

marginal man—scrutinizing his behavior as he responds to the world around him, the offers made in his presence, the duties he chooses to undertake—we also have to wonder whether, morally, such a person should dictate the shaping of our legal rules? After all, while the reasonable man, through sheer moral blindness and undaunted commonness, may be representative of the community, is he our model citizen? Should we mirror our behavior in the same way that he would? The reasonable man sets the bar legally, but in doing so, does he actually lower it morally? This median personality—the average citizen playing it safe, tucked away in the middle of the pack—is not self-guided by a deep sense of moral courage and virtue. And yet this is the very person whose conduct establishes the standard for the rest of us in determining what passes for law in America.

In Harper Lee's novel *To Kill a Mockingbird*, Tom Robinson is on trial for raping a white woman in a small Alabama town in the 1930s. Tom is falsely accused, but it's not hard to convict a black man in a Southern courthouse, particularly in the decades before the civil rights movement. In finding a basis upon which to convict Tom, the jury seems persuaded by the fact that Tom fled the scene of the alleged crime. Surely a reasonable man, innocent of any crime, would not have absconded from the home of a woman crying rape when the accused never laid a hand on her. Even in fiction, the reasonable man test controls the legal outcome of the case. Since Tom ran, and a reasonable man would not have, Tom must be guilty.

Of course, the problem here is that the reasonable man test is being employed to measure what a reasonable *white* man would have done in this situation. The reasonable *black* man, however, in the Deep South, finding himself lured into the home of a white woman, would have fled rather than be caught in such a compromising place. The law equates lawfulness with reasonableness, yet in this instance, the accused is acting reasonably, but the result, tainted by the politics of racism, produces a horrifyingly immoral outcome, although it is logically framed in legal terms.

Albert Camus's novel *The Stranger* raises the same issue, though the setting for this encounter with immoral justice is not the Deep South, but rather French-occupied Algeria. Mersault, the existentially challenged protagonist, confesses to having killed an Arab in self-defense. The prosecution makes the case that since Mersault fired more than one bullet, and since he lacked remorse over the killing, his actions were more premeditated than reflexive, more heinous than innocent. Indeed, the prosecution succeeds in painting Mersault as a morally depraved man, based not on the crime itself but rather on his dubious behavior both during and after his mother's funeral, which opens the novel. Weeks before the shooting, Mersault failed to exhibit the kind of conventional grief that would have impressed an Algerian jury of his humanity. He shed no tears, nor showed any emotion. Later that same day he had gone skinny-dipping and had sex with his girlfriend. He also attended a French comedic film. The prosecution fixates on this evidence to show Mersault's callous indifference to the loss of his mother. And this somehow convinces the court that the same attitude holds true with regard to his murder of the Arab. Why else would he have fired so many bullets?

The Algerian court ultimately beheads Mersault, on the evidence not of the murder itself but of conventional character flaws that inexplicably, and arguably, constitute an indictable offense, apart from the actual murder. Given the moral standards of 1950s Algeria, Mersault apparently hasn't responded to the death of his mother in a conventionally appropriate way. And it is this crime, one of indifference, which has nothing to do with the murder but everything to do with Mersault's particular way of mourning his mother, that ultimately leads to his execution. Yet the actual evidence of the underlying crime clearly shows that he possessed neither the intent, nor the requisite malice to kill the Arab, and therefore it should never have been deemed a capital crime.

Mersault's lawyer failed to argue that his client's actions after his mother's death, and the discharging of multiple bullets in the murder of the Arab, may not have been evidence of moral depravity or indifference, but rather the delayed reactions to grief. Mersault was a man in mourning, in a state of shock, undergoing a crisis of existence. But the court insisted on standardizing Mersault's reactions so that they would be evaluated and compared to the actions of a reasonable man. The reasonable man of Algeria would have cried at his mother's funeral. He would not have had sex on that same day, nor would he have gone to see a French comedy. And he certainly wouldn't have fired more than one bullet in self-defense.

The fact that Mersault acted strangely in response to his mother's death should have had no bearing in elevating his intentions to one of cold-blooded murder. Even more important, just because Mersault mourned his mother—or perhaps failed to mourn her—not in a manner befitting a reasonable man of Algeria, doesn't mean that his actions with regard to the Arab were legally unreasonable, or that his character was presumptively suspicious. The court, relying on the reasonable man test, missed the deeper emotional complexities of mourning, and the uncertain, unpredictable conduct that human beings sometimes numbly undertake in expressing their grief in the aftermath of loss. The Algerian court regarded Mersault not so much as a stranger, but rather as someone who is strange, and peculiar. Most Algerians might have perhaps expressed their grief differently. The legal standard here, however, insisted on conformity—reasonableness that ultimately produced an immoral result.

Mersault undoubtedly committed a crime. But the very circumstances that should have been used to establish the extenuation and mitigation of his actions instead were manipulated to upgrade the crime to something that it clearly was not. As Camus points out, unconventional, idiosyncratic, and even strange behavior has a way of being misapplied and misunderstood by a court of law. In this case, the application of the reasonable man test desensitized the court to a defendant such as Mersault, someone emotionally numb and grief-stricken and not deliberative and depraved. But this misuse of the reasonable man test unduly influenced its decision in determining his guilt. The court regarded Mersault's behavior in the aftermath of his mother's funeral as immoral. But actually it was the court's application of the reasonable man test that produced the immoral outcome, and showed once more that in a contest between the legal and the moral, the legal always wins out.

In an American courtroom, such evidence of Mersault's moral failure to mourn his mother would have been inadmissible as inappropriate character evidence. Yet the question of the multiple bullets would have been highly relevant for evidentiary purposes, and would have been subjected to the moral vagaries, and presumed objective standards, of the reasonable man test.

A recent real-life example of the way in which the reasonable man test may result in an immoral outcome can be found in the case of West African immigrant Amadou Diallo, who, in 1999, was murdered in New York City by four plainclothes police officers who mistook him for a rape suspect. Like in the case of Mersault in *The Stranger*, the issue of self-defense was complicated by the fact that there was more than one bullet. Indeed, here the police officers, entering a dimly lit vestibule and seeing Diallo pull something out of his jacket, fired forty-one bullets, nineteen of which hit their target. Also, similar to Mersault's case, at trial the officers were observed as showing no emotion or remorse.

Yet this case resulted in the acquittal of the four officers, and not in their execution for the crime of murder. What made this situation different? Why was Mersault treated more harshly? In this instance, a jury, based in Albany where the case was transferred on the grounds that the police officers would not have received a fair trial in New York City, apparently took account of all the complexities of the situation: plainclothes police officers working undercover, at night, in a dangerous neighborhood, inside a building populated with drug dealers, faced with poor lighting and amplified acoustics that echoed with each ricocheted bullet, and a dark-skinned male who was reaching inside his coat and not responding to police warnings (Diallo understood little English). Despite the volume of firepower, the jury apparently concluded that a reasonable police officer, working under these extreme circumstances and the general stresses of the job, might have reasonably fired this number of shots in self-defense.

Without arguing whether the acquittal of those who had killed Diallo was unjust, what is clearly evident is that the jury appreciated the complexity of a police officer's job in a dangerous, high-crime area. The jury did not merely look at the nineteen lodged bullets, and forty-one fired ones, and reflexively conclude that the officers' conduct had moved well beyond reasonableness into the territory of cold-blooded murder. The Diallo case was a complicated, disturbing, and highly emotional one. Perhaps it was racism that motivated the Albany jury. These were people who did not live in New York City, and perhaps had an exaggerated fear of the inner-city sanctums that constitute the urban world. The jurors might have felt unduly sympathetic to white police officers who, as part of their civic responsibility, fearlessly trafficked in dire terrains on a daily basis. It's difficult to know why the case was decided this way, other than to conclude that the jury in Diallo regarded the reasonable man with more complexity, and allowed his actions more latitude than did the fictional juries in *To Kill a Mockingbird* and *The Stranger*. The Diallo case, however, does show once again how the reasonable man test can be deployed to produce a result that is appropriately legal but not necessarily moral.

When the law relies on reasonableness, it sometimes ends up rewarding moral failure.

In Nazi Germany, the reasonable man, given the inflamed passions and politics of the Third Reich, would have reasonably remained silent and done nothing to save Jews during the Holocaust. That's what most people could be counted on to do, and actually did, in that situation. Under extreme circumstances of fear and crisis, it's always more reasonable to simply shut the blinds and pretend that it will all go away or return to normal in the morning. When one faces risks to body, livelihood, reputation, and profession, it's surely easier to disable the conscience and ignore the larger, or smaller, world around you. At least that's how the average person would react.

But to stand apart from the crowd, and stand up for friends and neighbors—even if they are strangers—to oppose governmental authority when it lacks moral authority, to rescue fellow men from danger, may be the right thing to do morally, even if it's not reasonable to do so. The reasonable man standard doesn't always produce an immoral, albeit legal, result. But by focusing on reasonableness to the exclusion of other values, the test often fails when judged by moral criteria. The reasonable man standard shows the law's preference for zero-sum, bottom-line behavior and an indifference toward nobler, more spiritually enlightened human aspirations. The law becomes defined not by the example set by those who are the most virtuous and exemplary among us. Instead, legal standards become influenced by pedestrian tastes and mindsets, attitudes that reflect little ambition, initiative, and honor. It is the median, homogenized response, the guy snugly standing in line, the one who is part of the larger pack of anonymous men, the numb, unoriginal and unthinking who guides the legal standard for human conduct. Our model of legal behavior becomes the middle brow, the low bar of our most common denominators. We are required to do no more than what the reasonable person would do in a given situation, even though reasonable people are often cowardly, self-centered, and morally obtuse.

So what does that tell us about the law, its moral failings, and why the public generally regards it with so much suspicion and discontent? If the reasonable man is the arbiter of what is legal, then must we look to the irrational among us for moral guidance? The law's fixation on the objective, reasonable, physical, and external deprives legal standards of also being influenced by the subjective, irrational, spiritual, and internal dynamics of the human experience. And if courts of law are places where the full sweep of humanity coalesces and unravels into anguished trials of human vulnerability, then shouldn't such forums also find room to embrace man at his most irrational and emotional—indeed, when he or she is operating at his or her most human?

What we should want, in fact, what we should insist on, are individuals locked in moral struggles, refusing to settle for anything less than doing the right thing. A more morally centered legal system would place equal value on what the conscience-stricken man would do in a given situation. The reasonable man is not always to be emulated, because reasonableness sometimes can come across as spineless and soulless—the reasonableness of a sheep who follows the herd and whose conscience is always clear.

A NEW PARADIGM
OF MORAL JUSTICE

The irreconcilable split between the legal and the moral shatters the public's faith in the law. If lawyers inspire so much disdain, perhaps it has something to do with the perception—widely held and largely true—that they disregard moral considerations and find no place for them in the law. Most people take for granted that the law is moral, or they are resigned to accept that it is not. My own students, over the years, have been perplexed by this question: Is the legal system moral; are moral concerns on the minds of lawyers and judges? The question rarely arises in law school, and most law students, not to mention practicing lawyers, have conveniently avoided asking it of themselves. Doing the right thing is a noble aspiration, and it also sounds great, but it is generally not what motivates lawyers in the performance of their jobs.

Another way to examine the moral failings of the legal system is to consider the conventional legal paradigm, which works as follows:

1. The focus of the law is on the legal and what is legally correct.

2. The law is primarily interested in protecting tangible, material property and the human body, and scrutinizing human actors once they are in motion, taking their tortious or criminal steps toward causing harm.

3. The law offers remedies that are either punitive or monetary in nature, i.e., jail time for guilty defendants, damage awards for injured plaintiffs.

This conventional paradigm—inviolable, nonnegotiable, uncritically applied by the legal establishment—is regarded as an article of faith in an otherwise faithless institution.

LEGAL-BODY-PUNISHMENT/MONEY

Judges and lawyers have a very narrow vision of what the law can and should accomplish. What seemingly matters most is that final judgments comport with constitutional procedures, prior legal precedents, or statutory mandates. A rule gets applied to the facts. The result is justice. It may be morally wrong, but the focus on doing what's legal rather than on what's right overrides all other considerations and concerns.

But the conventional legal paradigm doesn't end there, because this obsession with the legal over the moral is also expressed in the law's preference for the body over the spirit. Legal rules are triggered when the human body sustains an injury, when property is stolen or damaged, when rights are infringed. Lawyers think in concrete, tangible terms. They are concerned with the physical and external, and not with the ambiguities of invisible, untraceable, unmarked wounds.

Indeed, the law becomes animated when there is a bruise on the body, and when damage is done to private possessions—the harm that leaves evidence of itself. The law becomes operational when damages are quantifiable. Before the law starts to take a serious interest in most cases, courts always ask: What are the damages? This essentially means: Show me the bill of repairs, a receipt for the damages incurred, the victimized witness, the visible scar, or the presentation of expert evidence showing that the body will never be the same again.

The same fixation on the body occurs when courts assess the culpability and liability of human conduct, i.e., not just in the case of people who are damaged or injured, but also those who are responsible for causing the damage. A defendant must have done something affirmative and physical in order for his conduct to be legally actionable. He or she must have acted and, in doing so, caused harm. Only when the body has taken its first step and gone into motion—for instance, in delivering a punch, trespassing on someone else's property, breaching a promise made under a contract, embezzling money, or performing surgery on the wrong limb—does the law become interested in punishing the criminal or assigning liability against a tortfeasor and requiring him to pay damages.

With the body as the focal point of the law's attention, is there any wonder that psychological wounds caused by humiliation and indignity, or harms aggravated by the neglect and indifference of bystanders—those who neither move a muscle nor say a word—are completely ignored in the American legal system? (The intentional infliction of emotional distress, which many people believe to be a tort action that addresses spiritual harm, is a largely empty legal theory, usually added on, if at all, to an existing physical injury rather than treated as a serious, independent tort that doesn't require evidence of some other more tangible harm. I will discuss this point further in chapter 16.)

As for remedies—what justice is capable of providing as an answer to an injury or crime—here, too, the paradigm has a limited vision of relief. The legal system operates under the assumption that justice is achieved only by way of material, retributive, or punitive relief. Prosecutions and punishments for crimes committed; damage awards as compensation for injuries sustained.

This is the fulfillment of justice in America, the only way that the legal system contemplates making people whole after loss.

This book, however, argues for a morally inspired transformation of the legal system, one that embraces the conventional paradigm and its legal-body-punishment/money equation, but also calls attention to other values, more spiritual and restorative in nature—an alternative paradigm, if you will, one that looks more like this:

MORAL-SOUL-ACKNOWLEDGMENT/RESTORATION

This new, alternative paradigm would work as follows:

1. The law would strive to achieve moral outcomes.

2. The human spirit would also receive protection under the law, and the law should scrutinize the actions of those who are responsible for causing spiritual violence, indignity, and neglect.

3. Courts would provide moral remedies, such as in acknowledging the harm that was done, seeking apologies for them, and restoring relationships—for the benefit of the entire community.

Under this new moral paradigm, achieving correct legal results would simply not be enough. Moral considerations would be reflected in legal decision-making as well; and the law would no longer insulate itself from moral concerns. What is legal and what is moral would intersect so that decisions that are legally correct would also be morally sound. What happens in a courthouse should feel right emotionally—both to the parties to the action, and to the community at large.

Moreover, the human body—whether in movement or as the recipient of the injury—shouldn't be the law's only focus of attention. The legal system should also protect the human spirit and soul. And those who commit spiritual harms, or engage in acts of spiritual violence and indifference, should be as answerable in a court of law as someone who injures the human body. Similarly, property damage should not be more actionable than other, less visible and tangible forms of loss. Stealing someone's wallet is a crime, but, for some reason, taking away their dignity is not.

There are harms that exist below the radar of physical measurement. Just because the interior world of the spirit is unseen, doesn't mean that what it experiences is unfelt. A great deal of suffering is visited on the intangible sphere of the spirit—whether in the form of humiliation, indignity, or basic neglect. But without physical evidence of the harm—incontestable proof—the legal system treats these injuries, hurts, and grievances as if they are undeserving of relief. The result is a justice system that rejects the full dimensions of the human experience. Our species has both physical and spiritual qualities. The law, however, takes account of one and completely ignores the other.

Finally, the law should expand its notion of remedies—how it seeks to punish some people for the harms they have inflicted, and compensate others for the harms they have sustained. Specifically, legal remedies should not be limited to jail sentences, cash settlements, and damage awards as the only relief available to those who have been victimized, harmed, or suffered losses. Remedies must also offer moral and spiritual relief, and be directed to both body and soul. In the same way that the spirit can't be quantified in material or measurable terms, spiritual and moral remedies transcend the dollars and cents of money, and the minimum/maximum sentences of jail-time punishments. Sometimes what an injured party requires is not simply a cash award, or the knowledge that a criminal has been sent to jail. Sometimes true relief comes by way of acknowledging the hurt, telling and retelling the full story, discovering the truth and memorializing it for the future. Moral acknowledgment is a process of elevating the story precisely for the sake of memorializing it, and thereby somewhat relieving the injury.

The more details of the story that are revealed in an open forum, the more possible it becomes for victims to reconcile themselves to what happened and find some measure of relief. They can then move forward without feeling the additional grievance of a legal system that failed them by failing to listen to them. All of us are better off when truths are told and grievances are properly acknowledged.

Victims need to speak of how they came to be victims—the way they were before, and how they have been changed. And civilization is always more civilized when the truth is unhidden and known. In spite of all the injustice in the world, in the end—often many years later—the truth always wins out. Truth is all part of the healing process of what it means to seek and receive relief. Ultimately, a grievance demands an opportunity for the injured party to grieve.

Remedies of a spiritual and moral nature, however, are not usually presented by lawyers to their clients as available options. Indeed, most lawyers have never considered them. And in criminal cases, prosecutors don't have moral outcomes in mind, nor do they explain to crime victims that the legal system is generally devoted to a brand of justice that might leave the victim ultimately feeling betrayed and unrepresented by the system. Putting people in jail is the endgame of criminal justice. Making the streets safe by keeping criminals off of them. But the victim might be seeking, or expecting, some kind of moral justice, even if he can't name it, or know what form it would take.

The victim only becomes aware of this discrepancy between the goals of the legal system and his own quest for justice when he experiences the emptiness that occurs during his day in court—the folly of the final judgment, the sense of abandonment that follows the dismissal. Only then does he realize that something is missing. The intervention of the law in his life never remedied his grievance. Indeed, in some cases, the court further aggravates the injury and causes its own injustice.

Individuals who lose before the law—whether victims of crimes or casualties of civil injury—came to court expecting and hoping for one thing, and departed through the metal detectors and revolving doors feeling as if they had been doubly robbed of something even more valuable: their faith. Faith in justice, faith in just treatment, faith that when you step before the ornate and gilded confines of a courthouse, a sense of right will dictate the outcome. Otherwise, why not resort to frontier justice, or self-help?

In the Oscar-nominated film *In the Bedroom* (2002), directed by Todd Field, a father cannot bear that his son's killer is free on bail and that there has been great delay in bringing the case to trial. Worse still, the prosecutor is concerned that the evidence is weak, and that an ultimate conviction of first-degree murder is in doubt. How can the parents live their lives in the same town as someone who murdered their son? Not only does the criminal go unpunished, but his murdered victim's parents are victimized further when they see him in town flaunting his freedom, which only reminds them of their pain. The parents must endure the loss of their son, and they must live with the knowledge that the legal system has compounded the injustice by so miserably failing to redress their loss. How can so many criminally guilty and tortiously liable people walk among us—innocent and not legally responsible in the eyes of the law? Where is someone to go to relieve wrongs when the legal system pretends to open its doors but in fact shuts them and, in doing so, causes even further pain?

The conventional reliance on legal penalties or damage awards only allows for the replacement of something of material or physical value, or the imposition of a commutable jail sentence: a check gets cashed, a service is required and performed, a person goes to jail. But in the vast majority of cases, the injured party cannot really be made whole—no matter how much money he receives or how many days the offender is imprisoned—because the underlying grievance has left an actual hole that can't be filled. The material damage—that which can be seen and examined—has resulted in psychic scar-tissue that is invisible and unhealable by conventional means. In such cases, nothing can be replaced and repaired materially, because what is ultimately needed is not something that can even be measured. The remedy is of a spiritual nature, the very kind that the legal system does not know how to provide.

As I will discuss later in this book, settlement checks don't relieve grief, they only fatten bank accounts. Maybe there is a short-term feeling of euphoria, but it is a fleeting and ephemeral one, pumped up by the lawyer, but inevitably deflated. Money may be desired, for all the reasons why net worth invariably elevates self-worth. Money, in fact, does solve many problems. But money is never a sufficient remedy for grief. It can't relieve the underlying ailment, because sometimes the loss is irreplaceable. Whether it is a life or a limb, the brokenness of a relationship or the fragility of the human spirit, money damages is never, alone, meaningfully compensatory, and limiting the remedy to money is tantamount to an insult. Settlement checks—operating purely in the material realm, having currency only in the universe of commerce—cannot bandage what otherwise should be exposed to the open air. This is the moral imperative of a public trial: the opportunity to tell your story in open court; to speak of the grievance and memorialize the hurt; to confront those who are responsible for the injury and have them account for their wrongdoing; to create an official record of the proceedings, a permanent place of memory so that the incident is not forgotten.

The focus here is on moral remedies that are neither prosecutorial nor retributive in nature, but rather spiritual and restorative. Justice should not define itself only by way of prosecutions, punishments, and the reallocation of private assets.

Sometimes these remedies work, but often they do not. Instead, the legal system should begin to regard itself as a healing profession, because a client with a grievance is not that much different from a patient in pain. Doctors and lawyers have more in common than they would otherwise imagine. Patients and clients generally visit them only during trying times. The inside mechanics of the anatomy, or the outside forces of the community, have caused them harm. We run into the arms of these professions looking for relief. It's just that doctors understand relief in the context of healing, always seeking to relieve the underlying pain, to remedy the sickness, to find an antidote, if not a complete cure. Lawyers, by contrast, believe that relief is simply what you get at the end of a legal action.

A legal remedy, however, isn't about cure, it's about restitution, compensation, punishment. For this reason, legal remedies are actually misnomers. They neither repair nor cure, nor remedy. Instead, they seek some pale substitute to give a victim or injured person as redress for the harm they suffered. (In later chapters I'll discuss how, in the criminal area, the goal isn't even about that, because the victim, or the victim's family, hardly enters into the court's consideration at all.)

In ordinary parlance, remedies and relief are usually thought of as being medicinal in nature. You have a headache, you take an aspirin to relieve the pain. If you're nervous, you swallow a tranquilizer. Your heart is racing, there's a pill to calm or relieve the palpitations. The whole point of seeing a doctor or taking medicine is to end up feeling better, not worse. But in the language of law, remedies and relief are not about making clients and victims feel better. In fact, the law doesn't concern itself with feelings at all. They are deemed irrelevant, a nuisance within the well-oiled machine. (This idea will be addressed more directly in chapters 8, 9, and 16). All that matters is what you are entitled to, what the law provides, what is possible as compensation for the injury.

The medical profession sees its task as aiding and curing the body. But judges are like doctors who absolutely refuse to touch their patients. The legal system ought to be in the business of curing as well, because, like medical patients, clients visit lawyers for the same reason: pain. Admittedly it's a different kind of pain, but it produces anguish nonetheless. And for this reason, the pain must be managed and relieved. The technical expertise that lawyers possess in navigating through the legal system—and the narrow vision of remedies that the law embraces—is simply not enough to relieve this pain. It is only a part of the job. The law, in fact, is a healing profession, it's just that those who are engaged in this line of work, for the most part, don't know it.

The origins of what brings many litigants to the courthouse are indignities done to the spirit. A broken promise is as much a betrayal as is a marriage or business transaction gone bad. And even when the damage has a clear material and physical component—a disfigured face, a broken fender, a breached contract, the nonpayment of one kind or another—the aftershocks of the experience are felt more deeply, and last longer, in the psyche and soul. This is where injuries fester and breed, which gives rise to the need for yet another remedy. But that remedy is never forthcoming, because the legal system has neither the imagination nor the will to grant it. These remedies would provide restorative relief, enabling parties to manage to reconcile, or at least reconcile themselves to a life without bitterness and rage.

Moral responsibility often supersedes what the law otherwise requires. And it's generally easier to follow the law than be guided by conscience. Most people, however, don't make these fine distinctions about human conduct. Yet one day they discover that moral justice has no counterpart in the law, and wonder why what's morally wrong sometimes is without legal consequence.

Sometimes, however, severe moral consequences ensue independent of, and in response to, the law's neglect. The community rallies to do the right thing even when the law is otherwise silent and imposes no legal duty to act. A recent book published in Germany, which recounted the extent to which Austrian citizens willfully and shamefully pillaged property that had once belonged to their deported Jewish neighbors, prompted the government of Austria to take appropriate steps toward making restitution.

"What's new is a consensus of moral responsibility," said Hans Winkler, a senior official of the Austrian Foreign Ministry who negotiated various restitution agreements, was quoted in the *New York Times*. "There is a consensus that we shouldn't look at the issue as purely a question of legal responsibility."

The legal system could integrate moral considerations into its legal decision-making. It's just that there is no impetus or impulse to do so. If there were, the entire experience of the law would feel more just. The public seeks more, and deserves more, because it has a broader, more imaginative concept of what justice is. Justice is not some abstract application of rules to a given set of facts, nor is it some law-school hypothetical. Rather, a sense of justice is life itself, played out in real time, with real people. And how it feels to people matters. Justice either contributes to or erodes the moral sense that resides in every human being. It speaks to what is just and right, intuitively heartfelt, soulful, and true.

Of course, I realize there are those, mostly lawyers themselves, who find it hard to adopt this way of thinking. They would argue that discussions about soul and morality are indeed absent from the conventional legal paradigm, and for very good reason: These are weird words, designed to give off a warm and fuzzy feeling, but they have no application to the law. Only those who can tolerate a certain level of ambiguity in their lives and live with the elusiveness of faith are comfortable thinking in purely moral, spiritual terms. Law, these critics would argue, succeeds on a completely different model and mindset. What people need and demand from the legal system is not faith, but something rigidly tangible and dependable, which comes in the form of rules, statutes, and the sternness and stoicism of objective, dispassionate judgment.

The law is not for the tender-hearted or weak-willed. The coldness is there for a reason. Humanizing the law would essentially rob it of its objective virtue. Faith and spirit constitute the language of the clergy. It is they who deal in such abstractions, whereas the law operates in the land of predictability and absolutes. Clergy teach morals; judges are mere arbiters, neither trained nor seized with the impulse to teach what is right. All they are required to do is regulate external conduct consistent with man-made laws. Moral righteousness is not part of their job.

But why cede to organized religion the domain over doing the right thing? Why insulate the legal system from the duty to exercise moral authority equal in force to its commitment to follow the law? A greater connection between moral values and legal rules will arise when the justice system searches for precedents not only inside law books, but within the moral universe as well.

This is not easy for lawyers to accept. In art and literature, one can see moral and emotional complexity in the legal profession. In fact, it is precisely these portraits of ambivalence and vulnerability that make fictional lawyers—particularly the ones on television and film—so appealing.

For example, attorneys routinely agonize over the troubling moral nature and dilemmas of practicing law in the darkly gothic television drama *The Practice*. The show, often written by its creator, David E. Kelley, depicts lawyers as trying to do the right thing with almost religious zeal. In order to do that, they sometimes have to cross the line, either because they become too involved emotionally with their clients—revealing their human qualities for empathy—or they have to challenge the superior resources of the prosecution, and this formidable mismatch requires them to do whatever is necessary, even if it is legally and ethically questionable. Moreover, since these lawyers are human beings, their past lives, memories, and experiences interfere with the objectivity demanded of their profession. Passions also get in the way, as do family conflicts and connections. The lawyers in *The Practice*, rather than becoming desensitized to the pain of their clients, turn the suffering on themselves. Often they don't sleep so well at night. And they insist on being able to look at themselves in the mirror in the morning. How many real lawyers do we know like that?

In the Oscar-winning film *Erin Brockovich* (2000), Julia Roberts, playing the title role as an untrained but people-savvy paralegal, reminds the lawyer for whom she works: "I admit, I don't know shit about shit, but I know the difference between right and wrong." Why is it so hard for actual legal practitioners to utter these words and believe that a sense of moral righteousness should influence and guide their professional conduct?

There are specific reasons for this moral void in the legal profession. For one thing, religion depends not just on faith, but on a leap of faith, which is not all that different from faith itself, because all faith, by definition, requires some form of a free fall, the suspension of disbelief, the arrest of the rational mind. Blind faith is nearly always practiced by those who otherwise have no trouble seeing. They selectively choose blindness, for this occasion, because faith won't work if it is examined too closely. There is no such thing as a leap of science, or the leap of law, because those disciplines are anchored to the temporal ground of certainty. They seek to find all answers and eliminate all doubt. Religion, by contrast, cannot sustain its adherents without the marshaling of faith to the invisible, magical strings that suspend those who have taken the leap.

Leaps are not for lawyers. In the legal profession, trust is invested in objectivity, not faith. Reliance is placed on the concrete certainties of the law, not on the cloudy quicksand of the infinite. But what's so reliable about the law, given its affinity for anguish and injustice? Why shouldn't faith in the law be rewarded with legal results that are deserving of that faith—the faith that judges, motivated by a moral consciousness and private conscience, will do the right thing?

All of us, regardless of religious affiliation or receptivity to the divine, are captives of faith. We are constitutionally commanded to have faith—not by an external rule, but by internal intuition. Like the air we breathe, faith is primal—necessary, in fact—to sustaining life. Eventually, at some point, we all exercise our faith, because we need to believe in something—something larger than ourselves. Otherwise the world would become intolerably threatening. And it operates even in situations where there is a breakdown in faith, because we all need to keep some trust in reserve.

This leads to a cruel paradox. As human beings, we are virtually programmed to have faith in the very things that we know, in the end, will frustrate and disappoint us. God is a good example of this; marriage is even a better one. In each instance we know that the chances are excellent that God won't grant our prayers, and that marriages, which are designed to create lasting unions, in more than half the cases actually fall apart. And yet we continue to have unremitting faith, despite the low odds and bad history. When it comes to our prayers, and our vows, we trust that they will be answered and honored. We return to churches and altars even when God and former spouses have given us all the reason in the world to stay away.

This is true of the law as well. Most people long for justice, and yet, given what they know, they don't really expect to receive it. We ask for justice knowing all the while that the legal system isn't interested in giving us what we want. And yet, as true creatures of faith, longing for righteousness, we keep coming back, hoping that next time the courts will finally get it right. Sometimes, however, even unshakable faith undergoes a trauma that is immense and unrecoverable. The leap of faith results in a catastrophic fall, and faith forever loses its power and allure.

My father had been a lawyer, in Poland, before the Holo-

THE MYTH OF MORAL JUSTICE

caust. After the liberation of the camps, he was never a lawyer again. Justice became a joke. Laws were used in the service of annihilation. Judges and lawyers were complicit in mass murder. Everything was perfectly legal. The profession showed itself to be unworthy. The law was as indifferent as God, and, for my father, neither was to be trusted again. With his loyalty to the law now gone, he would need to find another livelihood.

Of course, the Holocaust is an extreme example of everything. It tested faith beyond its natural limits. Indeed, atrocity is the truest test of faith. Faith, after Auschwitz, is surely only for the true believers. Most people, however, can withstand the ordinary frustrations that the law delivers without completely abandoning their faith. Disappointed. Cynical. But not faithless. That's how deep the longing and desire is to believe in the law.

We need faith. But faith requires a leap into the unknown, while the legal system depends on detached, objective certainty. Judges function best when their world is narrowly confined to the letter of the law. But life itself best resembles the spirit of the law—not inflexible but rather fluid, capable of change, and always emotionally complex. The spirit has a role to play, even in legal decision-making. And what a true consideration of the law's spirit offers that the conventional legal paradigm invariably rejects is a full appreciation of the moral universe.

When I teach my course in Law and Literature, I begin the first day's class by reading a children's story out loud. I've been doing this for years, and each semester a good number of the students are surprised by this opening lecture, even though, given my general attitudes about traditional legal education, it shouldn't come as much of a shock. Many of these students haven't been read to in years, if ever, and they haven't read or heard a children's story since then. The story I read is *In the Month of Kislev*, written by Nina Jaffe and illustrated by Louise August. It is a Jewish story, one for Hanukkah, but, actually, many variations of it exist in other cultures. The story, briefly summarized and without illustrations, goes something like this:

In a small shtetl in Poland, there are two families—one rich, the other poor. As Hanukkah approaches, the three children from the poor family have very little to eat; indeed, they don't have even a single potato for potato latkes, which are traditionally served on the holiday. Passing underneath the kitchen window of the rich family, the three poor children inhale the aroma of potato latkes, and somehow mysteriously, magically, they feel as though they have eaten. When they return home, the parents, knowing that there is no food, can't believe that their children are not hungry. They attribute this to a Hanukkah miracle. The children go on smelling the rich family's latkes for the entire eight days of the holiday.

But on the eighth day, the man who heads the household of the rich family discovers the poor children smelling his latkes outside his home. He is outraged, and claims that they have enjoyed the smell, and have taken it away from him, without paying just compensation. The next day he brings the poor family before the rabbi and demands eight rubles as payment for the eight days of Hanukkah in which the children stole the smell of his latkes. The community descends on the house of the rabbi, awaiting his wisdom and decree.

The rabbi asks everyone in the community to take all the coins they have in their possession and place them inside a bag that he provides. When the bag is full, the rabbi shakes the bag numerous times until it jingles like a music box. When he is finished, he turns to the rich man and pronounces his judgment: "What's right is right. You asked for fair payment and you have received it. We have paid for the smell of your Hanukkah latkes with the sound of Hanukkah gelt." The townspeople, who had wondered what their rabbi was up to—how jingling coins could possibly remedy a legal dispute—suddenly realize: "How wise our rabbi is."

This story is wonderful not just in the way it merges the spheres of religion and law, but also in the way in which what passes for a legal remedy works equally well as a moral one. In the mind of the child hearing the story, there is no split between the legal and moral. They are the same, both leading to the right outcome. The rich man seeks the conventional remedy of money as compensation for his presumed loss. But what he was arguably deprived of was not of the material world. The smell of his latkes could not be quantified. What he lost, if anything, was sensory. The wisdom of the rabbi's judgment is that the remedy is appropriately tailored to respond to this particular spiritual loss. Monetary damages would have been misapplied here. In order for there to be a just result, the relief would have had to be spiritual and sensory in nature—the sound of Hanukkah coins as compensation for the smell of Hanukkah latkes.

As the rabbi says, "What's right is right"—the ultimate moral, spiritual remedy. And like most children's stories, this one had a happy ending: The rich man went home and learned a moral lesson, and from there on began to enrich the world with his charity. And the community, with renewed faith in their rabbi's wisdom and upon being shown how legal judgments are worthy of faith, was able to rest knowing that justice—understood in both legal and moral terms—was done.

I always remind my students that stories are important precisely because they introduce children to the existence of a moral universe. The hope is that in their formative years, children can begin to develop a moral consciousness. The question in the end is always: "What is the moral of the story?" Embedded within the story are the seeds of right and wrong, and after hearing the story, children will hopefully be able to know and appreciate the difference and live their lives according to these values—not necessarily because it is the rule, but because it is right.

But at the conclusion of a legal opinion, reported in case books and studied by law students, when the judge writes his holding, he or she never asks: "What is the moral of this case?" There is no equivalent moral lesson, only a legal one. A rule is established and applied to a particular set of facts, a precedent is followed, a legal reason provided. The decision is correct because it can be analogized to, or it logically springs from, a prior case. At no point, however, does a judge ever seek to justify his decision in moral terms.

We can only wonder how much more righteous and sensible the legal system would be if judges wrote their opinions as if their readers were children and not other lawyers. Each opinion written with the moral of the story in mind, as if to teach children how to live a moral life. That day may never come. But in the meantime, it would be better if judges at least asked the question of themselves.

POUND OF FLESH

The face of grief usually has a mouth that is too numb to speak. In the aftermath of loss and betrayal, indignity and injustice, shock sets in, the stomach drops, limbs go limp, and it seems as though there is no place to turn. Sometimes anger is all there is. The primal instinct of our species is to scream out not only against the injustice, but at the emptiness that lies underneath the injury—what it means to be bereft, deprived, and unheard.

These are the complex emotions that exist independently of the catalytic harm itself. A psychic wound gets umbilically attached to the physical one, integral and ancillary to the original injury, and yet feeding off its own blood supply of rage and disappointment. And, if left untreated, the hurt that arises from this neglect becomes its own pathology.

Unfortunately, the legal system does not perceive itself as being in the healing business, and so it never occurs to lawyers that they should be treating the emotional injuries that accompany the legal ones. Yet we are all the ultimate victims of this disregard, and we pay a high price for our indifference. The pain of injustice and unacknowledged loss does not disappear within the colorless, soulless ether of silence. Instead, the pain returns renewed, in another form—with a vengeance, and in vengeance.

We see this in race riots and localized conflicts, when the prolonged suffering of an entire group leads its members to turn their experience with economic and ethnic injustice into riotous, sometimes murderous, rage. The result is broken glass, property damage, and sometimes dead bodies. And, of course, the law, recruited as a cleanup and enforcement crew, is brought in to establish order and hold guilty parties responsible. But many tragic episodes could have been avoided. Injuries that originate from neglect are later manifested in the physical world. But the law is interested in people only after the emotional hurt actualizes itself in physical injury, only when bodies are in destructive motion, and not when they are in smoldering unrest. And, of course, unmindful or ignorant of our own complicity, we reflexively turn to ourselves and say: "Savages, what kind of uncivilized people would act this way?"

Untreated emotional injuries get played out in legal settings all the time. The law becomes the hammer for a wounded person's misplaced rage. Lawyers rename the hurt and the indignity and call it something else—the breach of a contract or the failure to exercise due care—which doesn't at all speak to the underlying grievance. The character of the hurt materializes as a *legal* injury, even though it began as a *spiritual* one. But even in this new guise—particularly in this new guise—the grief remains.

The transformation of emotional injuries into legal complaints occurs frequently. Breached promises in commercial contract settings result in hostile lawsuits; the same with the breach of a marriage contract, which constitutes an even more inviolable broken promise. Just as former business partners make claims to clients and accounts that were once shared, so, too, do former spouses seek to hoard the most important assets of the marital alliance: the children. Battles over accounts or clients, or assets and children, even for the ultimate winner, is often an ex-

pression of powerlessness, the deep resentment that stems from a
union—one that was supposed to last forever—suddenly coming
undone. In divorces, the children and the assets are beside the
point. Spoils of war in a spoiled marriage. But they are surely
conduits in a legal system that allows no other way for once mar-
ried people to speak to one another at a time when they find
themselves broken and unbound. Yet, when the law reduces
healing to the hostile division of assets, this legal remedy results
not in healing, but in further breakage.

The legal system allows, if not encourages, people operating
in their most vulnerable and grievous states to march into court
and slug it out in misapplied, pathological, and ruinous ways.
Courthouses are legally sanctioned fight clubs, welcoming immoral, emotionally destructive contests that bring about little relief and tremendous suffering. In this way, the legal system is
morally not that much unlike the coliseums of Ancient Rome, or
the rings of the World Wrestling Federation.

When the legal case is over, the emotions remain very much
undischarged. The fighting won't end simply because a gavel has
been pounded. The parties will inevitably resume the fight elsewhere—perhaps with other people—and find other trophies to
fight over. Hard-fought victories are ultimately surrendered to
the other party, proving that what was at stake was not the
clients, the assets, or the children, but the indignity and the rav-
aged pride.

If we know only one thing about William Shakespeare's *Merchant of Venice*, it is that the tale has something to do with a
"pound of flesh." And, of course, most people, when they think
of the play, recall Shylock as being one of Shakespeare's supreme
villains. What kind of person, after all, would negotiate a pound
of flesh as satisfaction for an unpaid debt? Who would want
human flesh as damages for material harm done in a commer-

cial transaction? It seems especially absurd when you consider that Shylock is offered treble monetary damages in exchange for abandoning his claim to Antonio's anatomy. Shylock rejects this far more lucrative remedy, and rabidly, repeatedly exclaims: "I crave the law. . . . I want my bond! . . . I stand for judgment!"

As an archetypal figure in a Shakespearean tragedy, Shylock is a man uttering the language of law, yet he has no idea what he is saying, or, better yet, he believes that he is saying the right thing, because that's all he's been told to say. Shylock is only parroting the language that presumably leads to justice, and therefore he frames his grievance in unmistakably legal terms, transforming the emotions of deep hurt into the syntax of a broken contract. His words are misplaced, and his remedy is barbaric, but he has no other means to express his pain and make things right. But the justice system isn't about making things right, so ultimately the law is the wrong place for Shylock to turn.

Shylock demands his bond, and yet he repeatedly reminds the audience, and the other Venetians on stage, that he is very much aware that the pound of human flesh is useless and valueless to him. He is a moneylender, a successful and sophisticated businessman. He knows he would be better off accepting a pound of an animal's flesh rather than Antonio's, yet it is not the rational, sensible businessman who is speaking here, but rather a man who has been exposed to far too much indignity, humiliation, and shame. And that exposure has rendered him spiritually damaged, paralyzed with a sickness of the soul. Antonio's flesh, which can't be consumed, can at least feed Shylock's revenge. His pleas for justice are animated by rage but mistakenly expressed through the language of law.

So much of what passes for immoral justice in America is the failure of the legal system to appreciate that all clients, victims, and parties are, to some extent, variations on Shylock. They come to the law overwhelmed by a tremendous backstory of pain that is often unrelated to the causes before the court. The physical injury provides the excuse to seek restitution or revenge for spiritual harms that the legal system would otherwise never find actionable. Desperately they cling for a legal remedy when what they need is a moral one. Broken, dispirited, and alone, they are the human embodiment of the fictional character of Shylock. They may have been harmed mercilessly, and yet they are being asked to show mercy. They have experienced pain, but no one is acknowledging it, or is interested in providing them with any relief other than the legal equivalent of a placebo.

Most people visit lawyers because they need a place to cry, and they enter courtrooms because they believe they are venues in which to be heard. But while sitting in their lawyer's office, rather than being encouraged to cry, they are advised that the law provides no relief for this type of injury, or they are directed by their lawyers to sue. These are the only offered options. The lawsuit becomes the legal ritual that puts everything else in motion, while the nonsuit shows the law as being unwilling to hear anything at all. In either case, these technical features of the law set new fires without extinguishing old ones.

The lawyer hears the client speak, but he is not really listening. The language of grievance goes unheard. The lawyer's mind trails off into an internal hard drive of form files and a check list of tactical legal maneuverings. The individual is reduced to a nameless plaintiff or defendant, analogized to other forgotten individuals whose factual circumstances are similar. Soon he will receive a docket number to mark his case among the multitudes awaiting disposition in the courts. Individuality is lost. The lawyer relinquishes any instincts for empathy that he might have had. An aggressive stance is erected, a defensive posture assumed.

The attorney-client relationship usually begins with a classic case of two people speaking different languages. While the lawyer is thinking legal action, the client is feeling the hurt. The client doesn't start out knowing any legal lingo, but he quickly becomes fluent. By the end of the consultation, thanks to the lawyer's framing of the problem in entirely legal, rather than moral, terms, the client's cry of hurt has been redeployed—in the worst sort of way.

Most novices to the civil legal system only know about monetary settlements and jury awards as examples of relief. (And in the criminal area, victims believe that all they can look forward to is seeing the offender behind bars.) They have been told that this is what the law provides in the event of an injury. Maybe they have read a billboard with an 800 phone number and a catchphrase that reads: "You may be entitled to money damages..." The client arrives at his lawyer's office suffering from injury, yet filled with hope that relief is possible, and that justice can be done. The client's imagination is limitless. Any combination of remedies might address the hurt. But lawyers are among the worst people to visit in these situations, because they have no sense of alternative remedies or other paradigms of repair, and have a distorted sense of what a remedy even is. The lawyer's imagination is forever locked into a cruise control that leads to the courthouse. The language of law is not amenable to bilingual education.

What the client is desperately trying to do is express a grievance, a wound, a hurt. In many ways he suffers from a condition of insufficient grieving. He probably shouldn't see a lawyer, at least not yet. But he has been persuaded to seek relief, and lawyers are the purveyors of the false relief that the law provides.

Sometimes clients are articulate in their attempts at stating their case against those who have done them wrong. But often, incapacitated by grief, the client can't express what he or she is actually feeling. And sometimes the hurt is so deep—formed over a sustained period of time and calcified from repeated abuse—that the emotions completely hijack any intelligible thought.

And that's when the Shylock factor sets in. In *The Merchant of Venice*, the pound of flesh is presented as a legal remedy to a commercial dispute. But what's needed is actually a moral remedy to the indignities that preceded the contract and which were inflamed by its breach. No matter what Shylock says, he would forgive the debt if he were to receive respect and friendship in return. The failure of Antonio's ships to come in is a smokescreen that obscures Shylock's grief. It might have been the basis for his lawsuit, but his true grievance is not contractual in nature. What rankles Shylock to the brink of legal madness is a spiritual injury, one that the law could never fix in its rigidly formulaic, conventional way of thinking.

Shylock is not after money or flesh, or anything material for that matter. Shylock doesn't know his true ailment, and, tragically, the law doesn't wish to know it, either. The law offers no legal remedy for indignity and disrespect.*

The legal system and its servants, operating without moral vision and imagination, remain slaves to a narrow perspective of limiting remedies to cash and jail time—the conventional legal paradigm—and defining justice in either monetary, retributive, or punitive terms. This does little to relieve vast grievances that neighbors and strangers inflict upon one another, and which society largely ignores. As Lee Taft, an assistant dean at the Harvard Divinity School, wrote in the *Yale Law Journal*, "payments of large verdicts or settlement monies failed to heal the deep wounds of many clients; they continued to suffer and express lingering feelings of anger and resentment."

---

*Ironically, Portia's "mercy seasons justice" speech in Act IV, Scene I, is an attempt to offer Shylock an alternative remedy, but one that still doesn't acknowledge the spiritual injuries that he has, in fact, suffered. The court ultimately places the burden on him to show mercy in exchange for salvation. But the court doesn't require a reciprocal acknowledgment from the various merchants of Venice that they have caused Shylock great spiritual pain. In a case of true Venetian blinds, the merchants don't confront their own complicity in having created the conditions whereby Shylock believes that he has no choice other than to sue, and dismember, Antonio.

Legal complaints are inadequate to the task of remedying the interior world of simmering hurts. All those lifeless motions, mechanical answers, and far too affirmative defenses only testify to the law's spiritual impotence and lack of empathy. Yes, people wish to have remedies that are grounded in law, and money and jail sentences invariably play a role in the remedy process. But what they primarily need—at least in the first instance—is relief from their grief.

But grief conjures the interior world of the emotions, while the law defines itself as having only an external agenda, trafficking in the raw materials of physical evidence and tangible harms. For lawyers to assume the soul as a client would change the nature of their profession, which prides itself on emotional and professional detachment, a basic aloofness from the human experience. Lawyers deliberately stand apart from us—esquires with their fancy suits and high-bar affiliations.

Indeed, lawyers, like other professionals, have almost a pathological fear of commingling their professional and public spheres of existence with their moral and private ones. To do so would risk contaminating their objectivity, which would presumably compromise their effectiveness. When there is a job to be done there is no room for a private conscience. How else is it possible for people to build concentration camps during the day and read poetry at night, or to advocate vigorously on behalf of guilty people and return home to the innocence of a child?

The critically acclaimed television show *The Sopranos* is entirely about this idea: the banality of murder, the separation between the moral and professional selves, the way in which a grotesquely violent job can be completely divorced from the domestic responsibilities of a middle-class family man. What makes *The Sopranos* so compellingly interesting is not the violence, of which there is surprisingly little for a drama about the Mafia. America tunes in because we see something of ourselves oddly represented within its cast of mobsters: divided and relativistic in our moral perspectives and self-regard, feeling as though we do the right thing when in so many areas of our lives we do not. We manage to live our lives, marry and maintain families, attend churches and synagogues, without conflict about these other, emotionally set-aside contradictions.

But how can lawyers solve human problems while willfully removing themselves from the heartache that is humanity? Whether they like it or not, lawyers are in the healing business. It's just that their medicine bags are filled with the wrong instruments. They are like doctors still relying on leeching and unicorn horns as cures for human ailments, and this is why the alchemy of lawyering often leaves the patient empty, deracinated, and without relief.

The fact is, you can't heal someone if you won't hold them—in some cases, literally—and the legal system is simply not about holding anybody. I don't mean containing people in a jail, but embracing them as human beings. That's what frightened citizens require. And that's what decent people do when in the presence of human vulnerability. In the aftermath of loss, betrayal, and disappointment, most people need to be steadied and reassured. They need to have someone hold their hand, to dispel any fears that the world will go away and leave them abandoned and alone. A mere touch can feel like the weight of an anchor for someone who needs to be held.

Doctors have always known this. And, actually, they have only recently begun to relearn this magic cure of their profession after decades of impersonal, remote, and detached specialization. Hands-off medicine, with all its blinking mechanical gadgetry, has indeed led to medical miracles. But at the same time, the absence of the doctor's human touch has also given rise to deep resentment by patients who longed for the days when bedside manners was one of the tricks stored inside a doctor's medicine bag. There is little doubt that, as doctors became more specialized and cut off from the suffering of their patients, medical malpractice litigation increased, even though doctors had, in fact, become more skilled and capable of healing than ever before. Yet patient satisfaction declined, largely because patients reasonably believed that doctors neither cared about nor treated them as human beings. A national survey conducted in 1999 by the Association of American Medical Colleges learned that only 27 percent of patients felt that it mattered what medical school their doctor attended when it came to choosing their physicians, but 85 percent would select a doctor based on his or her communication skills or caring attitudes. When house calls and handholding ended, so, too, did an effective way of treating patients: the psychic, spiritual, and curative benefits that come from listening and laying your hands on a sick person who desperately wants to be touched.

Lawyers, however, are not trained in the art of empathy. What lawyers are trained to do is think like lawyers—emotionally withdrawn, narrowly focused, morally obtuse. But that alone makes them lousy hand-holders. The failure of the law to hold people, to acknowledge their hurt, to essentially say to them, "I've got you; you will not go through this process alone," even when the law fails—particularly when the law fails—is a moral crime in its own right, and one that accounts for much of the cynicism and discontent that the general public has toward the legal profession. If the lawyer is unwilling to hold his client in physical and emotional ways and to provide a forum in which the client can speak of his grief, then what good is he?

"All I desire is the ventilation of a public grievance," says Joseph K. in Franz Kafka's *Trial*.

Grief is what animates and inflames most lawsuits. And what defuses them, even before they begin, are acknowledgments and apologies. In any moral society, grievances, injuries, and indignities must be acknowledged. When someone has experienced loss, leaving him alone in his pain and pretending that it is better not to mention it lest he be reminded of his grief, is not a commendable moral gesture. It is our own selfish wish not to be disturbed, or to be made to feel uncomfortable. Because we all know that loss is not easily forgotten—certainly not by the aggrieved. They, specifically, want for us not to forget, as well. Loss has to be appropriately named, and remembered. It has to become part of a narrative, a story for the victims and survivors, and for ourselves. And if we can't acknowledge loss properly outside the courthouse, then it is the duty of the legal system to take account of these hurts and grievances in the application of the law itself.

Yet, there is such apparent difficulty in our species to acknowledge loss, or to apologize for actions that have harmed others. It is as though our human wiring prevents us from performing these essentially moral acts. Our DNA seems better conditioned for denial, and that's why our legal system is such an overworked, underachieving enterprise. Justice in America is a reality game show that involves sifting through tidal waves of denial and barricades of human defensiveness.

What judges and lawyers never seem to understand is how little the lay person cares about the evolution of rules and precedents, and how much he simply wants to tell his story. The best way to heal a grievance is to name it, to have it proclaimed, to discover the underlying truths, to unbury the silences, to find the facts that are true both literally and emotionally—so that the pain becomes acknowledged to the world.

Put simply: The story itself is and provides its own remedy. The story is what people come to the courthouse to recite, and it is as powerful as any punishment or judgment. If nothing else gets accomplished, if criminals go free and tortfeasors succeed in causing further negligence, the telling of the story, by itself, is still the morally correct outcome. Giving people an opportunity to speak about what happened to them, and to confront those who are responsible for their hurt, is an indispensable part of what it means to do justice, and to administer a legal system that is just. And that's why the community is brought in as witnesses, to serve as jurors and to listen not just to the proceedings, but, more important, to the pain. An official record is created and preserved, and the community maintains its own memory. And together this all provides temporary relief. The aggrieved have the right to shout their pain out to the world, and the courthouse must be their megaphone.

Yet the legal system has completely lost its bearings; lawyers have forgotten, or have never learned, what it is that clients are asking them to facilitate—not just some vindication, but a true resolution. What does it mean to be given a hearing if nothing is being said, because there is no trial, or when what's been expressed resulted in an incomplete and unfaithful telling of the story? If trials go dark, like Broadway theaters on Monday nights, then how can we expect truths to come to light? Truth is what trials are convened to accomplish, but we increasingly support and tolerate a legal system that supervises fewer and fewer trials. Over ninety-five percent of all civil and criminal cases end either in settlements or plea arrangements, without ever reaching a formal trial. How much truth is being sacrificed to the administration of a justice system that is more concerned about administration than it is about the actual delivery of justice?

A court of law should certainly be a place of judgment, vindication, and even retribution. But it also should function as a sanctuary for truth-telling, with remedies limited not just to law, but to personal healing, as well. Most lawyers, however, have never considered the idea that all a client might want is to be heard, to have the truth come out and the pain acknowledged, even if he or she winds up being uncompensated and uncured. From a lawyer's point of view, what's a remedy if it produces neither punishment nor compensation? At the end of a lawyer's day, all that matters is that a check get written, or that a criminal pay his debt to society or be declared innocent. Relief can't come from having a story merely told. This kind of collective lawyerly thinking demonstrates once more the legal system's blind spot to moral and spiritual relief as a way to ease human suffering.

When attorneys speak of themselves as counselors, they flatter themselves. Similar to their use of the words "remedy" and "relief," "counselor" also has an altogether different meaning from how laymen usually understand it. A counselor is not someone who simply advises people of their rights, or explains what can be done under the law. A counselor, instead, provides true counsel. He has to listen and be engaged, he must enter the attorney-client relationship as a human being, finding ways— even outside the parameters of what the law provides—of bringing about some measure of relief. A counselor at law knows that "a pound of flesh" is merely a code phrase for a client in pain. An attorney at law, by contrast, sees the same client but ignores the cry and goes directly to filing a legal complaint.

STORY AS REMEDY

A s a novelist, I appreciate the healing benefits that come from the telling of a story—even a fictional one. Actually, as a novelist, it is my prerogative to tell made-up stories in any way I choose—the front story and the back, told from beginning to end, without interruption, without objection, without being overruled or dismissed or censored in any way. This is far more than can be said for those who appear before the law, where stories and truth are often trumped by administrative, efficiency-promoting values. A novelist knows the freedom that comes with narration, the liberty that arises out of the unconscious self. It brings expression to the soul, putting words in its mouth and flesh on bones broken by despair.

Those wounded by business transactions gone bad, failed marriages and severed partnerships, negligent merchants, doctors, and service-providers, and the mischief of criminals, deserve an equivalent freedom. They need to be able to experience what the novelist already knows, and what the injured intuitively sense: that there is no way to heal emotionally from an injury if the story goes unheard and victims are denied their moral right to testify to their own pain. And the appropriate remedy to redress such harms often transcends the mere impulse toward retribution and revenge.

When the novelist or playwright—whether a Camus, Dickens, Melville, or Shakespeare—focuses on the legal system, what they so often observe is the way in which stories get stifled. The law, in its pursuit of justice, somehow winds up thwarting the telling of the tale. There is an irony in this, because while the novelist is a natural storyteller, so, too, is the lawyer. It is technically part of his job: framing the client's case in narrative terms, assisting him in what to say. The novelist has a similar task: laying out the story, strategically setting up the plot, putting words in the mouths of his characters—with readers playing the role of jurors.

Yet, this is only true in principle. While both the lawyer and the novelist tell stories, much of a lawyer's job is devoted to narrowing the story, keeping it simple and straightforward. The novelist seeks to expand the canvas of life, to account for the alleged facts and unrevealed emotions, to include as much of the human drama and dynamic as possible. The lawyer, on the other hand, fears that such open, liberal narration will only confuse the issues. For him, what matters most is what is played out in front of the judge—the external and immediate responses, the spontaneous gestures and slip-ups that might betray guilt or innocence. The lawyer is mostly linear in his approach to life, while the artist leans willingly into all the bends and curves, stepping over lines and never standing in them. The lawyer talks about motive, but only clinically and legally speaking. The novelist, by contrast, is obsessed with human motivation—in all phases, and regardless of legal consequence.

When a novelist turns to the law and transforms it into art, he or she wants to know what brought the characters to the courthouse and rendered them so fragile, and what will it take—morally and emotionally—to bring about true justice and relief. Artists, unlike lawyers, look beyond the external. They are much more comfortable with a human condition that leaves no finger-prints, hair follicles, blood samples, or evidentiary traces. The interior world is their domain, and in such recesses of life there are no Exhibit A's, nothing to document or substantiate, no signs of physical proof to be found.

But, if both lawyers and artists are natural storytellers, and lawyers have a moral duty to help tell the stories of their clients, then why would they abdicate what might be the most vital and essential calling of their profession?

I have had to, on occasion, tell my own story in a court of law, and experienced what most people feel in similar circumstances: that the court isn't listening, and that it doesn't really matter what you have to say. Oftentimes a trial is merely a show trial. It's there for everyone's amusement or boredom, except for those who need it the most—those who came to court seeking relief. Sometimes an appearance before a judge has no real bearing on the outcome. The court has already made up its mind, and nothing that might be said is going to change it. The injured person is only patronizingly allowed to say his piece, if at all, while everyone in the courtroom is doodling or day-dreaming, or staring at the clock, or biding time until recess. The official hearing is not accompanied by parallel listening. Instead of judgment there is prejudgment, which is just a variation on prejudice.

I can understand the frustrations and resentments that the public has with attorneys. We want something from them—their counsel, their sound judgment, their advocacy. But their vision of what they can do for us is so myopically constrained by professional habit that our screams become redirected toward them, instead of the world or those who have caused us harm. Yet, lawyers remain inured to both our words, and our screams.

As a lawyer, I see all the fault lines of the law—the way in which stories are swallowed up without ever having been heard.

As a novelist, I speak the language of people who, more than anything else, want to hear their stories told.

The case of the surviving victims and families of the September 11th tragedy is an excellent example of the law's emotional and moral insensitivity to storytelling. Soon after the World Trade Center collapse, Congress established the Victim Compensation Fund, which it created in order to place a cap on legal claims arising out of the tragedy. Families and victims who received compensation under the fund were required to relinquish any individual lawsuits against either the airlines or the Port Authority of New York and New Jersey (which owned the World Trade Center) that they may have otherwise contemplated. The fund essentially served to prevent the ruination of the airline industry by victims who might have chosen to pursue individual claims—relentlessly and without limitation.

But there is a problem here, one of immoral justice. In all situations involving mass-tort litigation and class actions, individual members of the class are deprived of an opportunity to tell their individual stories. This is the consequence of being part of a class. Everyone is reduced to a number, one claimant among many, with nothing special or unique other than their similar injuries and a common agent, enterprise, or product that caused them. The lawsuit offers no special attention—legal or otherwise—on how the harm specifically damaged individual lives, and the ongoing effect that the harm has had on those lives.

In any class action, the moral component of every lawsuit—providing a forum in which to speak to the injury and the loss—is completely undermined and defeated. The victims do not receive an opportunity to speak at all. Or, if they do, the privilege is granted only to the few whose stories of injury and pain are deemed most representative of the class, or who might make the best witnesses. What the court wishes to hear is simply a general narrative of how the harm occurred, what damages were generally caused, what damages might recur, and nothing further. The court is not interested in specific, individual tales of hardship, and does not wish to hear a recitation of the basic facts and stories of endured suffering over and over again. The point of certifying a class action is to avoid the needless, wasteful duplication of tedious lawsuits that each assert the same legal claims. Of course the problem is that while legal issues arguably are handled more efficiently in a class action, the emotional issues are not so seamlessly consolidated.

Each class member requires more than an assigned number and the promise of a fair allocation from the eventual damage award. There has to be the acknowledgment of individual suffering, a sense that, behind the number, some human loss has taken place. When remedies are limited to a fixed portion of a monetary pie, victims can't see any other way to value their loss and relieve their grief other than by demanding a larger share of that pie—even if the pie itself is not something that they, initially, cared so much about.

The Victim Compensation Fund will divide roughly six billion dollars among the victims of September 11th and their surviving families. To make this distribution, the relevant factors have been largely reduced to a table of numbers that measures loss and calculates damages based on life expectancy and future earning potential. More value is being placed on economic loss than on emotional loss; indeed, typical of the conventional legal paradigm, the fund provides no mechanism to measure emotional loss. Aside from some discretion that Kenneth Feinberg, the special master whom Congress appointed to preside over the fund, has reserved for himself, the tables and formulas pretty much dictate the numerical outcome.

Limited by these strict mathematical guidelines, there are great disparities and inequities in the way some surviving families have been treated. The surviving spouse of a young childless bond trader who earned several hundred thousand dollars a year was entitled to a larger recovery than the widow of a middle-aged fireman who had two children, but whose annual income was considerably less than that of the bond trader's. However, applying the formulas and tables strictly would entitle the bond trader's spouse to receive an even greater portion of the fund than would be ultimately awarded. Fearing the public outcry to such gaping disparities, Feinberg did not allow this to happen. The point is that, when the fund was allocated, the lives of firemen and bond traders were each undervalued, though for different reasons. With respect to firemen, the formula did not account for anything other than their lost earnings; and with bond traders, the shortchanging was due to a reckoning with political realities.

Aside from these inequities, it is clear that the creation of the fund itself—ultimately and predictably—was morally unjust. Depriving surviving families of their individual stories of loss, and reducing their suffering to lifeless numbers that measured nothing but earning potential, provided insufficient relief. Loss must always be accounted for in ways that transcend the cold calculations of an accountant. Monetary relief, while legally sound, does not provide emotional relief, because it doesn't speak individually and uniquely to a loss. The legal system, however, operates quite smugly on the assumption that it does.

Courthouses are not places to bury truths, but to uncover them. It is where the records are housed, and the transcripts maintained. It is where the proceedings are witnessed by as many people as possible. The more the public sees, the more likely the lessons will be learned. The long arm of the law should extend itself to producing long memories. The moral imperative of a courthouse is to put those echoey exteriors to good use: giving voice to all those raw feelings of implacable loss.

It is true that Congress did not intend to value all lives lost on September 11th equally—at least not economically. But the larger issue is that surviving victims and families were given no means to obtain relief other than to accept a dollar amount that morally undervalued their loss. Money is never sufficiently compensatory, no matter how high the amount. Bereavement requires healing, but the legal system's balm confuses people into thinking of money as curative, rather than what it is, simply remunerative.

In a legal system that is good with numbers but lousy with empathy, what can a surviving relative do to honor a loved one other than demand the highest payout possible? As one father of a fireman was quoted in the *New Yorker:*

"You'll hear it said many times here that people don't care about the money, and it's true, we don't. But somehow the higher the amount, the more value then put on your loved one's life, the more meaning it has."

Since legal justice measures life strictly in monetary terms, and offers no other remedy that responds to grief, it sends a lifeless, inexplicable message that only the largest number somehow compensates for loss. This is basically a problem of limited options, since the legal system offers no moral or emotional alternative.

That same *New Yorker* article reported the following hostile exchange between Feinberg and a woman who had lost her sister:

"We've suffered enough. Why are you making our lives even more complicated? Make something easy, make everyone happy. I know you're all about the numbers, and the statute, and the regulations, and this computation, and this deduction.... We don't need to make a plea. We're not begging for money. We want our people back."

"I can't make you happy."

"Yes, you can."

The woman was sure that the law, in response to perhaps this nation's greatest tragedy, could show some heart and find a decent and moral way to relieve the grief. She wanted the special master to do something special, to make the surviving relatives happy—or as happy as they could be under the circumstances—

and not to have them feel cheated, stifled, and humiliated. She didn't know exactly how to bring this about, but she was pretty certain that the law would fail if all it did was rely on crunched numbers, spread sheets, and the coldness of an abacus.

Feinberg, a quintessential mass tort specialist who had presided over many cases involving deaths from toxic substances, was equally sure that the law is not a provider of happiness, that it cannot resurrect or reclaim the dead. And spiritual relief—to the extent to which that was what the woman was seeking—was not something Feinberg was trained or empowered to provide, nor did he particularly know what it even meant. As special master, he is simply the man who divides up the money; he is not engaged in the service of mending or repair.

"I refuse to make distinctions," Feinberg said in an article in the *New York Times Magazine*. "I refuse to go down the road of 'He was on the 103rd floor and died a slow death; she was on the 84th floor and was killed instantly.' I'm not getting into that."

But if he wasn't going to get into those distinctions—the different ways in which people died; the uniqueness of their suffering; what kind of people they were while they were alive; what remains after they've gone—then who would?

In time, even Feinberg was forced to consider the incompatibility between grief and money. By September 2003, less than four months before the looming deadline for filing applications under the statute that created the Victim Compensation Fund, only 60 percent of the surviving families had sought compensation by filing claims. And only sixty-nine private lawsuits—those that rejected the presumed efficiency and tax incentives of the fund in favor of a potentially more risky, and lucrative, private remedy—had been filed. Since 3,016 people died in the attacks and only 1,309 total claims or lawsuits had been filed by their surviving relatives, one question remained: Where were all the litigants that lawyers would naturally have assumed to have surfaced? Indeed, if these people failed to file their applications by

December 22, they would end up being barred from seeking compensation under the fund altogether. Surely they would want to recover for their losses. So why were they waiting?

The answer, of course, is not one that the conventional legal paradigm is particularly good at supplying. The reason so many never filed their claims was not because of legal gamesmanship or neglect, but rather spiritual deprivation. Grief, not money, is what shadows the aftermath of loss. Grief is what dominates the minds of survivors—if their minds are functioning at all. Feinberg wondered publicly what happened to the surviving relatives he was instructed to compensate. What he didn't realize was that most were still grieving, too paralyzed to confront their emotional pain in a forum that would do nothing but reduce their broken hearts to whole numbers. Filing papers may be the first and necessary step to receiving material compensation, but reliving the memories all for the sake of money is not the way to relieve grief.

"I have met with thousands of families," Feinberg acknowledged in an article in the *New York Times*. "And you would be amazed at the number of people who, when I say the deadline is approaching, still come up to me in tears and say, 'I'm not ready.' "

Actually, he shouldn't have been that surprised at all.

In early 2003, in a German courtroom, five surviving relatives of the victims of September 11th confronted the man who was accused of supporting the plot. He was being prosecuted as an accessory to the crime, and the German court, unlike an American one, allowed the families to function as co-plaintiffs to the action, as opposed to mere quasi-witnesses. One of the witnesses on behalf of the co-plaintiffs, Stephen Push, whose wife died on the airplane that crashed into the Pentagon, said in the Hamburg courtroom: "I am testifying because I believe that before this court passes judgment and sentence on the defendant, the court should see the human face of the tragedy." Another witness, Michael Lowe, whose daughter was a flight attendant on the first plane that struck the World Trade Center, testified, "I have traveled a long distance to let the court know firsthand the extraordinary devastation my family experienced."

The German trial wasn't about money but rather emotion, healing, and truth. And, for this reason, the German court wanted to hear about the human experience of loss—not economic loss or actuarial loss, but simply what it feels like to lose someone you love.

What's clear is that the surviving families of September 11th were given insufficient legal options in which to grieve. There was no occasion for stirring up the individual stories, giving them life even amidst all that collective death. And so, without alternative remedies, the families were forced into the conventional legal paradigm, even though the tragedy that forever ruined their lives was anything but conventional, and required extra-delicate, extraordinarily uncommon relief. It compounded the loss, truly adding insult to injury.

In the aftermath of the World Trade Center tragedy, what was necessary was not merely legal justice, but moral and historical justice as well. Never before in our nation's history was it so morally crucial for the stories of the individual lives of the innocent and the heroic to be told. The larger drama had been carried around the clock on television, but it was silent in the courthouses. Given the specialness of this crime and the sadistic nature in which the attacks occurred, the legal system had the moral duty to offer relief on a human and emotional level, in addition to relief of the conventional, material kind.

Perhaps the September 11th tragedy provided the perfect moment to open the courthouses and let them function as public grieving grounds, enabling families to come in and speak of their losses, to present proof of the lives that were taken away from them, to try to express how empty and painful it is to forge ahead when everything that mattered has turned to dust. Courthouses would have become affiliate funeral parlors for extended eulogies,

and these courthouse confessions of grief should have been captured on national television. This is the true path to moral justice:
a legal system that is as much interested in grieving, healing, and
restoration as it is in compensation and punishment.

But, in response to a tragedy that more than anything else
cried out for spiritual relief and moral justice, again the system
failed. The victims of September 11th were speaking one language, while the law jabbered on in its own turgid, predictable,
untranslatable tongue.

With the Victim Compensation Fund essentially closing the
door on the courthouse as a place for surviving families to speak to
their loss in terms other than money, some families, beginning in
April 2003, testified before the National Commission on Terrorist
Attacks Upon the United States. Congress created this panel in
order to conduct a broad investigation on how the tragic events of
September 11th had been allowed to happen, with specific instructions to examine the failures of government agencies and the
intelligence community. Not surprisingly, however, when the
panel first convened to hear public testimony, victims and surviving family members appeared as either witnesses, or merely sat in
the audience, holding up pictures of their loved ones. Congress
may not have created the panel for this purpose, but in light of its
open, public nature, and its specific September 11th agenda, these
survivors were naturally drawn to the hearings. They would have
traveled anywhere to experience the moment and memorialize
the loss. For them, it was tantamount to a public vigil, a continuous act of mourning. They attended the hearing not to file claims
or to plead for money, but only to voice and seek truth, to tell their
stories, and to honor the dead—enabling their stories with some
immediate, narrative life. Indeed, given the legal system's failure
to provide a public forum for these damaged individuals to express
their grief, any audience that is created for a September 11th–
related purpose is where we should always expect to find them—
from now on and forever.

It is unfair to place too much blame on Kenneth Feinberg. After all, he was merely doing his job, and even in more ordinary loss scenarios (death by car accidents, negligent medical procedures), the legal system's insistence on quantifying economic loss rather than acknowledging the emotional void created by that loss, leads to similar examples of moral and emotional disgust. For instance, in most survivor actions, parents of grown children are discouraged from filing lawsuits, because damages are routinely based on economic loss. And such losses are recoverable by the parents of grown children only when the children had financially supported the parents. When children are young, courts find ways to quantify other intangible losses, such as the loss of enjoyment. Yet the same effort to put a number on the emotional loss of an adult child is not usually made, nor is it necessarily what the surviving parents would even want.

It has always been this way. Even in 1904, in the New York case of *Predmore v. Consumers' Light & Power Co.*, the court refused to place a dollar value on grief unless the loss could be tied to some economic harm. Many subsequent New York cases have relied on the language of this decision in denying wrongful-death claims to parent-survivors unless they are able to show either economic dependency or some tangible pecuniary loss from the demise of an adult child.

The court wrote its instruction to the jury as follows: "Here was a son twenty-one years old. The father is advanced in years. How much money or money's worth do you think, on your oaths, this plaintiff, this father, would have received from his son if he had lived? That is the measure of all the recovery that you are entitled to give the plaintiff. You must discard all sympathy. If you do not, you will do injustice. You must confine yourselves absolutely to what, in your conservative judgment, it can fairly be said that this plaintiff would, in all human probability, have received in the way of money or moneys worth from his son if he had lived."

Any consideration other than the economic injury to the father would be an injustice, the court ruled. All sympathy must be discarded, which effectively eliminates any legal acknowledgment of the emotional harm that is traceable to a broken heart.

Earlier I discussed the film, *In the Bedroom,* and how the parents of a murdered son have no place to take their grief when the legal system fails to provide justice. In the film, the parents resort to self-help, which perhaps gives them some ambivalent sense of relief, and leaves motion-picture audiences unsure of just how to feel. The parents, in good faith, first wait for the engine of law to run its course. When it sputters and then stops, they seek to complete the journey toward justice by taking their own route, on their own terms.

In the civil area, the law does not meaningfully provide surviving parents of adult children with even an initial option. There is functionally no role for the courthouse at all, and therefore not even a nominally acceptable way for these people to address their grief. In the usual case, even though money isn't necessarily what a claimant wants as a remedy, grief is strangely quantified in the law, and money is all the law conventionally allows. In civil cases in which an adult child has lost his or her life, money isn't even available as a possible remedy for the surviving parents. This leaves the surviving parents of grown children with no civil method to either speak to or recover from their loss—in either economic or spiritual terms.

What if *In the Bedroom* had been a film that dealt with the same issue in a civil rather than in a criminal context? Would audiences have been equally sympathetic to parents who lost their adult child not because of a crime, but due to someone's negligence, and were given no opportunity to bring a civil suit because their economic loss was negligible, even though their emotional loss was vast and unimaginable? Would we have granted them the moral right to seek retribution as justice, or would we have regarded them as cold-blooded murderers? When the legal system leaves victims feeling unrelieved and empty, they become capable of all manner of inspired, self-help relief.

Another example of a favorable legal result that did not necessarily provide an equally satisfying moral one was found in the recent Holocaust restitution initiatives. In 1995, more than forty years after Germany approved making restitution payments to the surviving victims of Nazi persecution, Jewish leaders traveled to Switzerland to meet with officials from the Swiss Bankers Association to discuss the status of dormant accounts once held by Holocaust victims, along with the trading of looted Jewish assets, including gold, which had been deposited in Swiss banks during World War II.

This meeting eventually led to the creation of a commission to investigate the conduct of Swiss banks during the war, and an Executive Monitoring Committee comprised of nine hundred state and city financial officers to force the Swiss, through sanctions and the halting of deposits, to respond to these allegations more seriously and forthrightly. In October 1996, the first of several class-action lawsuits was filed in the United States against Swiss banks on behalf of Holocaust survivors and their heirs.

President Bill Clinton appointed then undersecretary for international trade, later deputy treasury secretary, Stuart Eizenstat, to examine American archives and to negotiate with the Swiss, and other European countries, in an effort to reach an overall settlement. Through these diplomatic initiatives, government regulatory pressures, and class-action lawsuits, the Swiss banks agreed in 1998 to a $1.25 billion settlement. The challenge to the Swiss banks soon led to other lawsuits, diplomatic negotiations, and eventual settlements with the German government and private companies on behalf of those who were victims of forced and slave labor. What followed were additional negotiations with Austria, Norway, Britain, France, the Netherlands, as well as several major European insurance companies, for actions taken in connection with looted property, unpaid insurance policies, and the slave labor of Jewish victims of the Holocaust. Several of these initiatives resulted in settlements of varying success, the French case perhaps the most exemplary, often involving profound compromises with regard to the level of disclosure of victims' assets and formulas for compensation. A dozen countries also agreed to pay restitution for gold bars seized from the Nazis after the war—gold that had been obtained from melting down former Jewish assets, including tooth fillings. Restitution also included stolen art works taken from victims of the Holocaust. Together these various settlements totaled between $8 and $10 billion.

A terrific legal victory, right? But what of its moral significance? Sure, the payment of money as damages always contains some moral dimension. Money and moral relief are not always unaligned. In this instance, these offending nations should not have been permitted to profit all these years from their ill-gotten gains. (Actually, while $10 billion sounds like a lot of money, it represents only a fraction of what these countries should have been required to pay in order to account, accurately, and with interest, for all the misdeeds and theft traceable to their World War II endeavors.) Disgorging these nations of stolen assets was a morally righteous and just act.*

The problem with the Holocaust restitution initiatives was that there were inadequate provisions for historical or moral justice. The settlement, predictably, was often limited to money at

---

*Indeed, even the surviving families of September 11th would not have been satisfied with moral justice that included only the telling of stories—in courthouses and on national television—without some compensatory component. And they would have wanted those who had been arguably negligent—the airlines, the Port Authority, even the FBI and CIA—to be punished for their neglect. But money alone can never stand in for true moral relief.

the expense of a true and complete accounting that would have disclosed the magnitude of unjust enrichment. The pillaging enterprises, in most cases, purchased the silence of history for a few pennies on the dollar, thereby exploiting the unfortunate conspiracy of time. And there was no priority placed on establishing historical truth, or in prosecuting those who had gone unpunished.

The apologies were perfunctory, at best, not the kind of unequivocal acceptance of responsibility that constitutes a sincere, meaningful, and moral act of contrition. (Germany was, perhaps, the one notable but unsurprising example.) There was neither a proper tallying of the stolen assets, nor a reckoning of the misdeeds. These nations were far more willing to fork over a check than engage in the necessary gestures and rituals that signify a true expression of remorse. They were, in most instances, pressured into issuing formal statements of apology, the contrition totally stripped of sincerity because it did not speak, specifically, to the grotesque crimes committed by them. There were no mandates for a public airing of what these countries had done, how they had allowed this to happen, and who were the agents, abetters, and conspirators of these crimes. The settlements produced no explicit moral lessons for the offending nations, or the world community. Despite a formidable legal victory, we are morally no better able to comprehend this new historical record of humanity's failure in the face of unfettered greed.

These concerns were not addressed, and the answers to them will never be known. And without answers, there can be no moral justice. Worse, Holocaust survivors, already a depleted and near-extinct group, do not believe on the whole that they were meaningfully consulted by Jewish representatives, government negotiators, or most class-action lawyers as to what they would have liked to see arise from these restitution efforts. It is true that survivors had the opportunity to "tell their stories"—but, in most cases, only to their lawyers. The negotiations were then conducted by lawyers and organizational representatives, who, although sometimes including survivors, were not necessarily representative of the victim class. Unfortunately, most survivors believe that they were not given an opportunity—individually or as a group—to say their piece in front of those nations that had deceived and stolen from them, to speak about what had been done nearly sixty years earlier, and what their needs are today.

So, while a legal remedy of money was achieved, to a limited degree and for a limited number of claimants, the moral remedy of having the story of atrocity told and the historical truth revealed cannot be regarded as a major achievement of this recent endeavor at Holocaust restitution.

More recently, in the summer of 2003, after fourteen years of lawsuits and diplomatic negotiations, in a letter delivered to the United Nations, Libya acknowledged its role and accepted responsibility for the bombing of Pan Am flight 103 over Lockerbie, Scotland. Yet at the same time, for many surviving family members, the letter did not go far enough in admitting guilt for the 270 lives that were lost due to its act of international terrorism. Indeed, many of the family members were willing to hold off from accepting the settlement offer, which would have brought each family $10 million, because as a condition for their receiving the full value of the settlement, the United States and the United Nations would have had to lift economic sanctions that had been imposed on Libya, and have Libya removed from the list of states that sponsor terrorism.

Dan and Susan Cohen, who lost a daughter, Theodora, on Pan Am flight 103, were quoted in the *New York Times* challenging various features of the settlement. "[A]ll of the things in the letter about how they cooperated and how they oppose terrorism are utter nonsense," said Susan Cohen. "[T]here is nothing they can say, no amount of money, that can restore my loss." And her husband said, "This is supposed to be about justice and the truth. Instead, what the Libyans proposed amounted to a bribe."

Admittedly, the cases of the Holocaust and September 11th tragedies, and even the downing of Pan Am flight 103, are extreme and uncommon crimes that perhaps require moral relief as much as legal relief. Yet, that does not mean that moral justice is required only in cases of extremity and atrocity. The fact is that most people who come before the law are looking for justice that includes a narrative, truth-seeking, story-preserving dimension. It's just that the legal system, locked and loaded into its unflinching conventional paradigm, is either blind to this need or simply refuses to define relief in moral terms. And so courthouses remain cluttered with casualties of a legal system who have been denied what they needed most. The courthouse, despite all the resonant acoustics and amplifying devices, does not hear the pain that is brought into its halls from the outside world.

THE VARIOUS FACES
OF GRIEF

Generally speaking, lawyers and judges are not very good judges of human nature. That's why they fail to appreciate how much a legal action is driven by grievances grounded in emotion and not law. A complaint is merely a legal artifact; it's not what ordinary people come to court to lodge. They aren't thinking about legal forms and strategies. What they want is for their lawyers to help restore their dignity and to speak to the event that caused it so much damage. No price can be placed on dignity, a lesson learned in life that seemingly has no application in law.

In December 2002, the New York City Transit Union threatened to strike. This would have immobilized the city and caused severe economic hardship, as 7 million people depend on buses and subways each day. A Brooklyn supreme court judge signed an injunction preventing the transit workers from striking, but the union was prepared to ignore the order if the Metro Transit Authority failed to provide them with the concessions they were seeking. With the strike deadline looming, minutes to midnight, a union official held a press conference and, on behalf of his membership, decided to extend the clock, which kept the negotiations going even though a settlement had not yet been reached. Interestingly, the union's gesture of good faith was given without receiving even one extra dollar in financial benefits for its membership. While the union was negotiating principally for money, the progress that they had achieved, and that encouraged them to continue to negotiate, was in the "noneconomic areas of dignity and respect."

When the legendary 1960s Motown girl-group the Supremes was set to embark on a reunion tour in the spring of 2000, Mary Wilson, one of the group's two cofounders (the other being Diana Ross), refused to participate. Although she was offered $3 million for the engagement, she balked, largely because she was asked to join after plans for the tour had already been announced, and because of unresolved personal issues with Ms. Ross. "A lot of my friends said, 'Girl, you should just take the money and run,' " Ms. Wilson was quoted as saying in the *New York Times*. "But my heart has been broken; I've turned the cheek many, many times. I don't need to get myself back in that situation and make myself unhappy."

Similarly, former CNN news anchor Greta Van Susteren decided to leave CNN for the Fox News channel, even though CNN offered her more money to stay. The reason for her abrupt departure: hurt feelings. Among factors contributing to her decision, Ms. Susteren said, was her being upset that the network had been showering more attention on another anchor, Paula Zahn. Ms. Susteren apparently felt that she was being treated as a "second-class citizen." In a letter to the network from her lawyer, which was reported in the *New York Times*, she cited as an example the network's failure to obtain for her an invitation to the White House Christmas party.

While neither of these cases resulted in much legal wrangling, they reveal how deep is the undertow of hurt. Damaged pride is the dark, hovering shadow that settles above courthouses. Dignity is what drives the mind to seek justice, more so than broken bodies. And for this reason, wholly apart from conventional notions of justice, and of course, money, the telling of the story and the public acknowledgment of the wrong is an important value even if it produces nothing concrete, other than the story itself. The story as remedy has significant undervalued appeal. It is a primal need of our species, the first moral step in doing what is just.

Influenced by the legacy of Nuremberg, which I'll discuss more fully in chapter 12, Belgium enacted a law in 1993 (modified and diluted in June 2003 due to pressure from the United States), granting itself "universal jurisdiction" to prosecute perpetrators of war crimes, crimes against humanity, and genocide, even in cases where Belgium has no legal connection to the crime, its perpetrators, or its victims. The Nuremberg trials established that when it comes to genocide, the world is a small place and mass murderers cannot hide behind claims to absolute sovereignty, or invoke territorial borders as a curtain of protection to avoid prosecution. Genocide is a moral crime that requires a moral resolution, and Nuremberg stands for the principle that the world and its citizens have a moral responsibility to prosecute these crimes.

Belgium and some other nations—Israel, in its abduction of Adolf Eichmann, and Spain, in its attempt to extradite Chilean dictator Augusto Pinochet—took Nuremberg's legacy seriously. Victims of extreme human rights abuses availed themselves of Belgian courts to file cases against Saddam Hussein, Fidel Castro, and Yasir Arafat. They brought these lawsuits knowing that, regardless of the result, they would have no way to legally enforce the verdict. The defendants, in all of these instances, ignored the lawsuits and did not appear in the Belgian courthouse to submit to jurisdiction and answer the charges. Belgium, ultimately, had no legal authority to pursue or punish anyone who had been indicted for these crimes. Yet that doesn't mean that this law of universal jurisdiction was not without tremendous moral and symbolic significance.

Eric David, a law professor and an advocate of Belgium's genocide law, said in the *New York Times* "We shouldn't forget that people who have undergone extraordinary suffering have been able to find a country in the world capable of hearing their pain and following up on their demands, even if it is in a purely theoretical way."

When the legal system shuts itself off from the story, it cannot do moral justice. The artist is especially sensitive to this moral deficiency, particularly the way in which settlements, plea bargains, confidentiality agreements, attorney-client privileges, evidentiary rules, zealous advocacy, and statutes of limitations are all favored in the law over the story and the simple truth.

In Sidney Lumet's *Verdict*, Paul Newman's character, Frank Galvin, undergoes almost a religious conversion when he realizes that it is his moral duty to speak for his client, a woman resigned to a vegetative state, forever silenced by a medical procedure negligently performed by her surgeons. She breathes with the assistance of a respirator, and her story will be told only with the help of her lawyer, because she can no longer speak for herself—in the law or elsewhere. Galvin recognizes this as his ultimate duty of representation. (The same duty would be present even if she could function normally, but the point is even more strongly made with a client who is in a coma.)

That a lawyer has a duty, first and foremost, to speak for his client, or to provide an opportunity for the client to speak on his or her own behalf, does not sound like such an original idea. Yet in the civil-law system, in which the impulse to settle the case tramples all other values, it's easy to see how a lawyer might forget what is obvious to almost any layman. Galvin's epiphany, however, is not without conflict. To represent his client faithfully, and morally, Galvin ends up rejecting the advice of everyone else in the film—men of God, in the archdioceses of the Catholic Church; and men of law, comprising fellow attorneys and the presiding judge in the case—all of whom regard settlements with almost religious devotion, articles of faith within a faithless legal system. For them, the object of civil law is to receive compensation for injuries—and as much compensation as possible. And the easiest, most efficient way to accomplish that is to negotiate a settlement, even if that results in no trial and no truth.

By proceeding to trial and having his client's story told, Galvin hopes to persuade the jury to return a verdict that publicly assigns fault and compensates generously for the loss. However, in going forward with the trial, Galvin also risks the possibility of receiving no monetary reward at all. He could lose. His expert witness might not be convincing, or, as it happened, might not even show up. And even if all goes well, the jury might not believe his story. The doctors who harmed his client, among the most respected in their field, might come across as dedicated, sympathetic, and totally blameless. Receiving no money is no small risk, because Galvin's law practice has become a casualty of his excessive drinking. Clearly, accepting a settlement offer makes the most financial sense. In addition, it would satisfy his client's family members, who are the actual, putative clients in this action. This in itself is an absurd legal anomaly, since they are not the ones in a coma.

But Galvin ignores all this advice and instead risks all rewards by proceeding to trial. Because it is only at trial, and through a trial, that the truth can be known, heard, witnessed by others, and recorded for posterity. Galvin believes that it is morally necessary to put the story on the record. He is certain that this is what his comatose client would have wanted. And even if the jury returns a verdict against his client, the decision to bring the case to a public hearing is still a morally righteous act. And one message of the film is that by pursuing the moral path, Galvin still ends up achieving a lucrative material award.

A similar situation unfolds in the film *The Accused* (1988), directed by Jonathan Kaplan and loosely based on a true story. Jodie Foster plays the role of Sara Tobias, a waitress from the side of the tracks where trailers are parked, dreams are unfulfilled, and voices go unheard. Sara is gang-raped one evening in a bar, surrounded by witnesses who not only watch, but also cheer the rapists on. The prosecuting attorney, played by Kelly McGillis, believes that Sara would not be a sympathetic witness for the State in its case against the rapists. There are allegations of drug use, a prior conviction, and, on the night of the rape, Sara was drunk and dancing provocatively. In order to avoid the risks of a trial in which the rapists might be acquitted, and without consulting Sara, the prosecutor negotiates a plea agreement with the various defendants. Each pleads guilty to reckless endangerment rather than rape, and is sent to jail for that lesser crime, thereby receiving a reduced but certain sentence. Sara learns of the plea agreement while watching the news, and immediately confronts the prosecuting attorney, who, she had assumed, was her lawyer and advocate.

"You double-crossing bitch. You sold me out. . . . This is what
   you did. I wouldn't be a good witness! I'm too fragile! My
   past is too questionable! I'm drunk! . . . I'm a drug addict!
   I'm some slut who got bounced around in some bar! I never
   got raped!"
"Of course you were raped."
"How come it doesn't say that? How come it doesn't say
   'Sara Tobias was raped?' What the fuck is 'reckless
   endangerment'?"
"It's a felony that carries the same prison term as rape. You
   asked me to put them away and I did."
"Who the hell are you to decide that I ain't good enough to be a
   witness? I bet if I went to law school and I didn't live in
   some godawful dump, I would be good enough."
"I understand how you feel. I did my best."
"No, you don't understand how I feel. . . . I don't know what
   you got for selling me out, but I sure as shit hope it was
   worth it."

At this point in the film, the prosecutor undergoes an epiphany similar to the one experienced by the defense lawyer,

Galvin, in *The Verdict.* There is a moral duty owed to the victim of a crime, and that duty is satisfied only when justice *feels* like justice. Above anything else, this means having the story told.

Prior to this moment in *The Accused*, the prosecutor had operated—typically for her profession—under the assumption that justice is only achieved when a criminal goes to jail, and that this is all a victim essentially desires. Incarceration is deemed the ultimate victory and deterrent, depriving the offender of his liberty and keeping the streets safe from crime. Prosecutors are rewarded for their successful conviction rates—the ratio of assigned cases to convictions—and for making sure that defendants serve jail time.

Most people fail to understand that prosecutors are not the assigned attorneys for crime victims. Indeed, paradoxically, unlike the accused offenders, crime victims receive no representation during a criminal proceeding. Instead they are diminished to the role of mere witnesses. This is why Sara learns of the outcome of the rape case not from the prosecutor but from watching the news. She is no more favored than an impartial member of the general public.

Prosecutors work for the State, and victims essentially work for the State, as well—volunteering, without pay, as witnesses for the prosecution. Our legal system bizarrely regards the State as the putative victim of every crime. In a rape case, it is the State that was raped; the victim merely testifies to the crime because she was there. The jury hears the State's complaint and indictment. It's as if the State agrees to step into the shoes of the victim, to take on all the unpleasantries of prosecution and the search for justice. The State vicariously but disingenuously accepts the burdens of being the victim without having to endure the pain, loss, and humiliation that are experienced by an actual, real-life victim. The State, in fact, deludes itself into thinking that it *is* the victim, that the injury was inflicted on the fibers of the nation rather than on the flesh of a person.

The victim receives no center stage or top billing in a criminal proceeding. He or she is without legal representation, standing, or human dignity in a court of law. In fact, given the presumptions of innocence that govern our criminal-justice system, even when victims are permitted to tell their stories, they are often heard with skepticism, as if the burden is on them to be both believable and believed. They not only have to tell their story, they have to sell it as well. It's difficult enough for victims to recite their stories in a public setting; it's worse when they know that the focus is on the rights of the perpetrators and not on their right to just treatment, dignity, and respect.

Yet, as Jodie Foster's character in *The Accused* makes unequivocally clear, most victims would find it emotionally revolting, not to mention morally unconscionable, not only to be deprived of a chance to tell their story but, more important, to discover that the offender had been put in jail for something less than what he had actually done.

What makes *The Accused* a chilling example of immoral justice is that it shows a prosecutor at odds with the mandates of her profession. Prosecutors seek convictions and jail time for criminal defendants. The best way to maximize those objectives is to negotiate plea bargains at the expense of truth. Prior to this case, the prosecutor in *The Accused* had never considered the moral duty of simply establishing the truth and having the offenders punished for what they actually did, rather than what they ultimately pleaded down to.

Indeed, we are treated to very few images of the moral prosecutor, either in the courthouse or in popular culture. One cinematic exception is Brad Pitt's character in the 1996 film *Sleepers*, which was based on Lorenzo Carcaterra's memoir of the same name. Of course, in *Sleepers*, in an effort to seek revenge for himself and his best friends for having been tortured and raped when they were students at a reform school, Pitt's character essentially becomes both the government's lawyer and the defense counsel, offering clandestine assistance to Dustin Hoffman, who plays the dim, unsteady, alcoholic attorney assigned to defend Pitt's friends (they murdered one of the guards who raped them when they were children). The question here is whether rigging the trial in favor of his friends and allowing the murder of their childhood persecutor to go unpunished makes Pitt's character a moral prosecutor—albeit one who violates the law and ignores the ethics of his profession—or whether he is simply taking moral justice into his own hands as an insider, rather than as an outside vigilante. The answer is difficult. What is certain is that as a government lawyer with very compromising motives, Pitt's character pursues truth and achieves a moral victory by resorting to manipulation, which ultimately costs him his job.

Whatever happened to truth in the criminal-justice system? We tolerate the idea of putting people in jail for crimes for which they were willing to plead guilty but which they did not commit. Truth becomes hostage to the efficiencies gained from negotiated pleas. In fact, it is the untold truths that we sentence to jail, not just the criminals themselves. We incarcerate truth and reward mendacity. Criminals are behind bars, but under very false pretenses. The truth has been punished even more severely—locked up in solitary confinement, forever.

Indeed, as part of the plea bargain, criminal defendants are not required to testify as to what they did, or even to show remorse. And in some cases, defendants who are completely innocent plead guilty because they have been pressured into doing so by prosecutors who have threatened them with even more severe penalties should the case actually proceed to trial and the defendant is found guilty.

With this essentially immoral, albeit perfectly legal arrangement, we have surrounded ourselves with lies, and locked ourselves up within a system that perpetuates further lies. Our jails are filled with people who are incarcerated for all the wrong reasons, a miasmic haze of generalized guilt—unspecified and totally disconnected from the actual events themselves. They sit in jail, and the story of what happened sits with them. And no one seems to care, as long as jails have low vacancy rates. We have bargained away the sanctity of truth for the certainty of a jail sentence. Indeed, the official courthouse records of criminal dispositions are distorted, because they reflect false punishments. A rape is reduced to an assault. Something that is felonious suddenly, magically, becomes merely mischievous. A first-degree offense is lessened to a crime with a lower degree of culpability, stripped down to something less ominous—and less true. We are all ultimately the unwitting victims of a system that subordinates truths to its narrow vision of justice. But isn't justice all about discovering the truth? Moral and historical justice can't be accomplished without knowing what happened. This is what people assume courthouses are for: truth-telling, truth-seeking, justice embodied in the very nature, and in all the delicate nuances, of truth itself.

There are grave moral risks in living among lies. This is the central lesson in Sophocles's *Oedipus Rex*. The real Oedipal complex is not sexual but legal. Oedipus is the king of Thebes, which is crumbling at the very core of its Greek columns, collapsing under the moral weight of a silenced, unpunished crime. A truth has been buried, a story has not been told. The prior king, Laius, was murdered, but nothing was done or said about solving the crime, nor was it spoken of again. Oedipus seamlessly slipped into the former king's robe. Years of silence, however, had a way of exposing and enlarging the cracks in the moral foundation of the kingdom. The truth, and the telling of the story, is the only remedy that can save Thebes, because the consequences of such injustice will not be made to go away simply by not speaking of it.

All societies ultimately corrode and cannot endure when surrounded by so many untold stories and insufficiently punished crimes. That's what Oedipus discovers, and it sends him on his own journey to justice, one that begins with his blindness to the truth and ends with his actual blindness. The moral imperative to know the truth is inviolable. At the end of the play, Thebes can finally move forward. The future for Oedipus—as judge, juror, and principal defendant—is not as promising, however. In keeping with the spirit of a Greek tragedy, he searches for the truth with open eyes even though it brings about his own ruin and ultimate self-inflicted blindness.

If the acknowledgment of the story and the discovery of the truth are important moral values, why then does the legal system excel, almost systematically, at subverting truths and squashing stories? If the public believes that the hallmark of the justice system is to ensure that victims are given an opportunity to tell their stories and to confront those who have harmed them, then why does the legal system work overtime to do all that is possible to avoid the trials where stories can be told and truth can be discovered? Is it any wonder that the public has so little regard for the legal system when the law shows such disdain for what citizens actually expect and want? A moral and just legal system is not one that merely recites the language of law, but rather one that allows citizens to speak in their own words, to express their own feelings, all in the quest for truth.

If there is a moral component to having trials, then why are they so rare? The answer is obvious: too much civil litigation, fueled by the exponential increase in tort claims; too many crimes committed by people who should be in jail and not enough courthouses in which to try them all. All this litigiousness and criminality needs efficient resolution, otherwise it will overwhelm an already overburdened judiciary. The legal system is a prisoner of its own budgetary and practical constraints. There is simply not enough time for all the trials, not enough courthouses to house all the disputes, not enough judges to mete out the kind of moral justice that would make us feel as though we truly live in a just society.

But if it's simply a matter of money, why not allocate more of it to the judicial branch? Build more courthouses; appoint and elect more judges to the bench. We spare so little on national defense, why be so frugal on the one branch of government that deals, in an unacknowledged way, with the moral health of the nation? We insist on the finest explosives to ensure our physical safety but care so little about the spiritual immolation that occurs when people smolder in their hurts and bake in their grief because of the absence of real, meaningful justice.

Our moral health is healed when there is an official forum, one of unquiet reverence, in which to bring our grievances. Injustice and indignity are not corrected on psychotherapists' couches or in Catholic confessionals. There are times when people need to depend on the law, because it is only in the law, or through the law, that the sense of making things right—of learning the truth and the lessons learned from those truths— can become animated and real in the hearts and minds of men and women. And the resolution that people seek is mainly found in the justice that comes from the spectacle of a trial.

Trial is the way in which the legal system approximates and arrives at truth. Truth cannot be discovered in star chambers, drumhead courts, and closed-door proceedings. It must be found in the open air of a public trial. It is where the clearest picture of what happened can be seen. And it is also where the injured, betrayed, and violated receive their day in court—a real day, not some nominal, perfunctory, superficially ceremonial legal moment, but a true day, devoted entirely to the elevation of the injured party's story and the discovery of the truth. It is also at trial where the public watches with fascination and awaits the outcome with all the bated curiosity of a Greek chorus. And it is at trial where the legal system provides the most glaringly sympathetic double exposure on the face of grief.

This faith in the revelations of law, regrettably, is not rewarded in a person's real-life encounters with the legal system. It does flourish, however—undeservedly, perhaps—in the dreams of art.

In Harper Lee's *To Kill a Mockingbird*, Atticus Finch addresses the jury and says:

[T]here is one way in this country in which all men are created equal—there is one human institution that makes a pauper the equal of a Rockefeller, the stupid man the equal of an Einstein, and the ignorant man the equal of any college president. That institution, gentlemen, is a court. It can be the Supreme Court of the United States or the humblest J.P. court in the land, . . . Our courts have their faults, . . . but in this country our courts are our great levelers, and in our courts all men are created equal.

And Jacob Ascher, the kindly, avuncular, moral defense lawyer who represents the Isaacsons, fictional stand-ins for the Rosenbergs in E. L. Doctorow's *Book of Daniel*, says to the children whose parents sit in jail:

What can I tell you. Some people are singled out. The world lacks civilization. Men do not respect God. You are only children and you can't understand—it's natural. . . . Oh, my children. What can I tell you? Soon, soon we will be in court. We shall have our trial.

ABORTED TRIALS AND
LYING UNDER THE LAW

In drama, when we are treated to depictions of lawyers, we generally see them inside courtrooms. The courtroom is the lawyer's domain. It is there where they clear their throats and stroke their chins, and rise from behind tables to offer objections. They pace around, slowly and methodically, like matadors or tango dancers moving without partners. They approach witnesses and lean against railings, making necessary eye contact, speaking with as much body language as the words coming out of their mouths.

So profoundly is this image of lawyers embedded in our minds that many people go to law school precisely to live out this fantasy. They imagine themselves arguing in front of a jury, yet few lawyers ever step inside a courtroom, let alone speak in open court. And even most litigators rarely participate in actual trials. They do discovery and take depositions, but cases are settled long before any lawyer has to make an opening statement to the jury. This is a strange and relatively recent feature of the legal profession. The most interesting and dramatic part of a lawyer's job virtually never takes place. There is a great deal of preparation, but no grand moment. Litigators are like surgeons who don't operate, or fighter pilots who never actually fly any planes.

What civil lawyers do most is negotiate deals, draft agreements, review documents, and effect settlements. None of those enterprises, however, make for much drama, either in the lives of lawyers, or in our imaginations. And that's why fictional lawyers are rarely portrayed sitting in their offices late at night, combing through boxes of documents, red ropes, and file folders, preparing for the next day's meeting, conference, or deposition. That would never keep us tuned in, or turning the page.

But this paradox between what we think lawyers do and how they actually spend their time is not merely the cause of so much spiritual damage done to lawyers, or why so many hate their jobs (I'll talk more about this in chapter 17), but it has an even greater effect on our real-life experiences with the law. Because most people who visit a lawyer in order to have their stories told assume that the lawyer is capable of doing just that, and also of bringing about an actual day in court.

Yet if trials carry such moral authority and emotional significance, and if stories and truth are the centerpiece of what it means to ensure moral justice, then why has the legal system erected such elaborate practices that make story-telling and truth-seeking impossible? The practices and procedures of the legal system are at the very core of what passes for immoral justice in America. With them, moral justice is repeatedly and mercilessly trumped; without them, moral justice has a fighting chance.

SETTLEMENTS

In the area of civil law, nothing is more questionably moral than settlements—as conventionally applied and practiced in our legal system. While in some cases they do indeed reflect the best interests and personal wishes of the parties to the action, in most situations they merely serve to silence the story in return for a cashier's check. The reflexive impulse toward settlements has turned courtroom lawyers into backroom negotiators. It has removed face-to-face, direct encounters between the parties. And it has robbed the legal process of its therapeutic, healing potential of bringing together the community in the search for the truth and the moral lessons that are learned from those truths. There is enormous moral value in having parties to a legal action sit in a courtroom, surrounded by strangers, and swear to tell the truth to each other, and to the world. And in the telling of these stories and the release of anger, rather than its displacement elsewhere, there is the possibility for healing and repair.

The whole point of a settlement is to get the parties to compromise by taking less than what they might have received, or had hoped for, had they proceeded to trial and risked the possibility of losing in return for a greater windfall. Settlements are accommodations; they are rarely the preferred option. The parties are, in fact, settling for less. A settlement assumes that combatants are better off accepting a middle-ground position rather than demanding more and, perhaps, in the end, receiving nothing.

The problem is that lawyers who encourage settlements mistakenly presume that the telling of the story is of no consequence to providing relief. Settlements buy into the presumptions of the conventional legal paradigm by thinking of remedies exclusively in monetary, rather than moral, terms.

Settlements, by definition, deprive people of their day in court. A settlement involves no story-telling or truth-finding. It produces little, if any, preserved public record of facts or testimony. And when it does, such discoveries are made between the parties, without the presence of a jury, or witnesses to any formal proceeding. This is one of the moral objections to court-sealed documents, or court-imposed secrecy, which is becoming more common these days—and dangerously so. Sealed documents protect the parties from outside scrutiny, which would be lost if the case ultimately went to trial. This judicial practice motivates the parties to reach a settlement by giving them a secrecy incentive to do so. The parties are encouraged to settle in order to avoid making sensitive documents and information public. But in many cases, it's in the public interest to make those documents public. Courts shouldn't be suppressing information that might be useful in other lawsuits and might also avert some future harm. The public has the right to know about negligent service providers or defective or hazardous products. And discoveries made in earlier lawsuits should be available as both a public warning and as potential future evidence.

Settlements are silent affairs. Usually they take place only between lawyers who rarely meet. Settlement negotiations hardly ever include the parties to the action. The lawyers become their surrogates and proxies, except that the lawyers aren't feeling the same emotions, because the case is not personal to them and they are not easily disposed to become emotionally involved. Lawyers believe that keeping the parties distant from one another, and not allowing their emotions to intrude on the negotiations, is the best way to arrive at a settlement. For this reason, these negotiations take on all the dispassion of a business deal. Lawyers seek an objective calculation of what's ultimately in the best interest of the client, but always measured in monetary, cost-benefit terms— without all the backstory and front-loaded histrionics.

But histrionics is what brings clients to lawyers in the first place. The injury and loss is felt emotionally, and physically, long before it becomes material, or measurable as money damages. The breach of a contract, and the breach of a duty of care, are terms of legal art. Emotionally they mean nothing. Once settlement discussions are underway, the whole point of having an opportunity to express the underlying grievance is completely undermined. That's because settlements—expressly or implicitly—pretend that the story was never important enough to tell. A settlement already assumes that you're not going to get what you want. Whatever principles were once elevated to sacred positions have suddenly been brought down and deflated. They have been negotiated away, and all that remains is a bank check that presumably settles the issue once and for all.

But nothing could be further from the truth. Not only do settlements isolate parties from one another and deprive them of the necessary moral confrontation that would otherwise take place at trial, but the silence about the story continues in perpetuity. As a condition of most settlements, in exchange for receiving and cashing a check, the aggrieved party is prohibited from speaking about the terms of the settlement, and sometimes, even the injury or breach that gave rise to the lawsuit—forever.

A settlement is tantamount to an entirely lawful, economically efficient bribe. It is a gag order without a judge issuing an actual order. It is the white noise of the legal system drowning out all the heartache. What a settlement says, between the lines but very much in black and white, is the following:

> If you sign this agreement and cash this check, you can no longer carry a public grudge. Your legal complaint has now been neutered of accusation. You cannot speak ill of me. I know you came here to speak, but I am paying you to shut up. You cannot tell the world what I have done to you, or how I have failed you. In fact, the receipt of this check is in no way an admission of any fault on my part at all. It is simply offered to make you go away, along with your story, which I never wanted to hear anyway. Enjoy your money, because that's all the satisfaction you can take away from this lawsuit. And never, absolutely never, complain about this matter again—to me or to anyone.

What is moral about such a resolution? And the statistics on settlements are staggering. The vast majority of cases never reach trial, never leave conference rooms, never involve the parties, never create any atmosphere of acknowledgment, truth, confrontation, apology, or forgiveness.

When feature films turn to the law as a set piece for human drama, they usually take one position or another in attacking the way in which the legal system sabotages stories and ignores emotional truths.

In addition to *The Verdict*, a similar critique of settlements is offered in Francis Ford Coppola's *Rainmaker* (1997), which is based on a John Grisham novel of the same name. In it, a young attorney Rudy Baylor, played by Matt Damon, represents a poor family, whose son is dying of leukemia, against an insurance company that refused to pay for a bone-marrow transplant. Baylor sees the injustice of the company—accepting the premiums but disallowing the coverage—and the indignity and indifference with which it has treated the insured. The parents reject a settlement offer because they want "to expose those people" for denying their son's claim, and the claims of other families as well. When the verdict is announced in the insured's favor, which includes a large punitive-damage award—the insurance company shamelessly files for bankruptcy. But Baylor's client doesn't seem disappointed that there will be no monetary recovery, because what was recovered in the award, although economically valueless, was the family's self-respect. The mother says: "One little woman from Memphis, Tennessee, bankrupted those sons-a-bitches?" She then proudly explains that she's going to bring the good news to her son when she visits his grave.

In the film *A Civil Action* (1998), John Travolta plays a lawyer, Jan Schlichtmann, who represents the surviving families of children who died from drinking contaminated water. In a voice-over narration, he explains that settlements are what lawyers and judges work toward. The victory is in the settlement itself, almost regardless of outcome. According to Schlichtmann, a lawyer who fights to bring the case to trial is out to prove something—not about the case, but about himself. There is no other reason for a trial, because no sensible attorney actually believes that going to trial in any way serves the client's best interests.

Schlichtmann's sentiment captures the prevailing mindset quite well. But not going to trial forecloses any relief, other than money—or some other tangible, physical award. The lawyer who urges a settlement shuts himself off from envisioning other remedial possibilities. And the client is deprived of the one source of relief that he reasonably assumed the legal system could provide: a day in court. Settlements are more than mere financial concessions. It's not just less money that the client accepts in signing a settlement agreement. The client must also surrender his story and abandon any hope of achieving moral justice.

One of the mothers of the dead children in *A Civil Action* says specifically and pointedly to her lawyers that money is not what she wants out of the lawsuit. Indeed, none of the parents is focused on money. What they particularly want is truth—the truth of what happened to their children.

Yet in striving for a conventional, monetary settlement, the lawyers never discovered the truth, never obtained an acknowledgment or apology from the corporations who poisoned the water supply, and ultimately failed to honor their clients' wishes.

Erin Brockovich is a variation on the same theme. Julia Roberts stars as a layperson working on a lawsuit on behalf of a community whose family members were dying, or had already died of cancer from a contaminated water supply. Like the parents in *A Civil Action*, the surviving families here are afflicted with grief. What's different is that the lead character is not a lawyer. Brockovich understands the emotional layers that transcend all the machinations of the legal system, while the lawyers are predictably obtuse to the underlying emotional complexity of the case. She functions not so much as a paralegal, but as someone who understands the magnitude of the damage and the reasons why some issues, morally, can't be negotiated and settled away. She tells the opposing counsel:

"Now that pisses me off. . . . These people don't dream about being rich. They dream about being able to watch their kids swim in a pool without worrying that they'll have to have a hysterectomy at the age of twenty."

In *The Sweet Hereafter*, a novel written by Russell Banks, which was also made into a feature film, the lawyer representing the families of children who were killed in a school-bus accident acknowledges:

> Every year, though, I swear I'm not going to take any more cases involving children. No more dead kids. No more stunned grieving parents who really only want to be left alone to mourn in the darkness of their homes, for God's sake, to sit on their dead kids' beds with their blinds drawn against the curious world outside and weep in silence as they contemplate their permanent pain. I'm under no delusions—I know that in the end a million-dollar settlement makes no difference to them, that it probably only serves to sharpen their pain by constricting it with legal language and rewarding it with money, that it complicates the guilt they feel and forces them to question the authenticity of their own suffering. I know all that; I've seen it a hundred times.

How many real lawyers possess that kind of intellectual honesty about the role they play and the good they do in their clients' lives? Few lawyers would concede that settlements are at least possibly undesirable or ineffective. In the civil area, settlements are so ubiquitous that the practice isn't something that anyone even questions. Morally we want our lawyers in court, helping us to tell our stories and regain our dignity. Legally we know that they sit at their desks, encouraging us to keep quiet and take the money that sometimes we don't even want.

Ironically, most lawyers, even litigators, are afraid of even going to court. In a pure winner-take-all paradigm, settlements are simply safer—for everyone—even if spiritually unsatisfying. What lawyers do instead is horse trade with each other until they arrive at a dollar number that their clients can live with. But that's the problem: Their clients can't live with it. In order to live, they need more than just the money. Meanwhile, the legal system churns away like an implacable check-writing machine, oblivious to our longing for moral virtue in the law.

PLEA BARGAINS

In criminal cases, plea bargains have the same questionable morality as settlements in the civil area. And they also strike ordinary citizens as being at odds with the values and aspirations of truth and justice. It's not that we don't want to see perpetrators in jail. We want our laws to be enforced. We want our streets, homes, and possessions to be safe. We want our families unharmed.

But there is something fundamentally wrong in reducing the nature and severity of a crime and calling the entire practice a "bargain." If nothing else, plea arrangements undermine truth and subvert justice. If the law is supposed to be fair and reliable in its application, then how can a guilty plea arise not out of the truth, but out of a negotiation—essentially the making of a deal, the copping of a plea, the driving of a bargain that runs over the actual truth? And when there is a number of guilty defendants, why should one be treated more favorably for having ratted out the rest? It all may be a good arrangement for the accused, and the prosecutor. But it is hardly a bargain to the victim, and naming it as such only inflames the hurt, trivializes the crime, and reveals the insensitivity of the legal system. What citizens expect and deserve is for justice to be done and punishment meted out—in a truthful, just, and uncompromising way.

As discussed earlier in connection with the film *The Accused,* in criminal cases, the victim, unlike the criminal defendant, isn't even represented by a lawyer. In the civil area, at least, the client approves the settlement, on whose behalf the compromise is negotiated. But in a criminal case, a plea bargain generally arises without the victim being consulted, largely because the deal is made not for the victim's benefit, but for the State's.

Plea bargains sacrifice the truth in order to more efficiently administer an overburdened justice system. Prosecutors are not paid to represent victims; they are there to obtain guilty pleas and put criminals in jail. Unlike the moral prosecutor in *The Accused*, government lawyers do not think of themselves as storytellers on behalf of victims. Nor does it particularly matter to them if criminals are punished for the actual crimes they committed rather than for lesser crimes that they did not commit but to which they are willing to confess. But caseload management has no relationship to moral rightness.

In Rob Reiner's film *A Few Good Men* (1992), which was adapted from the play of the same name (both written by Aaron Sorkin), a naval defense attorney, played by Tom Cruise, is assigned to defend two marines accused of murdering another marine in their unit. The marines tell their lawyer that they were merely following orders, that they were instructed by a superior officer to give their fellow marine a "Code Red," an unregulated, unofficial beating that is performed to impose discipline, but in this case resulted in death. Cruise's character is nonchalant about negotiating and accepting plea bargains, and never having to go to court. But in this case, it is not the victim but the accused themselves who insist on telling their story and having the truth revealed. They are the ones willing to forgo a more lenient and certain plea arrangement in order to preserve their honor, self-respect, and dignity, and have an opportunity to proclaim their innocence.

During the now-famous courtroom scene, in which Jack Nicholson, who plays Colonel Nathan Jessup, the commanding officer who ordered the Code Red, says, "You want the truth? You can't handle the truth!" he's discussing the moral compromises that he has to make in order to protect this country. Ironically, however, it's not that we, as civilians—in both the military and legal contexts—can't handle the truth, it's more that we're simply not used to hearing it stated in a courtroom.

A moral criminal-justice system where cases go to trial and truths are discovered rather than negotiated would also expose prosecutors to the risks and likelihood of acquittals. With trials, the risk works both ways. Despite all the resources available to the State in its prosecution of defendants, sometimes the presumptions of innocence are too difficult to overcome in the minds of a jury. A guilty person might be set free even though the prosecutor successfully searched for the truth and told the victim's story in front of a community of witnesses. Moral justice, on some level, would have been served, and yet a travesty of legal justice would also take place if the guilty were to win their freedom. Our society demands that guilt be punished. Would we tolerate a system where historical justice (i.e., knowing the truth of what happened) and restorative justice (i.e., seeking to heal wounds and enable some reconciliation to occur) are valued as much as retributive justice (i.e., making sure that we punish the guilty)? As the criminal-justice system is presently constituted, the focus is entirely on retribution, which satisfies a legal agenda, and not on either truth or restoration, which embodies a moral one.

Surely there are many law-and-order absolutists who would be unwilling to accept the risk that criminals might avoid jail time. Moral and historical justice, no matter how laudable, would lose much of its moral authority if guilty criminals went unpunished.* The point is that the commitment to maximum incarceration has led to its own brand of injustice, and has undermined the moral integrity of our legal system. Reducing our dependence on plea bargains would certainly be the correct approach in righting this moral wrong. But it would require prosecutors to inte-

---

*Of course, under the conventional legal paradigm, there are many people sitting in jail who are, in fact, innocent of any crime, but pleaded guilty under a plea arrangement in order to avoid the risk of a worse fate had they gone to trial.

grate moral postures into their professional stance, and see their jobs as combining two representational duties: one for the State, and the other for the victim.

LYING UNDER THE LAW

On television and in feature films, whenever there is a dramatic trial scene, there is inevitably a moment when a liar takes the stand. Usually, this witness is not very convincing. Indeed, he or she is typically unctuous and nervous-looking. The attorney conducting the examination will invariably state: "Need I remind you that you are under oath and that there are severe penalties for committing perjury?" Soon the contradictions in the liar's testimony are exposed, or the witness cracks under the pressure of having given false testimony in a court of law—even if it means confessing to the crime.

But what of the perjury itself? What about these penalties of perjury that the attorney warns the witness about? Was the lawyer himself lying, tricking the witness with a threat that is unsupported in the law, or do the penalties exist but remain unenforced, like an uncracked whip?

Clearly, if justice has any moral legitimacy, it has to reveal truths, and there has to be an integrity to the way in which those truths are discovered. But when lying is tolerated and is seemingly permissible, then the legal system shows itself to be unworthy and unjust. Nothing thwarts truth more than lying witnesses. It undermines any sense of justice, and shows the law to be a sham. Lying is worse than the mere risks associated with the adversarial process. It's one thing to accept that the opposing side's trial strategy was superior. It's quite another to realize that the outcome would have been different had a witness simply told the truth.

Everyone knows that lying is endemic to the legal system, and that perjury is an epidemic in the law. During the O. J. Simpson trial, Detective Mark Fuhrman lied in front of the entire nation in denying that he had used the "n-word" with respect to African-Americans. Although ultimately he was charged with having committed perjury, even the Los Angeles district attorney believed that the lie had not been a "material" one. The presiding judge accepted Fuhrman's "no contest" plea and fined him a mere $200. In some ways this tiny punishment was a perfunctory victory for the cause of truth, because the vast majority of perjury cases are never prosecuted at all.

In a 1995 article that appeared in the *ABA Journal*, Mark Curriden quoted a prosecutor as saying, "Outside of income tax evasion, perjury is probably the most underprosecuted crime in America." And he also wrote: "[P]erjury is being committed with greater frequency and impunity than ever before," and yet its prosecution "is a low priority for resource-strapped prosecutors just when it is apparently on the rise." A judge added: "It's the justice system's dirty little secret that no one wants to admit or confront."

It's not that the justice system sanctions lying. The legal may be functionally split from the moral in the American justice system, but that doesn't mean that the law sees no value in witnesses telling the truth. It is clearly better for legal results to be supported by actual truths—if not for moral reasons, then for purely legal ones. But it does seem as if the legal system has neither the time nor the patience for truth, since there is apparently no consequence to lying.

There are, in fact, many rules that prohibit perjury. Under federal criminal law, a false statement made under oath can be viewed as an obstruction of justice, and a judge can find the lying witness in contempt, which can carry a fine, as well as a term of imprisonment. Under state criminal law, with most states having adopted the Model Penal Code, a material false statement made under oath in an official court proceeding is a felony of the third degree.

In addition to criminal penalties, there are professional ethical requirements that prohibit perjury as well. Based on the

Model Code of Professional Responsibility and the Model Rules of Professional Conduct, state bar associations impose rules on lawyers not to present testimony or evidence in court that the attorney either knows to be false, or reasonably believes to be false. The ethical duty extends even further by requiring attorneys to disclose when a client is about to commit perjury. If attorneys fail in their affirmative ethical duties to keep perjury out of the courtroom, they can be subject to criminal prosecution, and even disbarment from the practice of law.

Interestingly, however, there are no civil remedies against a witness who lies under oath to the prejudice of one of the parties to an action. In fact, in an effort to encourage witnesses to come forward and testify in an uncensored manner, the United States Supreme Court has provided an unqualified immunity from civil litigation to all witnesses who commit perjury, even when that perjury is undisputed. In 1983, the Court decided *Briscoe v. LaHue*, a case involving a convicted felon who asserted a claim for damages under the Civil Rights Act against a police officer who had offered perjured testimony against him. The Court ruled that under common law, the immunity of witnesses from subsequent damages related to their giving of testimony has always been well established in order to encourage witnesses to come forward and speak freely. Yet, ironically, in some cases it may have had the exact opposite effect: witnesses began to realize that they can lie, without their statements ever exposing them to future civil action, all because the courts were so desperate for testimony, ultimately it didn't matter so much whether it was true.

Why is lying under oath so prevalent in the law? One state court judge, Carl O. Bradford, was quoted in Mark Curriden's 1995 article in the *ABA Journal* as saying: "You can walk into court, take the oath, lie up a storm, and not have to worry about being punished for it." And Jason Pernick, an assistant district attorney in Michigan was quoted in a law review article as saying, "The last thing that you hear before the lying begins is, 'I do solemnly swear to tell the truth . . .' "

The problem is not that there are no rules against perjury, but rather that there is little moral conviction to enforcing them. Perjury goes unpunished, and lying is an accepted practice in American courtrooms. Despite all the precautions, penalties, and prohibitions, lying inside courtrooms takes place with the same frequency, and lack of ambivalence, as it does outside. Very few witnesses are ever prosecuted for having committed perjury, even when the proof of their crime is well substantiated. As for lawyers, state bar associations rarely if ever initiate disciplinary actions against attorneys who either commit perjury, or assist in its making.

Citizens wish to have faith in their legal system, but no justice can come from an institution that so readily looks away when in the presence of so many lies. Indeed, sometimes the system itself provides the necessary incentives to lie. For instance, criminal contingency-fee arrangements—whereby government witnesses are given either financial rewards, leniency, or freedom from imprisonment in return for their testimony—create all sorts of incentives to commit perjury.

The legal system has a high tolerance for lying, and it doesn't seem too concerned about the public's growing cynicism that justice lacks the institutional integrity to root out lies. The law accepts virtual truths for actual truths, statements that are admittedly and intentionally misleading. They are not technically perjurous, but not entirely true, either. The burden is placed on the examining attorney to get to the truth by asking the right questions. And if the witness is more clever than the attorney, and answers in an evasive, elliptical manner, so be it. Consistent with the conventional legal paradigm, with its sporting-contest, winner-take-all ground rules, judges and lawyers believe that it is ultimately the job of the jury to ascertain the truth. They are the finders of fact. They are the ones responsible for judging the credibility of witnesses. It almost doesn't matter whether witnesses are lying or telling the truth, because the finality of the trial will result in findings of facts, and those facts will stand in for the truth, even if they were derived from lies.

This is yet another example of the false closure that comes from a final judgment. The legal system mistakenly, and condescendingly, believes that judgments are final simply because a judge is finished with the case. But if the outcome is unjust, then there can be no emotional closure, only a legal finality that will bear the stamp of law, without the moral adhesive. The jury might have found facts, but those facts were founded on lies and therefore have no relationship to actual truths. And for this reason, they carry no moral weight. And even worse, these lies won't disappear. People can be dismissed from courtrooms, and they often leave willingly, but lies are not nearly as compliant. They tend to linger, and resurface, sometimes in the most pathological and ruinous of ways. Unjust verdicts and the deep mistrust of and moral disgust with the legal system sometimes cause riots in the streets. And in such instances, the law has nothing but itself to blame. When it fails to enforce its own rules prohibiting perjury, when it provides incentives to lie, and when it perpetuates a zero-sum, adversarial system where lying is trivialized as a consequence of litigation and not as a moral outrage, the legal system becomes complicit in all the lying, and the assault on truth.

EVIDENCE RULES

For the most part, evidence rules are seen as essential to the proper and dignified workings of a trial or hearing. They narrow the scope of the inquiry, simplify issues and narratives, set boundaries. They ensure that what gets presented inside the courtroom, and what the jury can permissibly hear, conforms to a set of efficient administrative rules that manage the proceedings and assist in justice.

But these efficiency-saving values also severely undermine

truth and storytelling. Indeed, in limiting the scope of the narrative, evidence rules only allow so much of the story to be told. When citizens come before the law, they wish to speak, and they don't wish to be interrupted when doing so. They also have no preconceived notion of the order in which the story should be relayed. They may be reliable, yet entirely disorganized witnesses. And since trials are emotionally taxing, and parties appear in court at their most vulnerable, they tend to repeat themselves on the witness stand. We may swear on the Bible, or simply swear to tell the truth, but after that, our responses are not always so measured, confident, and clear. Nervousness and anxiety are central to the witness's demeanor.

Yet evidence rules are frequently invoked to exclude testimony that is deemed "irrelevant," "immaterial," "not credible," "cumulative," or "hearsay." These are standard objections that lawyers rise to proclaim, with dramatic fanfare, in order to have certain damaging statements stricken or excluded from the record—essentially not considered as evidence. It is a strange scene that occurs in all courtrooms—cutting off a witness while he's speaking, objecting on the grounds of relevancy, as if to say: "What he's saying here simply doesn't matter." The judge rules on these objections while the witness waits to hear whether what he had just said will be included as testimony, even though he had already said it and has every reason to believe that it has meaning—that it is, indeed, very much relevant.

These objections, aside from being rude and insulting, also limit the story and rob it of all the nuance and emotion of the human experience. What kind of a legal system says to people testifying under oath, right in front of their faces, as if they are not there hearing the interruption, that their words are "irrelevant," or worse, "not credible"—simply not to be believed? Evidence rules turn the entire courtroom proceeding into something frigidly cold, artificial, and staid. This is absurd, given that courtrooms are filled with people at their most animated, alive, and infinitely nervous. In light of the extreme, raw emotions that attend these proceedings, you would think that the legal system would have figured out by now that, morally, you can't turn testimony on and off with a switch. If the whole point of the trial is to determine the truth by allowing people to describe, in their own words, what happened, then why are the rules governing evidence so committed to telling people to shut up, that the manner and order in which they are speaking, and its prescribed relevancy, is more important than what they have to say?

In 2002, Woody Allen was involved in a lawsuit with his former business partners. They had produced his last series of films and had also been among his closest friends. The courtroom proceeding, and all the emotion that was drained out of it, was reported in the *New York Times* as follows:

"Are you working on a new movie?" the defense attorney asked.
"Yes, and that's why I haven't been able to be here all the time,
    because—"
" 'Yes' is the answer," the judge said.
"Because I have a film crew out now, shooting on the streets of
    New York, and I'm trying to—"
"Stop talking," the judge said.
"Stop talking?" Allen replied, somewhat stunned by the
    encounter.
"Yes," the judge said, "I'm the director here."
A few questions later, the defense lawyer asked Allen whether
    he considered the plaintiff to be a close personal friend.
"Yes. He's a trusted friend who—"
" 'Yes' is the answer," the judge interrupted once more.

Even in a good-natured way, who is this judge to interrupt Woody Allen, or anyone for that matter, when he's trying to testify and clarify his answers? Especially in a case like this one, where the lawsuit was between friends, Allen should have been permitted to explain the nature, extent, and history of his friendship with those he had been forced to sue.

All lawsuits are emotionally stressful. There is natural stage fright, even for an acclaimed director. People on the witness stand tend to sweat. They appear terribly anxious and uncomfortable. They repeat themselves. Their composure is less than composed. And this is all the more magnified when the witness is testifying in a case in which he is a party. And in a case where the lawsuit itself is between friends, the emotions and hurt feelings are even more pronounced.

As a screenwriter, Allen was certainly aware of the complications involved in rehashing a story, or telling it from scratch. Yet he wasn't testifying as a screenwriter who could have written it better. He was there as a human being. This was his life he was talking about; his relationship that had soured, to his surprise; his money that was allegedly lost. Why not just let Woody speak, in his own words, letting him take his own time to compose and, if emotionally necessary, to veer off course for a while?

Judges may want stories to come out seamlessly, and in as few words as possible. But in real life, you can't choreograph the telling, or rip out the rawness of feeling. The stories that come out of trials can't be scripted. The narration is not neat, because nerves interrupt both the order of the words, and the witness's demeanor.

Based on his reaction, Allen was seemingly stunned by the court's officiousness and self-importance. The director probably doesn't exert as much control on a film set as the judge asserted in these proceedings. Allen knows that improvisation sometimes leads to compelling drama and truths. Keeping the story too tight would deprive his films of spontaneity and emotion. The judge, however, thought nothing of censuring and shaping Allen's testimony, deleting what he deemed unnecessary. Yet Allen's testimony was important—at least to him. It may not have been necessary to resolve the legal issues, but perhaps, in a tentative, halting, even stumbling way, his words addressed the emotional ones—the experience of having to bring a lawsuit against his former friends and business partners.

I must say that I, too, had an experience where I was told by a judge to stop speaking in a courtroom—not as a lawyer, but as a party to an action. I was trying to explain my feelings about the unfairness of a settlement that I was being pressured to accept by the court. I was also trying to call attention to other information and matters that were not being accounted for in the settlement, and that, if ignored, would render the result even more unjust than I felt it already was. Soon after I began speaking, the judge warned me: "If you say another word, we'll start all over, I'll put you back on the stand, and I promise that you will end up in an even worse position then you are in now."

I never was permitted to say another word, nor did I risk offering one. And this experience has no doubt influenced the courses I teach, and the writing of this book. Emotionally, the entire experience of that case has never left me. It continues to inform my relationships and dealings with the world, and my perceptions about justice. Despite my legal training, I was not trained to know how to respond to those feelings of silence, banishment, and deprivation that the legal system imposes on losing parties. Where is someone to go when the place of legal refuge is itself unsafe, sinister, and ultimately endangering?

There are numerous examples of evidence rules that make no sense morally, even though they have longstanding legal justifications. These are the kinds of uniform, strictly applied rules that make ordinary citizens wince and lose faith in the law. One such rule has to do with prior bad acts, or evidence of past crimes or conduct. The rule is quite clear that such evidence is inadmissible because it might prejudice the defendant from obtaining a fair trial. The jury might assume that since the accused had done the act at least once before, there is a propensity that he or she might have done it again. The only way to correct for this presumption is to insulate the jury from this possible undue prejudice. Judges routinely exclude evidence of prior bad acts from the proceedings, although there are some exceptions that can override the rule.

While the goal of keeping the jury free from prejudice is a noble one, this rule, in particular, isolates the jury from hearing the entire story. In the case of a pickpocket or a shoplifter, evidence that the accused had committed these acts on prior occasions cannot be admitted to show propensity. Yet, aside from the possible prejudice, isn't this exactly the kind of full disclosure that the jury should hear in deciding guilt and innocence? Why can't the jury be instructed that, in hearing this evidence, they must not automatically infer guilt? It is possible that, after having committed five robberies, a defendant may not have been involved in this most recent one, but why should the jury not hear about the prior five? The prejudice might still remain after the instruction, but what we have now is truth-seeking with many of the truths in permanent lockup. The rights reserved for the accused have trumped our moral entitlement to the truth. But since juries are already asked to disregard certain statements made in court, why can't they similarly be trusted to temper whatever prejudice arises from evidence of bad character?

In the films *The Verdict* and *The Rainmaker*, crucial documentary evidence—on doctored hospital records and the denial of claim letters from the insurance company, respectively—were excluded from the trial and withheld from the jury because of overly narrow, formulaic, and senseless evidence rules. The evidence tells essential aspects of the story and discloses vital truths. But the loopholes in the law—supported by evidence rules that are legal but immoral—are manipulated to keep the evidence out and the story insufficiently narrated. Nevertheless, in both films, the jury overrides the court's instructions and considers the evidence anyway, ultimately awarding the claimants exorbitant punitive damages.

Evidence rules maintain such a tight lid on the story that trials lose their common meaning as places where truths are honored and told. The story becomes incidental to the administration of legal justice. If we end up hearing the entire tale, it's more by way of accident than design. Stories are introduced and redacted in synthesis alone, the cold Cliff's Notes version rather than the director's cut. Far from being an open forum, courtrooms are places where we are mostly told to shut up, to stop talking. Relevancy becomes an entirely external process. It's not what you want to say but what we need to hear. Stories are deemed useful only in resolving the legal issues, without elaboration or repetition, and without any consideration of human feelings. They have a limited purpose at trial—to serve the law rather than the other way around.

THE BEST-KEPT SECRETS
OF ZEALOUS ADVOCATES

I t's not just in courtrooms where lawyers fail to tell our stories and seek out truths. Even at work and in their offices, lawyers are engaged in a practice of law that often undermines the possibility for moral resolution. Full disclosure is a misnomer almost everywhere in the law. Most of what lawyers do is silence and squelch, spin and fudge, eviscerate or explain away the very stories that must be told and preserved. We are besieged by crazed advocates who are at their best when keeping secrets, who deal in rules riddled with loopholes, and in statutes that immorally close off the filing of claims.

TECHNICALITIES, LOOPHOLES,
AND PROCEDURAL IRREGULARITIES

Moral justice is further undermined by technicalities, loopholes, and procedural irregularities in the law. Lawyers look out for loopholes with almost laser precision—obscuring and skirting, erecting obstacles, blowing smoke, playing fast and loose in a game of three-card monte with the truth. Lawyers develop a nose for technicalities, and the way in which procedures can be

manipulated for the sake of winning a legal contest without regard to whether justice is done. These artifacts of the legal system are almost clichés of moral abuse. They promote mistrust
and bad faith, and reinforce the belief that courts aren't interested in truth at all.

A technicality allows you to avoid responsibility because the
conduct doesn't—literally or technically—rise to the level of an
infraction, or something else intervenes to cancel it out. Technicalities also have a way of obliterating the story when a court of
law gets overly bogged down in bureaucratic minutia and becomes more interested in going by route rather than doing
what's right. The grinding administration of justice then takes
on a life of its own, a life lived solely in the service of steering
the machine. And when the law looks more like a soulless apparatus than a safe haven, there is little wonder that actual breathing bodies of human life get crushed under the technical,
by-the-book maintenance of the justice system.

The law as big bureaucracy, complete with its own red tape:
the form files, the endless, repetitive pleadings, discovery dates,
adjournments, and continuances. This is precisely what Franz
Kafka, in *The Trial*, and Charles Dickens, in *Bleak House*, understood as the lifeless, absurdist machinations of the law. Both novels, written in different centuries and countries, and by entirely
different literary stylists, offer broadside assaults against the way
in which the law saps the life out of citizens who come before it.
In *The Trial*, Joseph K. seeks to exonerate himself from a nameless crime as he freely wanders the streets of Prague unarrested
but captive to the law's imprisoning light. In Charles Dickens's
Victorian masterpiece *Bleak House*, lives are lost and an entire
estate is squandered over the course of many years. Yet the cause
of this spiritual depletion and wealth extinction is a lawsuit with
no purpose other than to exhaust itself and everyone around it.
The law, as depicted in both of these novels, has a way of justifying its own bureaucratic agenda rather than servicing the public

good. Individuals enter the halls of justice believing that their day in court won't last an eternity, that there is some imminent and just resolution awaiting them. They often don't expect the indignity and frustration of the wait, brought upon by a technical obedience to the machine.

A procedural irregularity in the law occurs when someone violates a rule or regulation governing procedure—the way in which a task is supposed to be carried out—and this violation, in turn, ends any further inquiry into the substance or merits of what the court was initially asked to decide. This violation can take any number of forms, but the public is most familiar with those dealing with constitutional protections, such as when a police officer fails to read the Miranda warnings to a person taken into custody, unlawfully coerces a confession, or improperly searches a home or the trunk of a car. These procedural objections involve the Fourth Amendment and its exclusionary rule, because it results in evidence—whether it is an inanimate object or an uttered statement—being withheld or excluded from consideration because it was obtained unlawfully.

Procedural lapses are not always, or necessarily, a result of constitutional violations. Sometimes they come about during legal proceedings, such as when the case is dismissed on procedural, legal, or technical grounds. This can seem particularly anomalous in the civil area. Indeed, Rule 12(b)(6) of the Federal Rules of Civil Procedure, which is a motion to dismiss, demands that a case be dismissed, as a matter of law, because of the plaintiff's failure to state a legal claim upon which relief can be granted—even if everything that the plaintiff is alleging is true. Although the allegations are true, the claim may not actually violate the law, or is framed in a technically improper way. In order to proceed with his case, the plaintiff is required to go back and reshape his story, if he can, so that it resembles and establishes a legal claim.

To those without law degrees, and hopefully to some who have them, Rule 12(b)(6) naturally seems absurd. If the plaintiff is telling the truth, why shouldn't he be allowed to tell his story in front of a judge and jury? A 12(b)(6) motion to dismiss is the ultimate "dis," because it results in the opposite of storytelling. The plaintiff is prevented from speaking, regardless of how truthful or important his tale may be. Indeed, the story and the grievance are summarily rejected, even if we know that it is true.

Such procedural, overly narrow and technical applications of the law always come across as immoral to those who believe that the legal system should honor truths and do what's just. Loopholes undermine the faith and certainty in the law. And when criminals go unprosecuted because of a technical infraction or a procedural irregularity, the story goes untold and justice remains undone. Indeed, the story of the procedural lapse itself becomes the only story, superseding entirely the underlying, substantive events that gave rise to the crime or action. Such legal maneuvers operate outside the boundaries of moral justice, breeding enormous resentment and discontent and influencing negative attitudes about the legal system in the general public. If courts of law are supposed to do justice and discover truths, then why should loopholes, technicalities, and procedural irregularities deprive the ultimate truths from being known and the stories that give rise to them from being told?

Each of these diversions from truth reveals general imperfections of our constitutional system. A nation built upon democratic ideals, civil liberties, and a romantic vision of freedom is bound to discover that legal outcomes will occasionally come across as plain wrong. Presumptions of innocence, the equal and due process clauses of the Constitution, and the exclusionary rule, each, in their own way, provide rights but are also, at times, responsible for moral wrongs. While we generally luxuriate in these rights, judges, lawyers, and law professors seem to be unmindful about the way immoral outcomes—and the trampling of truth—completely sabotage the faith that the public should have in the law as an institution.

Loopholes, technicalities, and procedural irregularities make
us think that lawyers are more interested in paper, forms, and
procedures than they are in the everyday struggles of human
beings. We want counselors, not bureaucrats; we want lawyers
who possess legal knowledge but who are not mere legal machines. Clients come to lawyers because they are regarded—or
they regard themselves—as problem solvers. But it so often
feels as if the problems remain unattended to, or worse, that
the lawyer's intervention ends up creating more problems—not
putting out smoke, but instead kindling the flames, or starting
new fires altogether. Lawyers are often perceived as being self-
congratulatory in their own uselessness and the wreckage they
cause.

In the final chapters of *Bleak House*, with the case of
Jarndyce v. Jarndyce finally over and with nothing to show for it
other than financial ruination and spiritual death, Dickens describes the Chancery courthouse and its lawyers in the following
way:

> [P]eople came streaming out looking flushed and hot,
> and bringing a quantity of bad air with them. Still they
> were all exceedingly amused, and were more like people
> coming out from a Farce or a Juggler than from a court
> of Justice. . . . [G]reat bundles of paper began to be car-
> ried out—bundles in bags, bundles too large to be got
> into any bags, immense masses of papers of all shapes
> and no shapes, which the bearers staggered under, and
> threw down for the time being, . . . Even these clerks
> were laughing.
>
>   . . . .
>
> [Mr. Kenge, one of the lawyers, says:] "[T]his has
> been a great cause, this has been a protracted cause, this
> has been a complex cause. Jarndyce and Jarndyce has
> been termed, not inaptly, a Monument of Chancery prac-

tice. . . . on the numerous difficulties, contingencies, masterly fictions, and forms of procedure in this great cause, there has been expended study, ability, eloquence, knowledge, intellect, . . . high intellect. For many years the—a—I would say that the flower of the Bar . . . have been lavished upon Jarndyce and Jarndyce. . . ."

[Allan, the narrator's husband, then asks:] ". . . Do I understand that the whole estate is found to have been absorbed in costs?"

"Hem! I believe so."

"And that thus the suit lapses and melts away?"

"Probably."

And in Franz Kafka's *The Trial*, the conversation between the client, Joseph K., and his attorney, Huld, is presented this way:

> "I was never so much plagued by my case as I have been since engaging you to represent me. When I stood alone I did nothing at all, yet it hardly bothered me; after acquiring a lawyer, on the other hand, I felt that the stage was set for something to happen, I waited with unceasing and growing expectancy for your intervention, and you did nothing whatever. . . ."
>
> "After a certain stage in one's practice," said the lawyer quietly in a low voice, "nothing really new ever happens."

ATTORNEY-CLIENT PRIVILEGE

Another example of the way in which the public trust in lawyers is shaken by the stigma of immoral justice is found in the area of the attorney-client privilege. This piety of the profession—that confidences are privileged and cannot be revealed—is an un-

challenged ethical requirement among lawyers, uncompromising and sacrosanct, an absolute duty owed by an attorney to his
client.

But in faithfully carrying out this duty, lawyers, in essence,
become secret keepers, their clients' confidences secured, each
resting on top of one another. In the lawyer's mind, the privilege
is an essential service they provide; it's what makes them special.

In *Bleak House*, Tulkinghorn, the attorney who represents
Sir Leicester and harbors the dark secret of his client's wife,
Lady Dedlock, is referred to throughout the novel as a bloodless,
calculating, sinister secret-keeper. He's good at his job, but everyone winces when he enters a room. Lawyers maintain that the
attorney-client privilege is necessary. It ensures that they are
fully informed of everything relevant to their client's case, which
in turn enables them to assemble the best legal strategy. And
lawyers, because they are emotionally detached and objective
professionals, insist that these confidences are critical only for
representational purposes. They claim to have no personal in-
vestment in knowing a client's private business. Yet Dickens is
not so sure. Tulkinghorn, for instance, is depicted as a man who
enjoys knowing the intimate details of a good secret. He gathers
them up for his own amusement, and for use as possible leverage
against his clients or others. The privilege may, therefore, truly
be the lawyer's privilege to exercise, cunningly gathered with the
pretense of professional duty, but, like Tulkinghorn, retained and
manipulated with sheer glee, hardly forgotten at the end of the
business day.

In *Morales v. Portuondo*, a 2001 case brought before a federal
district court judge in New York, the court wisely and morally
overturned a conviction and undid a horrible injustice. Morales
was finally released from prison after serving thirteen years. As
teenagers, he and a codefendant had been convicted of murder.
Just prior to their sentencing, however, another teenager, Fornes,
confessed to both a priest and a Legal Aid attorney that it was he

who had committed the murder, and not Morales. The priest never revealed the confession, nor did the Legal Aid attorney, even though Fornes stated clearly and unequivocally, "I am here because I can't sleep, can't eat, no one has forced me or paid me or told me to do this, just something wrong has happened." Bound by the ethics of their respective callings, they believed that they were prevented from disclosing this information, even at the risk of furthering an injustice and committing their own moral crimes of complicity and neglect.

In fact, the Legal Aid attorney ultimately advised Fornes not to testify and implicate himself. In the lawyer's judgment, Fornes's testimony would not have altered the disposition against Morales, and would have certainly resulted in prejudice to Fornes, because he, too, would now have to be prosecuted for the crime. Morales was convicted in 1988 and went to jail. Fornes died in an unrelated incident in 1997. Yet the Legal Aid attorney still maintained the privilege and never came forward with the truth, even though his client was dead and two innocent men had been in jail for over a decade. Only recently did the attorney, as well as the priest, decide to reveal what they had known all along. It is true that both the attorney and the priest eventually did come forward, and, in doing so, they each chose to violate the ethical and sacred duties of their professions, thereby risking disbarment and excommunication. But neither of those consequences ensued. And in the thirteen years that preceded their decision to break their vows and speak, their silence assisted in destroying a young man's life.*

The *Morales* decision is an extreme but not unfamiliar example of how privileges show the law to be morally unjust. Con-

*A similar critique can be directed at the judiciary. This case went through various stages of appeals at the state and federal levels, in addition to the trial itself. In each instance, the presiding judges were aware of this exculpatory evidence, but chose to ignore it, or explain it away in order to achieve a presumptively legal result regardless of its severe moral implications.

fidentiality remains, unquestionably, a source of pride within the legal profession, and an acceptably lawful and ethical practice. But among those who are not lawyers, there is something palpably creepy about people who are ethically bound not to reveal the secrets that they treasure, regardless of the consequences that might spill from their silence. The safeguarding of secrets ultimately compromises truths. While the duty to the client is clear, the moral abuse of the privilege violates the public trust. Moral justice becomes impossible to achieve when attorneys fail to reveal what they know when it is morally wrong not to. The attorney-client privilege serves the interest of clients who wish to speak frankly with their attorneys, but it also has the social and moral consequence of perpetuating secrets and lies. And sometimes these secrets harbor an injustice that violates a much larger principle than the mere attorney-client privilege.

In 2003 an attorney in Washington State was suspended from the practice of law for six months by the Washington Supreme Court for having violated a client confidence, even though his disclosure led to the removal of a corrupt state-court judge. In 1992, attorney Douglas Schaefer was informed by one of his less scrupulous clients that Grant Anderson, who was soon to become a state-court judge, was about to engage in improper, unlawful conduct. Three years later, perhaps in retaliation for Judge Anderson's having sanctioned Schaefer for bringing a frivolous lawsuit, Schaefer notified the state bar of Judge Anderson's earlier misconduct. The Washington Supreme Court ruled: "Because of Schaefer's actions, a corrupt judge was exposed and the public was served by the judge's removal from office." Yet, the court determined that Schaefer should nonetheless be punished for having violated his client's trust. Following this decision, Schaefer was quoted in the *New York Times*, responding to the court's ruling: "They are clearly delivering the message that the secrets of a corrupt client who conspired with a corrupt judge are more important than the restoration of the integrity of the judicial system."

Schaefer is right; morally, such a ruling makes no sense. And most laymen would agree. Most lawyers, unfortunately, would not.

The American Bar Association's rules regarding the keeping of client confidences—as embodied in its Model Code of Conduct—mandates that in all cases the privilege should be maintained, but allows for disclosure "only to prevent a criminal act that the lawyer believes is likely to result in imminent death or substantial bodily harm." Under this rigidly narrow standard, very few confidences would have fallen outside the privilege. In 2001, the ABA relaxed the privilege slightly by allowing lawyers to breach client confidentiality "to prevent reasonably certain death or substantial bodily harm."

The new rule is an improvement, morally, over the original language, because it removes the words "imminent" and "criminal." Thus it reduces somewhat the range of confidences that an attorney is required to keep, because it permits the disclosure of noncriminal acts that may take place in the future. (This new rule still would not have changed the outcome in the Schaefer case.) But at the same time, the disclosure of the confidence is allowed only when harm might come to the body, and not the spirit. Typical of the conventional legal paradigm, there is no duty to disclose contemplated acts of spiritual violence, such as emotional harm, or the causing of humiliation or indignity. Financial misdeeds, fraud, and misrepresentations were also not excluded from the protection of the privilege. In all instances, it was clear that the basic principle of the rule remained intact—short of causing physical harm to another person, anything that a client discusses with his lawyer is privileged and cannot be revealed.

More recently, however, in the summer of 2003, during its annual meeting, the ABA once again examined the boundaries of the privilege and ultimately decided to give lawyers greater latitude in revealing client confidences. Unfortunately, the relaxing of the rule was not done for a moral purpose, but rather a political one. The new rule permits, but does not require, an attorney to disclose client confidences to prevent or rectify a crime or fraud that might cause substantial financial harm to others when the attorney's services assisted in furthering the crime. In addressing financial injury rather than purely bodily harm, the new rule contemplates a wider range of confidences where the privilege is forfeited. Yet, at the same time, the new rule is merely permissive rather than mandatory, and functions only when the attorney is complicit in the crime or fraud, rather than merely has knowledge of it. In adopting this new rule to its Model Code of Conduct, however, the ABA was apparently influenced less by doing the right thing, and more by the incentive to avoid political pressure from governmental regulators.

Ronald M. George, the chief justice of the California Supreme Court, acknowledged in the *New York Times* that "[t]o the extent the legal profession polices itself, it makes itself less susceptible to outside regulation." And M. Peter Moser, an attorney at Piper Rudnick in Baltimore, explained in another *New York Times* article that the modified rules were necessary so "we can avoid further intrusions into state regulation of lawyer discipline and conduct, which is what this is all about." Sensing that his colleagues were tragically undermining the attorney-client privilege, William G. Paul, an attorney with Crowe & Dunlevy in Oklahoma City, said, in yet another *New York Times* article, that the proposal would "barter away a piece of our professional soul to gain some hoped-for public approval."

Even if these new rules are morally superior to the stifling, protectionist language of the Model Code of Conduct that preceded them, it's clear that in making these modifications, lawyers were not driven by the impulse to introduce a new moral clarity to their profession.

This fear of regulatory intervention is a real one, even if cynically motivated. In response to an embarrassing and financially ruinous spate of corporate scandals on Wall Street—from Enron to WorldCom to Global Crossing—and as required by Section

307 of the Sarbanes-Oxley Act, in 2003 the Securities and Exchange Commission (SEC) adopted new rules requiring lawyers to disclose instances in which the companies they represent are violating securities laws.

The new rule mandates that a lawyer report a violation of the securities law to either executive management or the board of directors. It reads as follows: "Evidence of a material violation means credible evidence, based upon which it would be unreasonable, under the circumstances, for a prudent and competent attorney not to conclude that it is reasonably likely that a material violation has occurred, is ongoing, or is about to occur."

What does all that mean? Why can't the rule be stated in English, and framed without all those double negatives? The main reason, perhaps, is the impulse to keep the attorney-client privilege intact—even when it is presumably being modified by outside regulators. While the rule is mandatory, it also seems to be quite easy to ignore. The way the rule is written, a lawyer will never have to override the sanctity of the privilege in the name of a higher morality. Under the rule, if an attorney knows that his client has violated the securities laws, he still doesn't have to disclose this information if a different attorney would not have been unreasonable in believing that the rule had not been violated. It's clear that the SEC chose language that enables the attorney-client privilege to remain inviolable even in the face of a public demand for lawyers to consider the public good while simultaneously serving the client's best interest.*

Strike another victory for secrecy in the law.

---

*The actions taken by the ABA in the summer of 2003 dealing with the disclosure of fraud or other financial crimes committed by a client, as well as another provision that imposed a reporting requirement similar to the SEC rule, demonstrates just how sensitive and fearful lawyers are to outside regulation. But why is regulatory interference more compelling than a moral imperative? If what the client is doing or has done is a crime that could cause harm—to the body, the spirit, or someone's bankbook—then why should lawyers allow themselves to be in a position to conceal the truth and compound the injury?

Yet if a lawyer knows the truth but must advocate on behalf of his client in a way that obscures, falsifies, or diverts attention away from that truth—leading the court or corporate shareholders to draw false conclusions and reach judgments that are tantamount to lies—how is that serving the interests of society and justice? Doctors and psychotherapists, for instance, also have a duty to maintain patient confidences, but not at the expense of a higher duty owed to the general public. In these professions, the ethical duty to disclose a doctor-patient privilege is mandated in certain instances (to prevent harm or injury), while in the legal profession, the rule is only that the attorney may reveal the secret, and not that he should or must.

Practicing attorneys maintain that the legal and medical professions are not similar in this regard, and that's why the privilege rules operate differently. After all, patients don't visit doctors because they are suffering from a secret (although they may wish to keep their illness a secret), nor do they seek out doctors on the basis of how well the doctor can keep a secret. But a person who needs a lawyer will not visit one who cannot be trusted to maintain a confidence.

In an article in the *New York Times*, Lawrence J. Fox, a lawyer in Philadelphia, was quoted as saying, "Confidentiality is where the rubber meets the road. If clients aren't assured of confidentiality, they tend to withhold information. If they don't share everything, we won't be able to defend them as well."

But is that really true? Do people visit lawyers only because they have a secret and want to be able to confide in someone who can give them advice on how to ensure that the secret remain secreted, forever? Or do they come to lawyers because they have a problem, and they are hoping that the attorney will be able to find a solution to the problem, and one of those solutions might actually be the unburdening of the secret itself? Lawyers mistakenly overestimate the importance of the privilege to their clients. Many people aren't even aware of the privilege until their attorney advises them of it. Despite what lawyers believe, the privilege isn't the main draw of their profession. It's only an ethical byproduct of the job, supported by self-governing rules that distance lawyers from decent-thinking, moral men and women.

So then why should legal ethics override private morality? The ethical duties of the legal profession are being shamelessly abused in ways that prevent lawyers from doing the right thing.

David E. Kelley, the creator of the award-winning, critically acclaimed television drama *The Practice*, has a particular interest in storylines that deal with the attorney-client privilege. Many episodes have involved an attorney with privileged but damaging and morally compromising information about his or her client. The attorney knows that, ethically, the secret can't be revealed. Yet he is tormented by an intuitive awareness that a lawyer should not abandon his private conscience simply because the ethical rules of the profession shift the moral obligations elsewhere.

"At some point lawyers inevitably become desensitized to moral quandaries," Kelley said in an interview for an article for the *New York Times*. "Privileges are a good example of this, because the keeping and protecting of secrets come at the blatant expense of morality. It's a given not to reveal client confidences. But in *The Practice*, our lawyers, on a weekly basis, question rules that lawyers have to follow in the real world. Our characters examine ethical conundrums that real lawyers don't ever question."

The characters in *The Practice* are in a constant struggle with moral dilemmas inspired by ethical rules that don't seem all that ethical. Indeed, the show is compelling precisely because the low-rent law firm that is depicted in *The Practice* oftentimes represents the most unscrupulous, morally challenged clients. This results in weekly collisions between lawyers who want to do the right thing but are hemmed in by the procedural constraints of the legal system, the moral failings of their clients, and the ethical duty of faithful representation.

Indeed, legal ethics is actually a misnomer, because the ethics that it speaks to is not a general sense of propriety, but rather something that is specific to lawyers alone. Like the words "remedy" and "relief," lawyers use the word "ethics" in a completely different context, separate from its ordinary meaning. Most people think of ethical conduct as being essentially the same thing as moral behavior. But legal ethics doesn't mean "doing the right thing." It means representing clients faithfully, according to the self-regulating ethical requirements of the profession: the rules of the game rather than the moral standards of right and wrong.

Helen Gamble, an assistant district attorney played by Lara Flynn Boyle on *The Practice*, said: "Legal ethics and morality are two different things; sometimes they fly in the face of each other." This statement is made during an episode involving a woman who had kidnapped a baby girl sixteen years earlier. Another woman was accused of the crime, and while she was never convicted, she continues to suffer from the stigma of having been accused. Meanwhile, the kidnapped child's mother is desperate to know whether her daughter is still alive. The kidnapper hires a law firm to communicate with both the accused and the mother, in order to assure the former that she indeed was not guilty, and the latter that her daughter is safe and well. She also wants to give each of them a cashier's check for $70,000, but has no interest in making herself known, or in revealing the whereabouts of the child, who is now a teenager, living happily with the kidnapper, unaware of her true identity. All the kidnapper seeks to do is provide some measure of emotional relief to the people she harmed. Meanwhile, the law firm is ethically bound by the attorney-client privilege not to disclose the name of their client—the kidnapper—even though that means the true mother will forever be deprived of her daughter.

Clearly, the assistant district attorney on *The Practice* is right: there is a great difference between legal ethics and private morality. When legal ethics starts to resemble moral behavior, it will go a long way toward restoring confidence in a legal system that unsparingly perpetuates immoral justice under the guise of law.

ZEALOUS ADVOCACY

We live in an age where we are understandably suspicious of zealots. Religious fanaticism and zealotry have been responsible for all sorts of recent tragedies, atrocities, mass murders, acts of terrorism, not to mention ordinary crimes committed in the name of something so presumably holy, it has to be expressed in unremorsefully pathological ways. Unchecked extremism in business practices have led to the financial collapse of world markets and the ruination of millions.

Zealotry is bad. It is a source of evil. Actually, it is the highest fulfillment of evil, because whatever form evil takes, and to whatever reason it owes its existence, it is harmless without the engine of zealotry that turns it from mere suppressed feelings into animated, irrepressible rage. Most of us would say that moderation, tolerance, and unselfish acts of caring and connection are values to which people should aspire. Zealotry is for people who are out of control in their beliefs, completely locked into their own truths, and out of touch with the rest of the planet. They place value only on their own values. Their loyalties are unshakeable within their secret societies. The world makes no sense to them without the nicotine kick that comes from attaching a healthy dose of zeal to a mission otherwise benign.

But obviously this mindset of caution when it comes to zealotry doesn't carry forward into the legal profession. Among lawyers, a distinctive badge of honor is the zealousness of an attorney's representation. The ABA Model Code of Professional Responsibility, which was enacted in 1969, stated that "a lawyer should represent a client zealously within the bounds of the law." While the entire code was replaced in 1983 by the Model Rules of Professional Conduct, the essence of zealousness has never left the hearts of practitioners. Even in law school—all throughout moot court and mock trial—young lawyers are trained to be aggressive fighters on behalf of their clients. They are taught that advocacy must be fierce and unrelenting. That in order to serve the client well, the lawyer must provide focused, unreserved, and unyielding representation.

This satisfies the winner-take-all dimensions of the legal system quite well. Lawsuits are always framed as one party versus the other. Once the lawsuit commences—even before then—interests are automatically deemed adverse, hostile, and colliding. And in a contest in which one side is always pitted against the other, there are no external, extenuating considerations—no common or public values. All that matters is securing an ultimate victory—regardless of truth, regardless of honor, regardless of what's right. And it is the zealous advocate, sharp teeth gleaming, nostrils flaring, an intemperate dose of zeal in evident display, who is singularly capable of winning the contests that the legal system instigates.

From a moral perspective, it is not the advocacy, or the representation, that is the problem. It's the particularly loaded, elevated noun that precedes it—zealotry. Zealousness is insatiable in its passion for victory and vindication. Zealotry will stop at nothing to win. Zealotry has a way of trampling over any respect for the truth.

So much of what passes for zealous advocacy in the law is all about fudging, spinning, and explaining away the unflattering elements of a client's story. And in the worst cases, the lawyer engages in outright lying. Truth is beside the point, achieving the right moral outcome even more so. The zealous advocate wants to know what actually happened, but doesn't want the rest of us to know. Truth is important only as a way to maintain damage control. Truth, it seems, is the best weapon for waging a preemptive strike. The zealous attorney is not interested in truth per se, just in its exploitation. While a client is speaking, the attorney is contemplating the best light in which to characterize the story.

And that light is a false light. It isn't beamed in order to illuminate the truth, but rather to blind and distort it.

In the law, zealotry leads to lies. One story is as good as any other; each expendable, easily unreliable. In the mind of a zealot, truth is always subject to manipulation. Find one truth, assert it passionately, and ignore the rest. The fuzzier the story, the better. Honesty is corrupted by gamesmanship. The attorney may be the mouthpiece and storyteller of his client. But zealous representation gives license to the telling of entirely fictional, but legally more palatable, tales. Throw up as many possibilities as the mind can imagine, and then let the jury trudge through the assembled confusion. Attorneys will often do whatever is necessary to claim victory, including not listening to the wishes of their clients, or fabricating new truths to replace actual ones that prejudice the client's case. Prosecutors in the criminal area zealously focus on conviction rates and jail time because it awards them an ultimate victory. Zealousness leads some prosecutors to withhold evidence, mislead witnesses, or cut deals with dangerous criminals in exchange for their testimony. Remedies that are moral and spiritual in nature, however, can be accomplished without having to resort much to zeal. But the absence of zeal somehow also makes them less interesting.

The zero-sum nature of the legal system, combined with the universal adoption of zealotry as the marching orders of practitioners and prosecutors, transforms the moral mission of the legal system from one of truth-seeking, storytelling, and justice, to one of fabrication, distortion, and manipulation in pursuit of victory. These victories, however, make us all the losers.

A lawyer should advocate for his or her client faithfully, should seek out the best result, and function as the client's representative before the law. But legal representation should not operate at the expense of truth, and never to the extent that the lawyer has actively participated in a miscarriage of justice—conducting himself in a way that violates the moral standards of the community. In *Nix v. Whiteside*, the Supreme Court ruled that lawyers cannot "advocate or passively tolerate a client's giving false testimony." In a law review article, Yale law professor Akhil Reed Amar speculated whether *Nix* should be applied in situations not only when attorneys put on perjured testimony, but also where, through cross-examination, they harass or deceive witnesses who they know to be telling the truth. In the name of zealotry and brash advocacy, how much confrontation does the confrontation clause of the 6th Amendment actually permit? Professor Amar also pondered why is it proper for attorneys to spin false theories and facts during their opening statements, knowing that its only purpose is to distract jurors, throwing them off the scent for the truth.

We all have our stereotypical image of lawyers, especially litigators, as pure Type A personalities, raw-meat eaters, crazed and maniacal, easily volatile, eager to uncork, aggressive and competitive to the core, squinting through their ever shrinking tunnel vision. They are referred to, respectfully, as bulldogs who know how to play hardball. These are the people who rise to any challenge, accept any dare, walk away fuming from any contest in which they do not win. They are generally sore losers, but they are always willing to play for double or nothing—doubling down forever until they get the result they want.

But the fact is, nobody likes people like these. You don't invite them to your house. You don't want them near your children. You don't want them breathing too close next to you. So why does the legal system hold open casting calls for, and reward so handsomely, the zealots among us? They are given the privileged position as the guardians of our most intimate secrets and purveyors of our necessary truths. But they have never received our trust, nor do they deserve it.

There is such a thing as advocacy without zealotry—principled advocacy, honorable advocacy, moral advocacy, but without the rage and gamesmanship that is being played out presumably on our behalf, but mostly to our detriment.

STATUTES OF LIMITATION

Truth should never be time-barred. Yet there are truths that never come to light, and injustices that go uncorrected, all because of limitations placed on the time period in which lawsuits can be brought. Some of these statutes of limitation vary by state, or by the type of action being contemplated, but the basic principle remains the same: After a certain period of time, if the case has not yet been filed, the claimant is prevented by the passage of time from doing so.

What moral justification is there to prevent truth-seeking and storytelling on account of an arbitrary bureaucratic date that bars claims? If the claim is otherwise legitimate, then preventing its telling neither serves justice nor instills any confidence in the legal system. Instead, given the reliance on statutes of limitation, the opposite conclusion is reached: When the legal system can find an excuse not to hear a case—to have it excluded or dismissed—it will do so rather than undertake the more moral, truth-seeking path where full, uninhibited, uninterrupted stories can be heard.

In 2003, in *Stogner v. California*, the United State Supreme Court, citing the Ex Post Facto Clause of the Constitution, which bars retroactive punishments, modified a California law that extended the statute of limitations for sex crimes committed against children under the age of eighteen. The new state law enabled prosecutors to bring sexual assault cases, regardless of the passage of time, so long as less than a year had elapsed since the victim first gave evidence of the crime to the police. The idea behind the law is that while children might be afraid to come forward because of their age and vulnerability, these same intimidations and hesitations may wither once they reach adulthood. The California legislature also made the law apply retroactively, which the Supreme Court rejected, because it effectively revived the statute of limitations for those for whom it had already expired, exposing accused individuals to criminal prosecutions decades after having committed the crime. Interestingly, in hearing oral argument on this case, consistent with its ultimate ruling, the Supreme Court was far more concerned about the retroactive implications of the law than on the revival of the statute of limitations for future offenders. This perhaps shows that, in some circumstances, courts recognize that imposing a statute of limitations is inappropriate, if not immoral, if it means closing off otherwise meritorious claims.

The Holocaust restitution cases are illustrative once more. Fifty years had passed since the liberation of the concentration camps, when the full extent of the evidence regarding concealed Swiss bank accounts and looted Nazi gold, paintings, and other assets finally became known. Pursuant to the Luxembourg agreements in the 1950s, Germany had been making ongoing restitution to the Jewish people in the form of monthly payments to survivors. But these new disclosures, for the most part, did not involve the past activities of the German government, and therefore were not covered by the Luxembourg accords. Given this new information about swindled Jewish assets that became known in the 1990s, it was now time for other nations to make restitution in connection with their role in the Holocaust. But after fifty years, should those claims still have legal standing?

The answer, morally, of course, is yes. Morally these nations were required to provide restitution as a way to acknowledge their past crimes. That's why they were compelled to ultimately join in the settlement. There were no tolling provisions in the aftermath of Nuremberg, no sense that after a period of time, if one could escape prosecution long enough, or if the truth of one's participation and complicity remained concealed, there could legally be no punishment. The story doesn't go away simply because it remains unknown or untold. And the passage of time should not act as a bar to the telling of that story.

In 2003, Kurt Werner Schaechter, an eighty-two-year-old Austrian-born French Jew, filed suit in France against its national railroad company, the National Railroad Service (SNCF), for having transported his parents, and thousands of other French Jews, to Nazi death camps. Between 1942 and 1944, the company in fact had transported 76,000 French Jews to various death camps in Poland. Only 2,500 ultimately survived. Schaechter sought merely a symbolic remedy in his lawsuit—just one euro as compensation. Obviously he wasn't after money. What he did want was for the SNCF to acknowledge its complicity in the deportation and death of these former French citizens, to accept responsibility and express remorse for its actions. What Schaechter wanted was not monetary relief, but moral relief, achieved through historical and restorative justice.

"I am doing this out of responsibility to history," Schaechter said. "What distinguishes us from animals is our memory. Humanity cannot forget its history."

Not surprisingly, the SNCF had its own ideas about legal liability, moral responsibility, and even about whether the company had any duty at all to memory and history. Yves Baudelot, the company's lawyer, argued that because the ten-year statute of limitations had expired for the filing of such claims, the entire case should be dismissed. And, legally at least, he turned out to be right. A two-member Paris court ultimately agreed with him, ruling that this civil case could only have been brought within ten years from the date when Mr. Schaechter's parents were killed.

It is true, of course, that the Holocaust was a special crime, and those who committed genocide, profited from ill-gotten gains, or engaged in complicit acts, should not, morally, have been able to escape prosecution and punishment on account of a statute that limited the time period for the filing of claims. This is precisely what makes the French court's decision in the Schaechter case so morally repugnant. But perhaps the principle should be applied more broadly, essentially eliminating statutes of limitation altogether in many extreme cases of inhumanity and unconscionable fraud. Meritorious claims should not be defeated by arbitrary cutoff dates, particularly when the claims had been unknown—and could not have been previously brought—because the evidence itself had been concealed. No one should be rewarded for suppressing the truth, and time should never run out on the truth. And, morally, no limitation should ever be placed on the telling of the truth.

As Mr. Schaechter's lawyer, Joseph Roubache, stated, "They have chosen the easy path. Crimes against humanity should not be subject to proscription under either civil or criminal law."

An unfortunate example of many of these themes at work involves the following tragic incident. The venue was German, and the claimants were Israeli, but the impulse to squelch the story was universally legal, and human nature was once again forced to absorb the grief without any justice from the law.

In 1972, during the Summer Olympics in Munich, eight members of the Palestinian terrorist group, Black September, entered the Olympic compound and killed an Israeli wrestling coach and one of his wrestlers, and then captured and held hostage nine members of the Israeli Olympic team. (The others had escaped through the back door or had gone out the window.) Eventually each of these hostages was killed at Furstenfeldbruck Airfield when the combined ineptitude of German policemen and snipers failed miserably in their rescue efforts. An Academy Award–winning documentary *One Day in September* (2000), made by filmmaker Kevin MacDonald, recorded the emotional intensity of the day and the aftermath of injustice that ensued. For years the German government covered up its mismanagement of the rescue operation. Indeed, they claimed that they had kept no records of the incident, which later turned out to be false.

Nearly twenty years later, the surviving relatives of the men who were murdered in Munich brought an action against the

Federal Republic of Germany, the Free State of Bavaria, and the regional capital of Munich for their misconduct and negligence in failing to take all appropriate steps to protect and save the athletes' lives. The Munich court promptly dismissed the case, citing a three-year statute of limitations that barred claims not brought in a timely fashion. The problem was that the Germans had concealed their records for two decades, which made the bringing of an earlier, timely claim impossible.

The German government essentially hid behind a statute of limitations even when it was its own actions that prevented the surviving families from learning the full extent of mismanagement that preceded the murders. One of the surviving relatives, Ankie Spitzer, said: "I wanted from the Germans a full account of what happened.... I wanted to know, and I think I had a right to know, what happened to my husband. Who killed him? How did he die?... I want those who were criminally negligent to have to face up to it, to take responsibility.... I don't want money, I don't want revenge, I just want the truth to be known."

What the surviving relatives most want is an official, ceremonial acknowledgment that the murders occurred, and that their losses are real. For decades the families have asked the International Olympic Committee (IOC) for a moment of silence at each of the succeeding and future Summer Olympic games. This gesture is virtually costless, but it would be a significant step toward achieving meaningful moral justice and repair.

"We want official recognition that something happened in 1972," said Mimi Weinberg, one of the surviving widows. "For people to know that I sent my husband to Munich and he came back in a coffin."

The IOC has repeatedly and steadfastly refused.

Although this was a German case, the invocation of the statute of limitations in this situation embodied the very spirit of creative lawyering that American courtrooms prize above all else, the kind of slick legal maneuvering that provokes such widespread disgust. Lawyers will do everything and anything to find the loophole and exploit the technicality. And in the end, the dust never settles, even if the case does. All that's left is yet another exhaled collective groan at the indecency of the legal system, shamelessly accepting immoral outcomes under the protective cover of law.

FORBIDDEN EMOTIONS IN A WORLD OUT OF ORDER

One image has appeared so often on television legal dramas that it is virtually fixed in our minds as bound to happen at any trial—at least in fictional ones. We have yet to grow weary of this image; indeed, we have almost come to expect it.

Whether on *Perry Mason*, *Matlock*, or *L.A. Law*, or any soap opera that requires an occasional trial to invigorate the plot, the scene goes something like this: Someone is giving testimony in the witness box and testifies in a particularly damaging way about one of the parties to the action. Indeed, what he says is not only prejudicial, it is a lie. Hearing this testimony, the party prejudiced by the statement rises to his feet and pounds the table, screaming:

"He's lying, Your Honor! He's lying!"

And that point, the judge locates his gavel and pounds away on his bench, saying: "I'll have none of that in my courtroom! You are out of order! Please sit down!"

And then, to the attorney representing the shouting party, the judge says: "Please advise your client that if there are any further outbursts of this sort, he will be removed from my courtroom. I won't tolerate this."

And then, to the jury, the judge turns and says: "I'm going to ask the jury to disregard what you have just heard. This outburst will be stricken from the record, and you are to pay it no mind."

Even as a fictional encounter, a legal cliché, it is an emotional absurdity. Yet moments like this take place each day in courtrooms all over America. And as bizarre as this is, and as much as it reveals about the legal system, it is not something that people pay much attention to. It's simply taken for granted that this is what protocol in a courtroom looks like.

But even to assume this kind of decorum, or to insist on it, is nonsensical, if not plain immoral. Everything about life is out of order. Indeed, life is unmistakably messy and irresolute. Why should a courtroom, which is the gathering spot of life's unresolved conflicts, be a place that denies the essential humanity of those who wander inside it? Why insist on order when it so misrepresents the human experience? Given these tremulous beginnings, we should not be robbing the trial of the very oxygen that breathed life into the original dispute.

Obviously the law expects human beings to act not according to their nature, but rather pursuant to the design plans of a machine. What they want is for the party to the action to control himself, even though the witness just told a pernicious lie, under oath, with the party's life or livelihood on the line. And even though this was perhaps the most interesting and honest encounter that the jury has witnessed, they will ignore what they saw and heard—erase it from their minds—simply because the judge told them to do so. And finally, yes, even if the witness should lie so maliciously once again, the party to the action should comport himself in keeping with the formality of the occasion.

Who could possibly control himself in such a situation, and who would want to? More important, isn't the court even mildly curious whether the outburst itself—raw, explosive, and impassioned as it is—might actually reveal some essential truth about the case? Put simply: Doesn't the very existence of such unleashed emotion suggest that the witness might indeed have been lying? Courts are obviously willing to ignore fundamental truths all for the sake of preserving some imperial notion of courtroom decorum.

For laymen, a trial is a trial—not just a lever on a legal machine, but a test of faith, patience, and stamina. Trials are traumatizing. The whole point of a trial is to recapture the past—the sights, sounds, and feelings that existed at each vital stage of the recalled experience. Nothing is to be left out. This is what is meant by testimony. It is not idle talk, but ardent recollection. Yet while recollection is supposed to be healing, it also provokes terror, because to recall an event, one must also feel and reexperience the emotions that encircled and infused it. The memories and emotions are inseparable, and can't be sequestered or quarantined. You can't state the facts without resurrecting the feelings. Emotions always come attached, even to the coldest of facts. Trials don't allow the putting of the past behind us—nor should they—no matter how often courts speak about cases being closed and judgments being final.

Trials are, if nothing else, trying. Emotions can't be controlled, regardless of the judge's stern instructions. That's why witnesses tend to repeat themselves when testifying under oath. And it's also why trials engender outbursts of moral outrage. Going to trial is like going into surgery. The surgeon may be without butterflies, but the patient has much going on in his stomach, even though it is not the stomach that is the source of his medical problem. Only judges and lawyers actually believe that it's possible to curb desperation and keep it from bleeding openly in a court of law. The rest of us know better.

In Herman Melville's *Billy Budd, Sailor*, Billy Budd is so overcome by Claggert's false accusation that Billy had instigated a mutiny that he cannot contain his primal instinct to rebut the charge. But since Billy suffers from a speech impediment, his frustration over not being able to verbally challenge the lie leads to a physical blow, killing Claggert and dooming Billy to an expedited murder trial that takes no account of any mitigating or extenuating circumstances.*

When confronted with a lie, one that is hurtful and damaging, it is perfectly human to react with all the rawness and emotion of someone falsely accused. Instead of silencing these people and castigating them as lunatics, why not presume that those who are compelled to stand up and shout down a liar are in fact telling the truth? It is, of course, possible that such emotional outbursts can be cynically orchestrated for effect. Showboating in front of the jury, all in the guise of staged moral outrage. But why not at least allow the jury to consider the sincerity of the outburst? But because courts place no emotional trust in anyone, the law ends up favoring a facade of order and decorum to the detriment of intellectual and emotional honesty.

The fact is, the law has an absolute, unqualified disdain for emotion, regardless of how it is expressed. So much of the legal system is designed to squelch human emotion, to deny that it has any place in a court of law. Emotions are never mentioned in law school, and probably do not appear in any hornbook or legal treatise. As absurd as this sounds, people are expected to appear before a court without their emotions getting in the way. Hysteria is not an effective trial strategy. Instead, they are supposed to be able to engage in a calm-mannered, emotionally neutral discussion about the facts and their application to the law. But anybody who has ever been a party to an action knows how close to the surface looms the impulse to cry.

In 2003, Dr. Clara Harris, a Houston dentist, was sentenced to twenty years in prison for murdering her husband. She had run over him three times in her Mercedes-Benz. The husband, David Harris, also a dentist, who had been in private practice with his wife, had been having an affair with their receptionist.

---

*And the fact that Billy kills Claggert with one punch suggests how explosive a retaliation a lie can unleash.

Throughout the trial, Dr. Harris was seen crying and sobbing, and in each instance she was admonished by the judge, Carol G. Davies, to stop. After being convicted of murder, during the sentencing phase of the trial, Dr. Harris began to sob once again upon hearing her stepdaughter's testimony.

After this display, Judge Davies ordered and threatened: "Be quiet. I'm going to give you one more chance. Don't blow it, or you will be out of the courtroom."

At that moment, Dr. Harris's lawyer, George Parnham, rose to his feet and said: "She just got convicted of murder."

Later during the hearing, the judge explained that she was not being insensitive to the emotions of a defendant in a murder case, but that a courtroom was not the appropriate place in which to show them.

This is a simply ludicrous decree, which makes one wonder how this judge can be sitting in judgment of other human beings. A courtroom is exactly where delicate, disorderly emotions should be expressed. The trial naturally stirred up a variety of complicated emotions in a human being who had murdered her husband in the presence of her stepdaughter, and the jury should have been able to witness them. Dr. Harris is not a machine. Her primal feelings could not be turned off merely because a judge instructed her to do so. It was only the self-importance of this judge, and her inhuman sense of courtroom decorum, that deprived the defendant, and the jury, of the genuine human experience that would have been healing for the defendant and revealing for the jury.

This image of the lawyer inured to human emotion—totally disconnected to the pain of their clients—is a favorite subject among artists. In the film *Erin Brockovich*, a female attorney who has none of the powers of empathy of the title character, says to her grief-stricken clients: "We need specific details when the symptoms began. . . . If you could reserve sentimental embellishments I'd appreciate it, because it's not going to help you in court. I just need facts, dates, times."

This is what the law insists upon: stoics and Zen masters, men and women of dispassion, even amidst all the grief.

Novelists and filmmakers are drawn to courtrooms, in part, because the phenomenon of judgment—among peers and before a judge—and the emotions that get elicited at trials, are naturally compelling. There is no need to create dramatic moments when the setting automatically calls for them. Yet judges routinely ignore the maelstrom of emotion that accompanies the parties' anticipation of judgment. In fact, judges wish to will it all away so that it won't muck up the antiseptic sterility of their proceedings.

For this reason, the most emotional moments in a courtroom are generally found in art, not in life. The artist knows what to do with this raw material, while the judge acts like an insipid censor, dissecting facts that are totally divorced from feelings. Judges like to think of their courtrooms as operating rooms, as petri dishes of the human condition, observed only for clinical, legal purposes, and not out of any curiosity or to better understand the living tissues of life.

Many examples exist of the way in which the legal system shows its repugnance for human feeling. The law pretends that people walk into courtrooms without prejudices and preconceptions, have no right to react humanly to what they see there, and leave without having been transformed—if not made miserable—by their encounter with the law.

The selection of juries is one area where this unrealistic expectation and preference come into play. Courts operate under the presumption that jurors are blank-slate human beings, empty vessels of indifference, purely impartial and wholly objective. We need such people, the legal system insists. Indeed, they are our ideal citizens when serving on juries. Through the practice of voir dire, lawyers can strike from the jury those people who, through questioning, have shown themselves to have already formed an opinion, and not an indifferent one, about the very issue the court is preparing itself to hear.

For instance, in a criminal case involving drugs, it's important to know whether any of the potential jurors, or their families, have had experiences with drug use or drug dealers, or whether they may have special sensitivities on the issue. In cases where the police were involved, it's useful to know whether any of the prospective jurors have had unfavorable encounters with police officers, or whether they are related to one, or whether they have any predispositions toward believing that the police are always either law-abiding or predictably corrupt. In medical-malpractice cases, relatives of doctors, particularly surgeons, depending on the situation, might be excused from service on the jury. In copyright-infringement cases dealing with intellectual property, the relatives of an artist may possess a bias prejudicial enough to invoke a peremptory challenge.

What the courts want—what they believe to exist—are jurors who hold no strong opinions on or attachments to anything, and have no particular feelings or attitudes about the subject of the trial. The legal system presumes that objectivity is not only essential to a fair and unbiased examination of the facts, but that wholly objective people, in fact, exist in the world. They walk among us like wayward deer: obtuse to the world, oblivious to their surroundings, unaffected by the news of the day—and totally untainted by prejudice. Having somehow avoided all the unpleasantries and stresses of ordinary modern life, they come to us without any rage or resentment, without any past that could possibly intrude on their present responsibility to sit in judgment of other human beings. They will see the facts clearly, because their minds are miraculously unclouded by distraction. They are able to focus on the case and on nothing else. All we have to do is identify these fair-minded but empty-headed people from the pool of summoned applicants, and empanel them on the jury before they become contaminated and influenced by the outside world.

Most lawyers don't like to admit that what they're looking for in a jury is a group of people who represent the lowest common denominator of the community. For this reason, it is generally not an honor but an insult to be selected to serve on a jury. The most transparent expression of this preference was that there was a time when people with college educations had little chance of getting picked. And those with advanced degrees? Forget it. Lawyers themselves either could not, or would never be, selected to serve. Much of that has now changed, mostly because the education levels of the general population have increased, and advanced degrees are not all that uncommon.

What has not changed is that anyone who presents himself as too independent-minded, strong-willed, free-spirited, opinionated, or smart is likely to be removed, if for no other reason than his potential influence on the other jurors. When I clerked for a federal judge years ago in Miami, it became obvious to me that, in selecting their juries, lawyers were looking for people who worked for either Eastern Airlines or Burger King, both companies with corporate headquarters located in Miami. It wasn't just that these two large corporations were the primary employers in Miami, so that the jury pool was likely to include at least some of their employees. What made them attractive breeding grounds for jurors was that they already encouraged conformity. Whether their employees were working behind the counter or on the plane, each company had a specific uniform, and demanded an attention to rules. In the minds of most Miami lawyers, those who worked for such institutions would produce a perfect jury—not of peers, but of pure blandness and homogeneity.

Of course, lawyers often fail to get whom they want on their juries. And this happens not only because sometimes they select unwisely. It's just that what they are looking for doesn't truly exist in the general population. What they want are human beings who don't register human qualities. The *Stepford Wives*, after all, were engineered; they didn't just materialize from the suburbs without tremendous manipulation of the human anatomy. The same thing is true of jurors. If we want them to have no feelings and no past, we're going to have to start from scratch and create a new breed of unfeeling, unopinionated, desensitized men and women. They will need to be sequestered from the rest of humanity. Take away their newspapers and TVs. Deprive them of alliances and relationships. Give them no special skills, ardent hobbies, or past lives. In the end we'll get human clones who look like us but have no story of their own.

Human beings are not by nature blank, not even the most densely neutral among us. Every human being comes ready-assembled with the potential for bias and prejudgment. And we evolve into people who act on these predispositions, even if we don't admit to having them. If you are part of this world, then you have had at least some minimal, nominal encounter with an institution, enterprise, entity, or person that might have caused you harm or rubbed you the wrong way. There are faces that for some known or unknown reason you just can't, or won't, trust. You stroll around and carry the imprint of a moment inside you, like a bar code that gets scanned as you walk through life. People are naturally partial, even if they think of themselves as unflinchingly fair.

The Trial, by Franz Kafka, addresses the way nuanced prejudice is often part of the legal process. In his first bizarre conversation with Bloch, another man of Prague who has surrendered his life to defending himself in front of the law, Joseph K. learns that people already believe that he is guilty, simply because of the line of his lip:

> You must remember that in these proceedings things are always coming up for discussion that are simply beyond reason, people are too tired or distracted to think and so they take refuge in superstition. . . . And one of the superstitions is that you're supposed to tell from a man's face,

especially the line of his lips, how his case is going to turn out. Well, people declared that judging from the expression of your lips, you would be found guilty, and in the near future too.

If jurors were completely impartial, lawyers wouldn't tell their clients to wear a nice suit to court, or to cut their hair, or to stand straight and not stand out, or to look directly into the eyes of witnesses. It wouldn't matter to a jury that had no preconceived biases or expectations about what a party to an action should look like. The only impression of consequence would be the truth. The jury would be charged with finding the facts and nothing more, because they wouldn't be looking for anything else. Attractiveness, appearance, and likeability would have no bearing at all on the outcome.

Similarly, after a jury has been instructed to disregard an outburst, who actually believes that they can, and will, erase it from their minds? Surely it's going to linger in their memory and affect the outcome.

The film *Legally Blonde*, an otherwise silly movie, offered at least one truth about the legal system. Elle Wood, a Harvard law student played by Reese Witherspoon, delivers a speech on behalf of her graduating class, and quotes Aristotle: "The law is reason free from passion." Aristotle was not a lawyer, but he did give lawyers a good slogan to live by, because most lawyers and judges believe this statement to be true. But Elle, the L.A. beach babe, challenges Aristotle without resorting to the Socratic method, and says that, in her view, passion is essential for lawyers, whether they are practising law, or life. Elle is no doubt right. Whether they admit it or not, lawyers and judges are never free from passion, and neither are the clients and citizens they serve.

Indeed, a moral justice system is one in which lawyers and judges would openly embrace more passion, not less. Passion not for the law, which is pathetic, but passion for the human experience, which is essential. What our society needs is more compassionate, empathetic lawyers, not cut off from humanity and walled off from their emotional responses to life, but totally integrated within them. We need lawyers and judges who feel responsible not just to the law, but to their private, moral conscience, and their duties to the larger community. We must demand lawyers who are as capable with human feelings as they are with legal reasoning.

Everyone associated with the legal system has a lot to learn in adopting a greater sense of mutual caring and connection in dealing with those who come before it.

Despite the wisdom offered by Atticus Finch in *To Kill a Mockingbird*, lawyers generally refuse to walk in another man's shoes. Instead, they choose the predictable, sensible-shoe, comfortable path that leads strictly to the courthouse, with all its dizzying docket numbers and zigzag rituals, a place where the resulting mess can be filed away even though all those untidy emotions cannot. And instead of speaking plain English, they hold court only in the language of law.

Judges refuse to acknowledge their own biases, but they abhor the possibility that parties or witnesses might have biases of their own. Along with its disdain for emotion, the legal system has an even more exaggerated contempt for subjectivity. When a witness's testimony is deemed biased, lawyers invoke all sorts of procedural and evidentiary rules to either exclude the testimony, or to have it discredited or disregarded. But why should witness testimony be discounted simply because there might be subjectivity in the person but not necessarily in the testimony? Isn't it possible that the subjective witness may actually be telling the truth? When it comes to the parties to the action, or their immediate relatives, we are asked always to assume partiality. The legal system apparently assumes that similar to blank-slate jurors, witnesses won't have emotional or subjective responses to the case unless they have a personal stake in the outcome.

Evidence rules are often used to defeat the testimony of witnesses who are either parties to the action, or are deemed too emotionally and subjectively involved to speak factual truths. Because of the general assault on subjectivity in the law, the information these witnesses possess isn't taken seriously, and is ignored legally. What the legal system wants are eyewitnesses whose eyes remain clear of subjective interference. But in rooting out what would exist anyway—in nature, in the human soul—courtrooms are deprived of eyewitness veracity, truths of the best kind precisely because they involve the direct recounting of an event, along with the simultaneous emotion of having a life radically upended and altered.

Another area of the law that has no regard for emotional complexity involves findings of fact. In every case that ends in a court-imposed resolution, whether by way of a final judgment at the end of a trial, or through a motion for summary judgment before the trial ever gets underway, the judge will write an order or opinion that includes the findings of fact, which are usually determined by either the jury or the judge, or sometimes stipulated by the parties themselves. This is the factual story of the case, the final record that sets forth the facts of the dispute, which is now resolved. Anyone who wants to know what happened is welcome to visit the records division of the courthouse and read what the court found to be the facts—unless, of course, for some privacy reason, the court file and its contents have been sealed. The application of the law and the outcome of the case derive from these found facts. The presumption is that these facts have not only been found, but they are now unimpeachable. Absent an appeal, both sides agree that this is the final, unchallenged version of what happened—found by a jury, written by a judge, accepted by all. And even if subject to an appeal, these facts are seldom capable of being overturned, unless a new trial is ordered and new findings are made.

But it is a myth that the winners of a legal action depart from the courthouse feeling completely vindicated, luxuriating in the judgment that favored them on that particular day. And the myth about the losers is even greater. The defeated party never leaves the building enamored of the judgment, fully accepting that these found facts constitute the complete, final, and most truthful account of what occurred. These losers of the law are sent either home or to prison, disgruntled, far from chastened, sometimes even more aggrieved, not simply because of the loss, but the way in which it came about.

Calling something "findings of fact," with the imperial definiteness suggested by this phrase, reveals the intellectual arrogance of the legal system. Facts are actually hard to find, and even when you find them, you can't be so sure that they are indeed facts. Or perhaps they are facts, but there is no truth to them—emotionally and literally. They remain elusive, even when we believe we have pinned them down. They habituate naturally in gray zones. Sometimes they are obvious to the eye, but more often they are shadowy and abstract. Truth is more easily said than known. We are trash-talkers when it comes to truth, because it is really only our private, particular truths that we are sure of. And there are considerable doubts even about those.

We have all had arguments with family and friends when we can't believe the other's recollection of an event or conversation that took place. We wind up exasperated, saying: "Is that what you think happened? I can't believe that's how you see it!" Then we walk around for days, shocked and embittered by the obtuseness, or worse, disingenuousness of the people around us, the people we otherwise love. Are they maliciously denying us our stories and our truths, or are they simply locked into their own truths, which are equally complex, proprietary, and ultimately unknowable?

In E. L. Doctorow's *The Book of Daniel*, Daniel, whose parents were executed for allegedly providing the Soviets with classified information about the atomic bomb, confronts the daughter of the man who accused his parents of a crime no one could actually prove, and which probably did not even take place. Daniel expects Linda Mindish, the daughter, to feel remorseful and sympathetic, since her father was unpunished while his parents were sent to prison and then to the electric chair. But Daniel discovers that rather than being repentant, the other family remembers the story in an entirely different, accusatory, and self-exonerating way. Daniel, as narrator, says: "And then that moment passed and I saw her as locked into her family truths as we were locked in ours."

So why should we expect judges and juries—no matter how long or hard they deliberate—to be able to find facts when the actual witnesses and participants to the dispute have no clarity, just conflicting versions of the same story? And even when the facts are undisputed, incontrovertible, and clear, there are still emotional truths simmering within the parties themselves, hurts and grievances that are genuine and true to them even if they can't be found by a jury or relieved by a court. Facts need to be understood in the context of deeper emotional complexities that go beyond a simple determination of whether the traffic light was green or red when the car was passing underneath it. And it's precisely these complexities that resist being found by a court of law, or a court of anything else. Some truths transcend trials. They outlive verdicts. They are the phase two that follows the final judgment. It is folly to claim that a court has discovered the facts of the case when there is such irreconcilable disagreement among those who know better.

But that's not how the legal system sees itself. Judges believe that they get it right even when they focus on facts that have no connection to the emotional spheres of life. Emotional truths, after all, are wholly interior and internal, incapable of being truly exposed in the courthouse. You can't diagram emotions or subject them to cross-examination. They don't make for good exhibits.

And because judges have such disregard for emotion, there is no way to properly account for them. Judicial infallibility, mixed with blind faith in legal reasoning and the certainty of objective truths, leaves no room for emotional complexity at all.

Courts are once again kidding themselves. Emotionally, the individual spirit rebels against what is false, immoral, and unjust. The pounding of a gavel won't make it all go away, because the heartbeat of injustice will rage on even louder. Unresolved, unmediated grievances have a way of returning as pathology—both in the courthouse, in the form of appeals that churn without end, enriching lawyers and yet bringing no satisfaction to clients; and outside the courthouse, in the manner of damaged lives all too willing to express their disappointment in destructive ways. Parties appeal legal actions and misdirect their pain elsewhere simply because they wish to be relieved of the indignity of what happened when they came before the law and wound up so unceremoniously dismissed. Sometimes an appeal is a true appeal, not merely the seeking of a reversal, but something even more— the return of what had been lost emotionally at trial.

Near the end of Herman Melville's *Billy Budd, Sailor*, there is a description of how the case against Billy was reported in a naval journal that covered the news on the high seas. The report essentially represented the last word on the matter, the only account of the affair. For the reader of Melville's story, what's striking and horrifying is the realization that this report lives on as the official record of the proceedings—distorted and twisted though it may be. It is the truest fiction of the short story. The reader knows that Billy Budd's crime, and the actions that preceded it, cried out for mitigation and extenuation. The murder of Claggert was not a true capital crime, but an act of self-defense against Claggert's slander against Billy. Yet the report that gets written—the findings of fact about the murder case involving Billy Budd and his alleged murder of Claggert—tells a very different story from the one the reader is painfully aware of. The drumhead court didn't get it right. The ultimate facts are a lie, and the emotional complexity of the story is not accounted for either in the trial or the final report.

Of course, this happens all the time—not in literary fiction but in actual legal proceedings. An injustice takes place in the courthouse, the losing party is devastated, and the official record of the proceeding—the reported court decision—publishes specific findings of facts that bear no relationship to the actual truth. People reading the decision have no reason to doubt that this account accurately describes what had happened. And the defeated party must live with the knowledge that there is no way to correct the errors, to fill in the omissions, to redact those facts that should never have been found, because they are no better than untruths. These findings may have the imprimatur of the jury, but the audience for truth is much larger, and the stakes infinitely higher. How are losing parties to reconcile themselves not only to the indignity of the trial itself, but to the published falsehoods that masquerade as unimpeachable facts?

Such are the consequences of a legal system that abandons its people to harsh, rash, false, meaningless judgments. A justice system that is more interested in the system than in justice. But injustice always preserves its primal urgency, never letting go until some measure of right can intercede and replace the wrong.

Courthouses are stages where life gets played out in miniature, but life is a drama that simply can't be staged. Courts are in the business of compression; judges like to isolate the injury, mark it with an X, poke around until some approximate truth shakes loose. Yet, rather than humanizing the law, courts end up dehumanizing the human experience.

Sometimes defendants won't, or simply can't, speak. Whether due to incapacity or some other block, the defendant won't share his story. The truth is there, but it is too interior a truth, and so therefore the law won't go looking for it. The truth will require coaxing. The burden, nonetheless, remains on the party to tell his or her story, without the court's assistance.

Courts are also only interested in the story being told in a particular way. But truth sometimes shows up according to its own timetable. The story may not come out right on command, with a gun to its head and a stopwatch ticking by its side. Some parties are able to speak to their circumstances and others are not. Some are simply better storytellers; others lack the finesse or performance skills to say anything at all.

Yet since the law operates under an adversarial system, with one side pitted against the other, if one party is holding back, or is emotionally unable to speak, or is incapacitated in speaking, or is simply an ineffective speaker, the truth will be sacrificed to the inadequacy of the telling, even if the court is aware—or could be aware—of another, more truthful truth.

Novelists have long represented this tragic dynamic in the law. Mersault suffers from an existential crisis in Camus's *The Stranger*, a numbness, shock, and detachment traceable to his mother's recent death. He simply can't, or won't, defend himself in the way the court ordinarily would expect. He is unremorseful, and his response to grief unconventional. He refuses to explain the backstory that preceded his murder of the Arab. And his lawyer is incompetent in explaining it for him. What is a court to do when the defendant is blocked emotionally and cannot say what is necessary to gain either his freedom, or the court's sympathy?

In *Billy Budd, Sailor*, Billy Budd suffers from both a speech impediment and a deaf ear to suppressed spiritual places, and therefore cannot explain what would have motivated Claggert to spread such a rumor about him. Captain Vere knows the truth— Billy doesn't deserve to die a capital death. Yet Captain Vere chooses to apply martial law strictly, and immorally. Billy can't articulate the elements of mitigation in his favor, and so Captain Vere takes no account of them.

Similarly, in *The Merchant of Venice*, Shylock is blocked emotionally by his long-simmering, newly activated rage. And for this reason, he is unable to state his case in a civilized manner, other than to insist on receiving his pound of flesh. The court never hears the emotional trauma of the man making this demand, nor does it choose to look underneath the rage to find the backstory of hurt that animates it. Presented only with what it can see and hear, and taking Shylock literally at his word, the Venetian court misses the underlying truth and achieves the completely wrong moral result.

This is predictable, in both art and in life. What passes for direct examination in the law is neither direct, nor deep. By placing a blockade on human emotions, courts end up oblivious to so much. Courts need to look beyond what simply materializes on a given day, in a given moment, before their eyes. Anyone can make a finding of fact with that kind of unclouded visibility. And yet the law ultimately endows this easy evidence with sometimes undeserved legal meaning.

Emotional complexity requires magnified vision. What the artist knows to be true is the way in which the legal system denies the emotional experience of human beings. And without an appreciation of those interior worlds where emotional lives give way to legal actions, some truths will never actually be known, and the law will be the less wiser for it.

JUDGES WHO FEIGN
NOT HAVING FEELINGS

J udges like to think of themselves as inured to human feeling. Once the robe is on, the heart stops. What happens in the courtroom requires the utmost emotional detachment. Objectivity reigns. And, of course, judges should never admit their own error, or acknowledge that they have particular feelings or biases about a case.

Learned Hand, however, a legendary federal judge who sat on the Court of Appeals for the Second Circuit, was a good example of a jurist who offered some emotional and intellectual honesty in his opinions, particularly when those legal decisions may have seemed morally wrong. In *United States v. Dennis*, a case decided in 1950, the defendants were convicted under the Smith Act for having conspired to organize the Communist Party in order to overthrow the United States government. *Dennis* was one of many Red Scare cases in which people were convicted for their Communist activities and alliances, all the while asserting their First Amendment right to engage in political free speech. In this case, the court of appeals ultimately ruled that the Smith Act did not violate the free-speech principles of the Constitution, and therefore upheld the convictions against Dennis and his codefendants.

But when Dennis raised the argument that he could not receive a fair trial as an avowed Communist in America during the Cold War, Judge Hand wrote:

> [A]s it turns out, it is probable that the trial was at a less unpropitious time than any that has succeeded it, or is likely to follow. Certainly we must spare no effort to secure an impartial panel; but those who may have in fact committed a crime cannot secure immunity because it is possible that the jurors who may try them may not be exempt from the general feelings prevalent in the society in which they live; . . .

Judge Hand wrote what most judges would never admit. There are times when the objective man does not exist, or has gone on hiatus, and all who remain are the completely partial, subjective men among us. Muslim men after September 11th may not receive a fair trial in a courtroom at this time. The same would have been true of the Germans and Japanese during World War II, and it was certainly the case with Communists in the 1950s.

During the 1950s, most people in this country regarded communists with nothing but contempt. Only a few Americans were indifferent, and hardly any were sympathetic. And, as Judge Hand wrote, at the time, those feelings didn't fade quickly enough to untaint a jury. What Judge Hand essentially acknowledged was that feelings and emotions matter, and that they are always present—sometimes more keenly felt or widely shared than at other times, but present nonetheless. In doing so, Judge Hand admitted that Dennis and his codefendants perhaps had not received an impartial trial, even though courts are supposed to ensure fairness and fair play. Unfortunately, the sympathies in the country, at that time, simply didn't fall in their favor.

Judge Hand conceded: "We must do as best we can with the means we have."

Remarkably, Judge Hand's opinion didn't pretend that the general public's feelings against Communism was neutral, and that blank-slate jurors were available to serve. On the contrary, the times were sufficiently heated so as to make it impossible to select an impartial jury. But a jury had to be selected, and the prosecution had to proceed in spite of the prejudice. And the defendants were summarily found guilty.

Often we are ruled by our subjective experiences and perceptions, no matter how much we deny it and proclaim our fairness. Indeed, in the same opinion, Judge Hand provided a subtle attack against the entire process of *voir dire* and its promise to root out the subjectivities and biases of prospective jurors. In doing so, he adopted an emotionally honest approach, one that asserts that human nature will inevitably interfere with the pretenses of objectivity. He wrote: "*voir dire* is a clumsy and imperfect way of detecting suppressed emotional commitments to which all of us are to some extent subject, unconsciously or subconsciously. It is of the nature of our deepest antipathies that often we do not admit them even to ourselves."

What Judge Hand was saying—horrible for lawyers to read yet unassailably true—is that jurors are not blank-slate human beings. They have opinions on matters, even if they have never considered those opinions before. Through a trial the more self-aware jurors may come to learn that they actually don't like cops, or surgeons, or surfboard manufacturers. And they may discover, to their utter amazement, that they will casually give the benefit of the doubt to a white person but wouldn't extend the same presumption of innocence or good faith to a person of color. Even worse, Judge Hand reminds us that often during periods of great political fervor, upheaval, and paranoia, a jury is inexorably contaminated with bias and there may be no jurors sympathetic to the man on trial.

Sometimes the reverse is true: No matter what the evidence or the moral dimension of the case, the jury will not convict the defendant. This happened during the Civil Rights era in the Deep South, where Klansmen were acquitted of killing southern blacks and northern freedom riders even though the evidence against them, and what the jury heard, should have resulted in convictions. And, of course, the O. J. Simpson jury seemed to have such a disdain for the L.A. Police Department that the evidence pointing toward Simpson's guilt appeared to be immaterial. All that mattered was the jury's cynicism and mistrust toward those who gathered the evidence. There was no benefit of the doubt, no reason to shift the presumptions away from where everyone on the jury was leaning. A murder trial became a referendum on race, a guilty man was set free, and the resulting justice was legally correct but morally reprehensible. Sometimes the jury pool is comprised of people entirely like-minded against one side or the other. In those instances, the case is over before it even starts.

Attorney General John Ashcroft wasn't nearly as forthcoming as Judge Hand when he proposed sweeping investigative and prosecutorial initiatives to combat terrorism in the aftermath of the September 11th tragedy, pursuant to the Patriot Act. The attorney general routinely came across as tentative, and at times even squirming, when asked to explain how his fast-track, furtive procedures to interview, arrest, and interrogate Middle Eastern men was consistent with civil liberties. His concept of military tribunals provoked even greater discomfort—and for good reason. The fact is: Middle Eastern men with any links to Al Qaeda were going to receive a very different brand of justice from the rest of us, and it was absurd for the attorney general to make it seem as though these post–September 11th investigations and prosecutions complied with constitutional safeguards of justice.

These were indeed strange times and special circumstances. There might have been strong moral and political reasons to justify Ashcroft's various undertakings, as abhorrent as they may have sounded to civil libertarians. Ashcroft wasn't entirely truthful when he tried to suggest that his legal initiatives comported with the law. Because they didn't. Unfortunately, he tried to present his case in legal terms. But the constitutional ground on which he was standing was genuinely shaky. He would have been far better off, and more intellectually honest, had he instead rested on the moral foundation of Ground Zero. The hole in the ground where the World Trade Center once stood may have warranted an alternative path to justice, one perhaps that was legally suspect but morally sound.

Judge Learned Hand, by contrast, made a career of acknowledging fault lines in the law in ways that most judges, or attorney generals, would not. *Schmidt v. United States*, decided in 1949, is one of my favorite examples. Schmidt, a native of Germany and a City College professor of French and German, was denied citizenship because he failed to establish that he was a person of "good moral character" for the five years prior to petitioning for naturalization. In every other way he was qualified to become a citizen, except that, as Judge Hand wrote, "in a moment of what may have been unnecessary frankness," Schmidt admitted that from time to time he had had consensual sexual intercourse with unmarried women. He didn't have to reveal this information to the immigration authorities, and it obviously had a negative impact on his application. The issue for Judge Hand was whether this admission showed Schmidt to be not a person of good moral character.

The court ultimately ruled that casual sex had by an unmarried man with single women does not defeat a claim to having good moral character. Schmidt should not have been denied citizenship on account of these sexual experiences. But in arriving at this result, Judge Hand conceded that he wouldn't really know

how to decide what good moral character meant in this situation.
He wrote:

> It would not be practical—even if the parties had asked
> for it, which they did not—to conduct an inquiry as to
> what is the common conscience on the point. Even
> though we could take a poll, it would not be enough
> merely to count heads, without any appraisal of the
> voters. A majority of the votes of those in prisons and
> brothels, for instance, ought scarcely to outweigh the
> votes of accredited churchgoers. Nor can we see any rea-
> son to suppose that the opinion of clergymen would be
> a more reliable estimate than our own.... [We must]
> resort to our own conjecture, fallible as we recognize it
> to be.

There are two extraordinary acknowledgments in this decision that are rarely found in the published opinions of most
judges. First, no one has the last word on morality, or even on
knowing what is moral—including judges themselves. No one's
credentials on the question of good moral character are superior
to anyone else's, and no one person's opinion on the matter
should be more influential than another's. The second idea,
somewhat related to the first, is that judges themselves are falli-
ble, and that sometimes they make decisions that end up being
wrong. Since many decisions are based on conjecture, they invariably are subject and prone to judicial fallibility. This display
of intellectual and emotional honesty is quite unusual, because
judges rarely, if ever, admit when they are wrong, or when the
law is wrong. Nor is it typical for a judge to acknowledge that
there are some things that are simply unknowable, no matter
whom you ask or what criteria you use. Judge Hand basically
wrote that morality is subjective, judges make mistakes, and it
would have been far better for Schmidt to have kept his mouth

shut and not to have so candidly disclosed his sexual history. The naturalization authorities didn't actually have to know this information in order to decide on his fitness for citizenship.

Why do judges have difficulty admitting their own fallibility, or the fact that sometimes the law is simply wrong? It would go a long way toward instilling public confidence in the judiciary if judges acknowledged that they are capable of error, or admitted that sometimes the results of their decisions are legally correct yet might seem morally wrong to the public. Claimants would be more willing to admit their own faults if judges could do the same in their own courtrooms.

When the Supreme Court of the United States decided to hear the case of *Lawrence v. Texas* in the early winter of 2002, it gave itself an opportunity to admit that it had made a prior error in the 1986 decision of *Bowers v. Hardwick*. Both cases dealt with the constitutionality of state sodomy statutes, and whether the constitutional right to privacy extended to homosexual activity. In *Bowers*, in a 5-4 decision, the Supreme Court ruled that the right to privacy did not protect such conduct, and thereby upheld the constitutionality of the Georgia statute.

But one of the judges, who voted along with the slim majority, later admitted that he believed that he had made a mistake. Justice Lewis Powell, who had cast the deciding vote, said that he should have ruled the other way, finding the sodomy statute to be unconstitutional. Although he never had another opportunity to correct the error by ruling in a subsequent case on the same issue, Justice Powell publicly acknowledged that it was wrong not to have extended the right to privacy to homosexual conduct.

This was an uncommon and admirable gesture on the part of a sitting Supreme Court justice. Essentially, Powell did what most judges would never do: publicly admitted judicial error and showed regret for that decision. But why should this be so unusual? Isn't this what parents teach their children in order to foster a sense of integrity and personal responsibility? If judges aren't capable of admitting when they are wrong, what kind of an example does that set for the rest of us? Shouldn't judges be susceptible to being judged, and judging themselves?

The *Lawrence* case allowed the Court to change its mind and overrule itself, which it ultimately did in June 2003, when it found the Texas statute making sodomy a crime to be unconstitutional. Justice Anthony M. Kennedy wrote in his 6-3 majority opinion, "*Bowers* was not correct when it was decided, and it is not correct today. Its continuance as precedent demeans the lives of homosexual persons."

But the general rule that governs these situations is that a court should not overrule one of its precedents simply because it believes that it decided incorrectly the first time. For instance, in the 1992 case of *Planned Parenthood v. Casey*, the Supreme Court explained that "the decision to overrule should rest on some special reason over and above the belief that a prior case was wrongly decided." The Supreme Court set forth a series of factors that a court should consider before overturning a prior decision, but none of these factors dealt with the specific admission that a mistake had been made. Under *Casey*, the Supreme Court can overrule itself and change its mind without ever having to admit that its reasoning had been incorrect the first time. Similarly, the very existence of a prior error, by itself, is not even a factor in deciding whether a case should be overruled.

For this reason, given the low threshold for emotional and intellectual honesty that the Supreme Court has established for itself, Justice Powell's acknowledgment of his own error in the aftermath of *Bowers* was heroic. As Kenji Yoshino, a law professor at Yale Law School, wrote in an op-ed that appeared in the *New York Times:*

> It may be that it is easier for an individual to admit error
> than it is for an institution. This reluctance to confess
> past mistakes is especially pronounced in the judiciary,

whose legitimacy and power depend on public trust in its pronouncements. Yet it needn't be so. While acknowledging the importance of consistency, we can also ask whether the court's authority would be diminished through greater candor. The answer is no.

Of course this raises yet another question of whether judges can show themselves to be human beings while on the bench. Are they real people underneath those robes, or are they as sterilized and robbed of emotion and feelings as they wish their courtrooms to be? There is nothing that prevents judges from revealing their humanity, other than their exaggerated, proprietary sense of decorum.

Recently, Supreme Court Justice Clarence Thomas, during an oral argument in the case of *Virginia v. Black*, engaged in an uncharacteristic personal narrative from the bench. This case, which involved an incident of cross-burning on an African-American family's lawn, provoked the otherwise taciturn justice to comment on whether such conduct should be afforded protection under the First Amendment as legitimate political speech. Justice Thomas entered the conversation not by asking a question of the attorney making his argument, but rather by delivering his own impassioned, emotionally charged remarks. Speaking as an African-American and not as a judge, he reminded the Court of the horror that this provocative symbol signified to his persecuted community. He explained that a burned cross communicates "no particular message" other than to unleash a "reign of terror."

Given the fact that Justice Thomas is perhaps the most conservative judge on a Supreme Court that has distinguished itself as being pretty liberal on First Amendment issues, his words took everyone by surprise, including his own colleagues on the Court. For that moment, Thomas slipped out of his robe and stepped into the shoes of a black man. And, at least emotionally, the shoes fit far better than the robe, and he was humanized more than at any other time in his tenure on the bench, and more than anyone had ever seen him before.

Two interesting highlights resulted from Thomas's remarks. The first was that the other justices joined in, echoing their own feelings, attacking cross-burning as dangerous symbolic speech that should be outside the protection of the First Amendment. An uncharacteristic sentiment from such an otherwise free speech—oriented Court. (Consistent with these comments from the bench, the Court ultimately ruled later in 2003 that a properly drafted statute, which outlaws an act of cross-burning that is carried out with an intent to intimidate, is constitutional.) Perhaps they were made uncomfortable by their colleague's personal reflections of racial injustice and pain, and, as an expression of solidarity, wanted him to know that they understood how pernicious and harmful cross-burning was to the collective dignity of all African-Americans.

But outside of the Supreme Court, there were those who were upset with Justice Thomas for his unexpected, and ultimately digressive, personal narrative. By implicitly proclaiming his own experience as a black man in America, he had subverted the very essence of judicial decision-making, which requires the judge not to have a personal stake in the outcome, to rule with dispassion—from an emotional distance. In telling his own story, he had contaminated the sterile zone from which he is expected to judge as an otherwise disinterested man. His legal reasoning was now apparently compromised by his personal history.

Yet even if Justice Thomas had said nothing, shouldn't we expect that the one African-American on the Supreme Court would have had a special reaction to cross-burning, in so many ways different from the other justices? And aren't we all fortunate that he indeed has that perspective? Apparently those who insist on selecting blank-slate jurors are themselves blank-slate judges, or believe that neither jurors nor judges possess any feelings, past histories, or preformed opinions. Judges allow no more from themselves emotionally than they do from their jurors, or the parties to the action. But we should take no pride or comfort in knowing that the living legacy of the law is served by lifeless human beings. This is especially disconcerting in the case of the Supreme Court—the highest court in the judiciary. Do we want Justices on the bench who do not have the experience and empathy to understand the effect that a law has, or may have, on some particular community? Cross-burning may actually convey a twisted, odious political message, but Courts are better served when they are at least informed about the spiritual consequences that ensue from delivering that message.

The legal system believes that it is best when Supreme Court Justices are not individually invested in the legal matters before the Court. Justices should adjudicate the issues abstractly, clinically, like emotionally uninvolved lawyers. When Justice Thomas shared his legacy with his brethren in a way that illuminated their own feelings about cross-burning, the Court's ultimate decision benefited from his singular emotional perspective more so than from his legal wisdom.

I happen to be a child of Holocaust survivors. If I were an appellate judge, and the case on appeal involved the claimed First Amendment rights of a neo-Nazi group to march in a community of Holocaust survivors, how could I not speak up at the oral argument to explain how this alleged expression of symbolic, content-based speech would be tantamount to committing spiritual violence against an already traumatized group? And how could the legal reasoning of the court possibly be harmed by hearing me out? As I wrote in chapter 1, the conventional legal paradigm focuses exclusively on crimes to the body and not to the spirit. If the neo-Nazis had come swinging bats and shooting rifles, the law would not protect them, even if their physical conduct was intended to deliver a political message. Given this paradox, it's clear that this nation has allowed the principle of free speech to inflict a great deal of spiritual harm, and, in expanding the permissive reach of the Constitution, it has also left a legacy of immoral justice. The First Amendment, and its promise of granting unfettered discourse in the marketplace of ideas, is undeniably sacred. The presumption in our legal system is always in favor of granting more speech, not less. Yet, morally, why should that be the case when some professed ideas are not only odious but dubious, and the communication of them is as damaging and painful as any physical blow?

The scene of marching, parading Nazis—in the minds of Holocaust survivors—recalls a traumatic past and is an act of devastating violence. Just because it is communicated, or perhaps disguised, as a gesture of symbolic, ideological speech that theoretically doesn't leave a physical bruise, doesn't make it any less of a threatening, harmful act. Perhaps the case of *Virginia v. Black* will stand as a new precedent that speaks to how intimidating and threatening conduct is less about speech and more about violence, if not to the body, then to the soul.

The legal system fears that the introduction of a judge's emotional history into the framework of deciding cases will result in distorted decisions. Why is that necessarily true? And distorted by what: humanity? There can be no justice without emotional complexity. What's the point of a decision that is legally sound but morally and emotionally without reason? Judges believe that because of their legal training and facility with the rules evidence, their emotions will not interfere with their decision-making authority. They assume they can filter out the emotional noises, discounting and ignoring evidence that properly should not be considered at trial.

Judges developed these instincts for dispassion and walled-off emotions while they were still lawyers. In order to lawyer well, we are told, one must be hardened to life. Inured to human suffering. Unseduced by sympathy or moral conscience. Empathy and personal feeling should never be introduced into the attorney-client relationship. Keep it professional. No first-name basis. Actually, no real need even to remember the client's first name. Jan Schlichtmann, the character portrayed by John Travolta in the film *A Civil Action*, admits that lawyers are without feelings and compassion for their clients' suffering. But to do so, in his mind, would almost be tantamount to malpractice. Such sympathies and empathies only distract the lawyer from doing his job, and is no better than a doctor who is afraid of blood.

Better to remain aloof; the lawyer's emotional mindset distanced from the client's actual experience. But sometimes the emotional complexity of a situation should take precedence over legal precedent. The law obsesses over the external, superficial wound, never bothering to peek underneath, where the real damage lies.

Judges may insist that they are capable of insulating their legal opinions from their raw emotions, but, in actuality, such clear divisions occur only in a judge's dreams. This is why Judge Carolyn B. Kuhl, a California state court judge who testified before the Senate Judiciary Committee in connection with her nomination to become a federal appeals judge, came across so disingenuously when she said, "As a judge, I don't have personal views about cases anymore."

In real cases, there is a natural collision between the rules, precedents, and procedures of the law, and the greater world around it, made up of human failings, political pressures, and moral restraints. There have been those who have understood this shortcoming in the law's narrow vision for itself. In the 1920s and 1930s, a group of academics known as the legal realists argued that the law isn't always rational and objective, and that other forces—both personal and political—that exist outside of the courtroom can guide a legal result independent of what the actual law would otherwise require. Indeed, sometimes the social context of the situation, and the psychology of the actors, especially judges, can be as important as legal reasoning in determining the outcome of a case. In 1930, Jerome Frank wrote in *Law and the Modern Mind* that thinking about law only in rational terms is a mistake, mostly because, at bottom, "judges are human," and therefore, on occasion, predictably irrational.

No one would argue against this, other than perhaps judges themselves. Various recent studies have shown just how human, and therefore inherently biased, prejudging, and flawed judges actually are, although they would neither admit nor believe this to be true. Jeffrey J. Rachlinski, a law professor and psychologist from Cornell University, and Chris Guthrie, a law professor from the University of Missouri, asked 167 federal magistrates to answer a questionnaire that sought to show how judges often make systematic errors in judgment based on their own illusions about certain situations. The study revealed that these magistrates were likely to engage in often biased mental shortcuts that affected their decision-making and resulted in judicial errors. As the authors wrote in 2001 in the *Cornell Law Review*, "Wholly apart from political orientation and self-interest, the very nature of human thought can mislead judges confronted by particular types of situations into making consistent and predictable mistakes."

Stephen Landsman, a law professor at DePaul College of Law, and Richard F. Rakos, a psychologist, performed a study that sought to determine whether state judges in Ohio were capable of properly ignoring or discounting evidence that had been ruled to be inadmissible. One example of this would be evidence of a prior conviction or bad act, which was discussed in chapter 6. Under the rule, the jury would never be permitted to hear or see such evidence. But Landsman and Rakos wondered whether judges—knowing the evidence but excluding it from the jury's consideration—were emotionally and psychologically equipped to block it out of their own thought processes. Could they essentially instruct themselves to ignore what they already know, and not have it affect their objectivity?

Interestingly, the results of the research, reported in the *New York Times*, indicated that judges aren't nearly as good at detachment as they had assumed. Consciously or not, the prejudicial evidence against the defendant ultimately influenced the outcome, even though the evidence should have had no bearing on the decision. When the judge was informed about the defendant's prior bad act, he or she tended to prejudice the defendant, or rule against him. On the other hand, when the judge was not made aware of the prejudicial evidence, he tended to lean in the defendant's favor. With respect to these findings, Professor Landsman said, "[Judges] make decisions in the same way that other people make decisions, [but] getting that idea out and following up its implications has been very difficult because it threatens a judge's claim of authority and trustworthiness."

Judges also have complicated and differing emotional reactions to disgust. Some commentators have suggested that disgust and shame can influence a legal outcome, and, later in this book, I discuss the way shame and revulsion might be employed to provide spiritual relief, and to impose a spiritual penalty. We naturally tend to distance ourselves from those whose actions we find repellent, and the shame they experience from our moral outrage may compel them to reform their behavior and deter others from emulating that behavior. But if judges were entirely objective, their idiosyncratic reactions to certain human conduct would not influence their legal decisions. Dan M. Kahan, a law professor at Yale University, writing in 1998 in the *Michigan Law Review*, explained just how particular reactions to disgust may indeed impact a judge's ruling. In a case where a man killed two lesbians, the judge refused to admit testimony that the defendant was disgusted by their sexual conduct. Yet in another case, where a man murdered two homosexuals, a different judge acknowledged his own disgust toward gay cruisers, and accordingly mitigated the sentence.

Similarly, judges can be influenced by the myths and moral

tales that emanate out of the narrative tradition of a culture. This might include the legend of King Arthur, or other characters that exist in children's stories and fables. These tales shape the attitudes of judges no less than their legal training. In discussing his book *Minding the Law* (coauthored with Jerome Bruner, a psychologist), in the *New York Times*, Anthony Amsterdam, a capital defense attorney, said, "Much judicial decision-making is driven by psychological processes, . . . Our whole book, in a sense, is a treatise for the proposition that judges have choices they do not acknowledge to themselves and the world."

Edward R. Korman, a federal judge in Brooklyn, ironically the same judge who presided over the class-action lawsuit filed by Holocaust survivors in connection with the Swiss banking case, is also a judge who reportedly needs a box of Kleenex on the bench to wipe away tears that are brought on by some of his cases. Unlike many of his colleagues, he does not shy away from thinking of himself as an emotional man. Neither, apparently, does Archbishop Desmond Tutu, who headed the South African Truth and Reconciliation Commission, which I'll discuss in greater detail in chapter 13. The difference between a truth commission and a court of law is vast, but one sure difference is the emotional responses that Tutu had to hearing his countrymen speak about the horrors they had suffered under apartheid. Unlike a stoic, imperious courtroom judge, Tutu was known to bury his head in his hands and cry upon hearing particularly gruesome testimony of torture, death, indignity, and deprivation. Most courtroom judges would never reveal the way in which a case was affecting them emotionally. A judge generally wears the expression of a sphinx, and on his sleeves all is robe and no heart. Justice Albie Sachs of the South African Constitutional Court said, emphatically, "Tutu cries. A judge does not cry."

But why is this something in which judges take such perverse pride? As human beings first and judges second, why shouldn't they feel the freedom to cry? Why isn't it incumbent upon them to show that in order to be able to impose judgments on humanity, they have to live among us, and feel what we are feeling?

Judge Korman, for one, apparently believes that there is a connection between a judge and a human being.

"The notion that judges don't have private views about the matters before them is unrealistic," he was quoted as saying in a profile of him in the *New York Times*. "The question is how to put all of that aside without letting it cloud your thinking or stand in the way."

Judges obviously have subjective, private opinions, because they recently won the legal right to express them off the bench. In the 2002 case of *Republican Party of Minnesota v. White*, the United States Supreme Court ruled that candidates who run for judicial office have the same right to free speech as do candidates who run for political office. And, in 2003, a federal court in New York ruled that a Republican state court judge, Thomas J. Spargo, could not be disciplined for having, among other things, participated in demonstrations in Florida against the recount process following the 2000 presidential election.

In both instances, those opposing the decisions argued that rules preventing judges from engaging in politics and expressing their political opinions were necessary to ensure that the judiciary remain free from bias. This argument, however, absurdly assumes that as long as judges do not articulate their political opinions outside of the courtroom, then either these opinions won't exist inside, or they'll be sufficiently suppressed. But the very fact that the Supreme Court, and a federal district court, ruled that judges have the right to express political opinions is tantamount to saying that judges are human and therefore have opinions on politics and other matters not before the court.

It is an unacknowledged truth of the legal system that judges are not indifferent to certain outcomes. They are neither blind nor free from bias. They pick favorites; they secretly want one side to win, rooting all the way, sometimes rigging the result. In *The Merchant of Venice*, Portia is surely not an impartial jurist. Indeed, the conflict of interest couldn't be greater. Antonio, who is bound to Shylock legally and whose flesh is the subject of the lawsuit, is her husband's best friend. In fact, it was precisely because Bassanio, her husband, needed hard cash in order to win her hand in marriage that Antonio got himself into Shylock's debt in the first place. Yet here she is, the presiding judge in an action in which the debt of her husband's best friend will either be discharged, or a pound of his flesh removed.

E. L. Doctorow's *The Book of Daniel*, introduces the idea that some cases can enhance the careers of those who preside over them. Jack Fein, a fictional *New York Times* reporter who, in the novel, covered the trial, tells Daniel—the son of the executed Isaacsons—that for the judge and the prosecution, "it was a career-making case, baby, everybody did well."

In the actual Rosenberg case, the presiding judge, Irving Kaufman, eventually became the chief judge of the Court of Appeals for the Second Circuit. At the time of the Rosenberg trial, Judge Kaufman was no doubt aware of the hostile climate that existed in the United States for Communists. The execution of the Rosenbergs, as opposed to sentencing them to life imprisonment, may have made him notorious in some circles and patriotic in others. Whether his sentencing decision was motivated by legal principle or cynical, self-serving politics, he wound up profiting personally from the electricity that unplugged the life out of Julius and Ethel Rosenberg—although he claimed that the case had the opposite effect, prejudicing him professionally.

Judges very often depart from legal reasoning—or cleverly manipulate their reasoning—in order to achieve a certain outcome that may be influenced by a personal or emotional agenda. In 2003, Chief Justice William H. Rehnquist wrote the majority opinion rejecting the claim made by states that they were immune from having to enforce the Family and Medical Leave Act.

Most women's rights groups were surprised that Rehnquist, among the Supreme Court's most conservative Justices, would adopt this position and write that the Act was necessary to eliminate the "pervasive sex-role stereotype that caring for family members is women's work." What Justice Rehnquist didn't say was that his daughter was a single working mother with childcare problems of her own, and occasionally she had to recruit the Chief Justice of the United States Supreme Court to pick up his granddaughters from school.

While some biases humanize a judge's application of the law, not all do. In contested child custody cases throughout America, judges work overtime to romanticize mothers and demonize fathers in order to ensure that mothers are granted full custody in divorce actions. This is true even when the evidence is neutral on who would make the better custodial parent, or when the advantage should favor the father. Perhaps guided by narrative childhood myths about the sacredness of mothers, or by sexist stereotypes, judges reflexively believe that children—particularly small ones—should be with their mothers. And they revert to that mindset—invoking the best-interest-of-the-child standard—as if it logically follows that the child's best interest could never be served by granting the father custody.

The language of the law, in almost every state, actually mandates even-handedness. Mothers are not supposed to receive any presumptions of being the better parent in child-custody cases. Yet, in the vast majority of cases, unless the mother has a criminal record, is engaged in illicit behavior, has been institutionalized, or is a drug abuser, she will be deemed the primary custodial parent. It's not the law that is creating this legal abuse; it's the misapplication of the law by judges who are impermissibly guided by archaic gender stereotypes and the mythology of motherhood. If judges were entirely objective and unbiased, as they claim, then this result would not happen so systematically and pervasively.

But when parents divorce, judges routinely conventionalize the family dynamic, consigning traditional roles to mothers and fathers. For legal purposes, the custodial time machine is set to the 1950s stereotype of working fathers and stay-at-home mothers. The legal consequences that arise from the cynical exploitation of this stereotype deprive children of their fathers, reduce men to mere child-support providers, and fosters an atmosphere of obvious inequality. Such a poisonously discriminatory application of rules create immoral precedents and destroy human relationships.

All too often unacknowledged preferences tip the scales of justice. For example, in addition to rooting for one side, judges sometimes favor certain lawyers. They enjoy seeing them in their courtrooms, and they are more likely to reward them with a favorable result. Familiarity proves to be a distinct advantage. Sometimes this favoritism is related to the attorney's reputation; the judge simply knows that the lawyer's skill level is superior. More often it has to do with personal chemistry, likeability, and affection. It doesn't hurt if the lawyer and judge are graduates of the same alma mater, or attend the same church or synagogue, or occasionally see each other in the neighborhood or country club. Maybe their children have gone to the same schools. If the outcome is anywhere in doubt, these nuanced associations are likely to influence the outcome. Other lawyers will have to work that much harder, because they are, from the outset, prejudiced by emotional remoteness. But if judges are truly objective and impartial, then none of these intimacies and associations would ever matter or come into play.

In *The Trial*, Joseph K.'s lawyer, Huld, pointedly justifies his particular value to the case by claiming that he is especially connected to judges who like him and who favor his clients. "Nothing was of any real value but respectable personal connections with the higher officials," Huld explains to Joseph K., "that was to say, higher officials of subordinate rank, naturally. Only through these could the course of the proceedings be influenced."

Sometimes the bias is subtle; at other times it is unabashedly explicit. In *The Verdict*, there is a terrific scene in which the high-priced lawyer representing the archdiocese, played by James Mason, is in the judge's chambers, sitting comfortably as if he had been in that room many times before, speaking with the judge about matters presumably unrelated to the case. (Theoretically, *ex parte* communications—those outside the presence of opposing counsel—are improper.) When Frank Galvin, the plaintiff's attorney, arrives, he doesn't know where to put his coat, and he looks like a man who feels unwelcome and uneasy about joining the discussion. Galvin's intuition turns out to be correct. Throughout the trial the judge's demeanor could not have been more hostile to Galvin, or more supportive of the archdiocese and its lawyer.

Judges have all the power to will an outcome. As human beings, they have their own hang-ups, preferences, emotional history. They like some people, dislike others, and those attitudes do not go into escrow simply because they're wearing their robes. Prejudicial attitudes find their way inside legal decisions without acknowledgment, influenced by all that is human about a judge—both on and off the bench.

What's required is an infusion of tenderness and empathy into the judicial process. This doesn't mean more lenient sentences, or weak-kneed spineless judges. It does mean that judges should admit when they are wrong, or when the law fails, or when the law is being correctly applied but the result is morally hard to swallow. There is nothing that prohibits judges from proclaiming this directly from the bench, or writing it into their opinions. Something like: "I am required by law to do what I must do today, even though I realize that it will strike some, including me, as immoral. I can't disguise my own emotions about this unjust result, nor should I have to. Neither can I pretend that the result is just, because I know that it is not. Nonetheless, I am bound to apply the law in this way, which will, paradoxically, produce both the correct legal result and the wrong moral outcome." The only thing that prevents a judge from writing or saying such words is either false pride or plain emotional dishonesty.

APOLOGY
AS MORAL ANTIDOTE
TO THE LEGAL DISEASE

One of the dirty little secrets of the legal system is that if people could simply learn how to apologize, lawyers and judges would be out of work. Completely shut down with virtually nothing left to do, like a plant closing because it failed to modernize, a product that had become obsolete, or a job that had been downsized out of existence. Courtrooms would go the way of typewriters, tanning oils, and eight-track cassettes. Lawyers would be forced to retrain themselves, or put their skills to an entirely different use.

Well, maybe not exactly, but close. Sometimes what the injured party wants to receive most is an apology, and once he or she receives it, the impulse to file a lawsuit, and the rage that arises out of the injury and fuels so much of the animus, is almost entirely dissipated. Apologies have enormous value, independent of any monetary settlement. They are both remedial and compensatory. And they are extremely cheap to deliver. Indeed, an apology can come at no cost to the one making it, other than in the price of swallowed pride. And, of course, an apology can be not only costless to make, but enriching to the maker. The person apologizing can find himself spiritually ennobled by his assumption of responsibility. Saying you're sorry has infinite value to both the party who needs to hear it, and the one who needs to say it. And in creating this reciprocal exchange, the eventual payment of money becomes less loaded, and, in some cases, no longer necessary.

Doing the right thing can result in tremendous spiritual reward. And once it's over, once the apology has been made and accepted, there aren't any papers to file or motions to argue or juries to select or evidence to introduce. Resolution comes simply from saying: "I'm sorry. I know I was wrong. I would like to acknowledge that. I feel very bad about what I have done, and I realize that I have caused you great hurt. And now let me hear you speak, so I can get a fuller sense of what I have done to you. And after you have finished, let me prove that you have been heard, and let me try to make things right and restore our relationship and earn back, or gain, your friendship and respect."

Case closed. Now doesn't that make you feel better?

We all make mistakes each day. Some are harmful, others benign. Sometimes our actions result in damage—to the body, the spirit, or to someone's physical possessions or property. Yet when that happens, the idea of accepting blame, taking responsibility, expressing regret, and acknowledging the harm and the pain that the actions have caused, is foreign to our species. We are an inflexibly, incurably defensive people. We are loath to admit fault. We will go to any lengths to defend our honor and to save face, proclaiming our innocence no matter what the cost, no matter whether our foolishly defensive resolve results in protracted and financially ruinous litigation.

Some cultures are better than others at acknowledging fault and accepting responsibility. In Japan, when a plane crashes and produces casualties, the president of an airline will go to the homes of each of the families who suffered loss, and virtually beg for forgiveness. In Holland, in 2002, the entire Dutch government resigned as an act of atonement for the murder of seven thousand people in Srebrenica, because Dutch peacekeepers, in 1995, failed to prevent the massacre. Holland's acting government took responsibility for its neglect while no other country that had forces present was similarly inclined to acknowledge its moral complicity in this crime. In May 2002, South Korean president Kim Dae-jung resigned from office in connection with scandals and corruption related to the activities of his sons and confidants. His words of resignation were: "I can't find words to describe my apologetic feeling. I and my wife spend every day in agony."

You won't find such exemplary, moral acts of virtue expressed very often. They are rare, not just in their occurrence, but also in perceived obligation, because most people simply don't feel obligated to apologize, no matter what they may have done, no matter how obvious their fault. They dig themselves in and drag their feet, pretending that the dispute, or the indignity, will go away on its own. If it doesn't, they will retain a lawyer to ensure that they are vindicated, even if the transparent, unmanipulated truth would otherwise show them to be responsible.

That's because, for the most part, human beings—Americans especially, with their impulses toward autonomy and individuality over community values and social bonds—are not wired to apologize. Somehow it's not part of our DNA, the genetic material that not only controls eye and hair color, but apparently moral temperament, as well. Worse still, apologies are perceived not as gestures of human virtue, but weakness. Saying you're sorry is for those who can't stand up for themselves and defend their honor. Indeed, accepting blame and offering an immediate, untempered apology of shame and regret is regarded not as honorable but as foolish and cowardly.

The failure of human beings to accept moral responsibility and apologize for their wrongs contributes to a burning, implacable resentment that finds its way into legal complaints. When the guilty and the responsible, the complicit and the neglectful, do not acknowledge that damage was done, do not express their regret and sympathy, and do not take account of their actions, insult is added to injury. And the resulting alchemy is lethal and toxic. Without an apology, why would anyone not resort to legal measures? The burden shifts to them to find their own means to reconcile—to stew, by themselves, without a word of compassion or repentance from the very people whom they need to hear it from the most.

If the story itself is capable of providing its own remedy, then the absence of an apology makes the telling of that story even more crucial. Otherwise not a word will be said, those responsible will walk away with a clear conscience, and those who have been harmed will rightly conclude that the truth will disappear unless they take legal action. Faced with nowhere else to bring their grievance, they will initiate a lawsuit, if not in search of a spiritually healing apology, then at least as a way to achieve some conventional courthouse justice.

In an article about apologies and how underused they are in dispute resolution, Teresa J. Ayling, an employment lawyer from Minnesota, was quoted as saying: "I have dealt with many employees who have experienced difficulties in the workplace—harassment and other types of bad behavior—and they will say, 'If only they said they were sorry and wouldn't do it again, it would have been just fine.' "

In 1995, the syndicated columnist Art Buchwald prevailed after a seven-year legal battle against Paramount Pictures, claiming that he had submitted the idea, and the original script, for the Eddie Murphy film, *Coming to America*, without ever being properly compensated or acknowledged for his efforts. The trial court eventually agreed with Buchwald, although the damage award that he received was considerably less than what he had sought, and even less than what he eventually had to pay out in legal fees. But Buchwald never wished to have his life consumed by a long-term litigation. "When I got involved," he wrote in a book about his experience, "I expected to be in a business dispute that I assumed would be resolved early in the game for a minimal sum of money and, hopefully, an apology."

In 1985, a Holocaust survivor living in Los Angeles brought suit against several neo-Nazi groups for libel and emotional distress in connection with their statements denying the existence of the Holocaust. The ultimate settlement agreement included the payment of monetary damages, along with the following language: "Do hereby officially and formally apologize to Mr. Mel Mermelstein, a survivor of Auschwitz-Birkenau and Buchenwald, and all other survivors of Auschwitz for the pain, anguish and suffering he and other Auschwitz survivors have sustained relating to the $50,000 reward offer of proof that 'Jews were gassed in gas chambers at Auschwitz.' "

Relatives of the Israeli athletes murdered during the 1972 Summer Olympic games filed a lawsuit against Germany for failing to provide for their safety. In the Academy Award–winning documentary *One Day in September*, one of the surviving relatives, Ankie Spitzer, said: "If they would only say to us, 'Look, we tried, we didn't know what we were doing, we didn't mean for what happened to happen, we're sorry'—that would be the end of it." Another surviving spouse, Ilana Romano, said: "The real struggle is for somebody to say: 'We are responsible. We made a mistake and want to be forgiven.' "

In the film *A Civil Action*, which was based on a true story, the surviving families of children who died from contaminated water sued the corporations that were negligently responsible. One of the mothers says that what the parents want is an apology, to have some responsible party come to their homes, accept responsibility, and say they're sorry.

What this mother wanted was for the CEOs of these companies to do what a Japanese airline president would do automatically: show up, pay respects, apologize, express sorrow over the loss, do what's necessary to repair the situation short of bringing the children back. The Japanese corporate executive would undertake this gesture regardless of legal consequences. He would do it simply because it is the right, responsible, moral thing to do. In Japan, interestingly, during such moments of head-bowing, tear-shedding remorse, the executive is loath to discuss money or settlements. Doing so might disrespectfully suggest that his ultimate goal is to dispose of the matter quickly through restitution, when in fact the proper moral message is to allow the families to grieve, and to recognize the vastness of their loss, which cannot be reversed through money. Money will be forthcoming. And the Japanese executive knows this all along. But unlike in the American legal system, where money is the only objective—where the only way to express loss is to quantify it—in Japan money has its proper time and place. Mixing money and an apology during the same conversation is crude and undignified, and any talk of money undermines the force and sincerity of the apology. Most important, there is a cultural understanding that money alone is not an effective means of repair. Before hastily cutting any checks, there must come a freely given and sincere apology.

This is what the grieving mother in *A Civil Action* viscerally understood. This is what she had hoped would happen; as a remedy this is what she most wanted. Although an apology wouldn't bring back her child, it would provide the unfiltered, moral acknowledgment of loss, and the acceptance of responsibility. What she needed—and what she was morally entitled to—was to make a human connection with the person or entity that robbed her of her child, and for that person to stare grief in the face and try to imagine the knee-buckling horror of her loss.

But that necessary human interaction never took place—neither in real life, nor in the film. Early on in *A Civil Action*, the lawyer representing the families, Jan Schlichtmann, explains that apologies in the American legal system come by way of having companies pay a lot of money. Obviously that explanation didn't convince any of the family members, for whom money—regardless of amount—was no substitute for what was for them even more material: an apology. And toward the end of the film, in a dramatic scene where Schlichtmann announces to the families how much each of them will receive as part of the settlement, their faces are underwhelmed, and one by one each parent reminds the lawyer that this meager settlement in money alone does not feel to them like an apology, nor will it prevent future abuses for others, since the defendants are not required to clean up the contamination. And receiving an apology from their own lawyer, which Schlictmann offers as a concession to their disappointment, doesn't cut it either.

The desire to hear words of repentance never leaves, even after years of litigation and the receipt of a virtually meaningless check. The road to forgiveness—if forgiveness is even possible—doesn't pass through banks but makes various slow-moving detours through alleyways of apologies and remorse.

The healing power of an apology is morally vital, but seldom seen. In an essay in the *New York Times*, Bill Keller observed how Americans have "refined the art of the apologetic-sounding non-apology to near perfection. I'm sorry *if* I've offended you." This is what can be described as the apology of the passive-aggressive. In the United States, apologies are cynically applied, given as an excuse or justification for less than exemplary conduct, and not as sincere gestures of contrition. When Americans apologize, they do it grudgingly so as to avoid having to pay some other price, or in order to mitigate their punishment, and not out of a sense of social or moral responsibility—not because they should, but because they have to.

Bill Clinton never admitted any wrongdoing until impeachment proceedings made him finally realize that lawyerly denials threatened his presidency. Richard Nixon reassured us that he was not a crook, but his reassurances also confirmed that he wasn't any good at apologies, either. Senator Ted Kennedy never acknowledged his responsibility, or displayed any real contrition, for the death of Mary Jo Kopechne. Senator Trent Lott apologized for his racist statements made in good fun but in bad taste, but he did so in a failed effort to preserve his majority leadership of the Senate. He might not have done so otherwise. When his comments were first disclosed, he was full of excuses and self-righteous justifications, but empty of remorse. In the squirming end, he promised to reform his past behavior. Even with all the cynicism that surrounded his strategic acts of regret, at least the senator apologized, which sets him apart from most politicians, who would never do so unless they had to—and by then, morally, it's too late.

Make no mistake. This three-card monte in the game of contrition is not limited only to politicians. Baseball players seemingly round the bases of denial endlessly, as well. Pete Rose continues, defiantly, to stand behind his career achievements as baseball's all-time hit leader. But he makes absolutely no contact in the apology game, having become a pathological avoider of responsibility for betting on baseball. Since he's obviously a gambling man, what are the odds that Rose will ever sincerely apologize? Interestingly, public opinion nowadays seems to support Rose's candidacy for admission into the Hall of Fame, despite the fact that he only recently admitted wrongdoing after over a decade of denial. Americans obviously have low expectations on apologetic behavior, and have come to expect excuses and denials in place of true regret. We would have reelected Bill Clinton faster than you can say "Al Gore," and I bet we'll see Pete Rose inducted into the Hall of Fame fairly soon.

Apologies are yet another example of the law's forced separation between the legal and the moral. Morally we know we should apologize; legally we know that we are not obligated to, and that there may even be legal consequences to doing so. As individualistic, autonomy-obsessed Americans, we don't like to be asked to do more than legally necessary. It's one thing to have to obey the law, it's quite another to be required to do the right, moral thing. For this reason, we have no need for apologies. They are extra-legal. They reduce our freedom and crimp our styles. An apology compels us to stop what we're doing and assess the moral dimensions of the damage rather than merely pay the fine.

Guilt and liability are legal terms; responsibility is a moral one. The legal system perks up when laws get violated, not when moral duties get shirked. We send people to jail for their guilt in breaking the law; their moral crime adds no time to the sentence, nor does contrition change the outcome of their punishment. And the wider culture is equally underwhelmed by apologetic, moral gestures. As a nation, collectively, we don't seem to care whether those who are either guilty or liable do anything other than sit in jail, or pay damages. We don't punish people for not offering apologies; in fact, we're quite comfortable with punishments that are unattached to remorse.

Ultimately, we are a nation of easy forgivers. It's uncool to hold grudges, but it's okay for people to cause unapologetic harm. And we insist that the injured quickly get over their suffering and grievance, to move on so that they don't hold the rest of us back.

"Sorry" is obviously a sucker's game, not for smooth-operating, fast-talking, street-hustling Americans. In addition to Pete Rose's lack of remorse, we can add all of those former Enron executives, including CEO Kenneth Lay, none of whom have come forward to issue an apology for the decimation of the company, the deceit of their investors and lenders, and the ruination of the financial lives of so many Enron employees and shareholders. Corporate America always clams up and invokes the Fifth Amendment when financial and ethical laws are broken. The breach of fiduciary duty and the public trust apparently doesn't deserve an explanation. The very people who owe us some answers can never find the personal integrity to speak.

And they always remind us that their silence is not of their own choosing. If it were up to them, they would tell us what we need to know, they would proclaim and prove their innocence. But they can't speak, or won't, on the advice of counsel.

In 2002, in connection with the sexual abuse scandals in the Catholic Church, Cardinal Bernard Law of Boston came forward late, and unconvincingly, in his statements of accountability. Most Church officials didn't even do that—unapologetically squirming and fudging, but never acknowledging the damage, and the unpardonable violence, done to their parishioners. Apparently they feared that any expression of fault, any gesture of regret, would expose the Church to liability. But since when do priests—professionally moral men, concerned with salvation and redemption—worry themselves with liability rules? Aren't they, spiritually and metaphorically, above that? The exposure to liability is a matter for the temporal world. Judgment is reserved elsewhere, on a much higher plane, where such calculating, strategic, self-exonerating pursuits—at the expense of moral virtue—would otherwise invoke the wrath of God.

As for the responses of the Pope with respect to these recent sexual abuse scandals, he has said very little other than to express his "sadness and shame" for the actions of "some priests," as if these priests were actually working for some other rival organization that didn't ultimately answer to him. Where does the buck stop at the Catholic Church if not with the Pope, and is papal infallibility any less egregious than the smugness of the judiciary? Of course, the Church—the institution that presumably speaks with the greatest moral authority in the world—has, historically, not shown much of a willingness to accept moral responsibility for its own misdeeds. As a number of recent books, including Daniel Jonah Goldhagen's *Moral Reckoning: The Role of the Catholic Church in the Holocaust and Its Unfulfilled Duty of Repair*, James Carroll's *Constantine's Sword: The Church and the Jews: A History*, Garry Wills's *Papal Sin: Structures of Deceit*, David I. Kertzer's *Popes Against the Jews: The Vatican's Role in the Rise of Modern Anti-Semitism*, and Susan Zuccotti's *Under His Very Windows: The Vatican and the Holocaust in Italy*, have all pointed out, the Church's official conduct during the Holocaust was a moral disgrace at best, and a tacit contribution to the mass murders at worst.

Because apologies serve as much as a source of spiritual relief as anything else, it is troublesome when religious institutions fail in the very areas that we would assume them to lead by example. Men and women of God preach doing the right thing. To apologize for one's personal failing and error is a moral duty. And the sense of moral failure from not apologizing is the price one pays for living with a conscience. It is what a righteous person, or someone who aspires to righteousness, would naturally do. An apology should be given not merely for damage control or the defense of a lawsuit, but because it is the path of the morally virtuous and spiritually evolved. And the Vatican, more than any other institution, should know that and practice it.

Acknowledgments and apologies offer moral relief, whereas purely legal remedies, which compensate mostly for economic loss, provide only a very small spiritual dimension. It's not that money, as restitution, isn't without some moral significance. But without words of acknowledgment and contrition, the value of a remedy is limited to only a material gain rather than a spiritual one. The legal system, which tragically divides the moral and legal, shows no interest in integrating the compensatory aspects of a remedy with its spiritual opposite. And if religious institutions—the models of moral conduct—fail to uphold these virtues in their own affairs, then the legal system will have neither the incentive nor the direction to reform itself.

Doing the right thing shouldn't be so alien to justice. If apologies serve such a necessary moral purpose, why then should they be so absent from the law?

The problem, of course, is not limited only to faceless corporations, soulless religious institutions, feckless ballplayers, manipulative politicians, and obtuse legal systems. Few people are able to accept moral responsibility and simply say they're sorry. Somehow it's not in us to do so. But what is in us is the spiritual longing to hear from the people who have caused us harm, to hear in their own words, and with their own voices, their acknowledgment of how much pain they have caused, and their sincere regret and desire for moral repair. And what is also in us is the deep resentment that comes from hearing no words of contrition from those who are morally obligated to speak. The law seemingly welcomes and encourages blamelessness and silence. Such a legal system is guilty of many things—most especially, of supplanting moral justice in the name of legal justice.

The conventional legal paradigm provides mostly disincentives to apologize, and, in most cases, actively discourages it. This was clearly evident in the Houston murder trial of Dr. Clara Harris. At one point during the sentencing phase, she cried out an apology to her stepdaughter. The judge ordered the defendant to remain quiet.

As Erin Brockovich appropriately reprimands the lawyer for whom she works in the film *Erin Brockovich*: "Do they teach lawyers to apologize? Because you suck at it."

Well, there is a reason why lawyers admittedly suck at it. It's not part of their mindset, training, or legal education. They are not compensated for getting people to apologize. Indeed, it's not in their financial interest to do so. An apology takes little time to say, and therefore never comes close to exhausting a retainer, or demanding numerous billable hours. Getting things over and done with hardly complements the adversarial process, which churns away and drags along like a lumbering behemoth, moving just for the sake of moving, getting nowhere but crushing everything that gets in its way. Attorneys are trained to file actions, to submit papers and request documents, to research the law, to advance the client's cause, which, roughly translated, means: turning up the heat, intimidating the other side, escalating the emotions, creating misunderstandings, making any hope of reconciliation impossible. A once-resolvable dispute gets transformed into a lifelong grudge that will carry on as a transgenerational family injustice. Lawyers instinctively know that the straightest line to litigation is not traveled by way of an apology, but rather through denying responsibility altogether.

A longtime plaintiff's lawyer from Chicago, Philip H. Corboy, was quoted in the *ABA Journal* as saying that he never asks for apologies on behalf of his clients: "We're in the business of redress, the business of seeking justice under the justice system. The role of the tort system is compensation, not apology."

To most lawyers, an apology is anathema, too simple a solution to a problem that an attorney is paid to complexify. Saying you're sorry is the kind of homespun, common-sense resolution that is more associated with the values of Middle America and the South. Actually, apologetic behavior does take place with greater frequency outside of the major metropolitan areas. The people of Middle America initiate fewer lawsuits than the rest of the nation, perhaps because their grievances are diffused before they reach the critical mass of resentment that precipitates the calling of an attorney. Where the social bonds are strongest, the impulse to protect those bonds, and to forge new ones, is at its greatest. Those who fester away in large, isolating, civically rude, socially alienating cosmopolitan cities seem to have a harder time accepting fault. In the American legal system, the fusion of disconnected communities, wounded psyches, and proliferating attorneys becomes a cauldron of heated antagonism. And in such an unhealthy environment, all the proclaimed aims of vindication are misplaced, and self-righteousness locks everyone in as enemies and adversaries. Hardly an atmosphere where a simple apology will do.

The law is about the adjudication of rights, the assignment of liability, the determination of guilt and innocence, the serving of jail time, the payment of compensation. This is what the law means by a legal resolution. Law is not about the repair of relationships, the moral duties owed to and shared by our fellow human beings. These would constitute moral resolutions. In our legal system, and in our culture, apologies are regarded as the last resort, a way to gain extra leverage or to press an advantage, and not because it is the right thing to do in and of itself. Not morally corrective but cynically coercive.

But if the job of an attorney is essentially to resolve conflicts, then why not exploit the greatest secret weapon in the arsenal of repair? Why hold back on the ultimate antidote to a legal dispute? One reason is that lawyers themselves, in their personal and professional lives, have no aptitude for apologies. Perhaps they are self-selected and drawn toward a profession that is implacably defensive, one that encourages blamelessness and denial. It is in their very nature to be argumentative. They don't like to be proven wrong, and they derive far too much pleasure from small, petty victories.

The organizing principles of the legal profession only reinforce these values. In the film *Regarding Henry* (1991), Harrison Ford plays a high-powered, chain-smoking, short-fused, emotionally abusive Wall Street litigator who needs to get shot in the head in order to rediscover his humanity. Early in the film, his wife asks him to apologize to their daughter for needlessly punishing her for having spilled juice on the piano. The father instead justifies the punishment by offering a principled, reasoned analogy, just like a lawyer would do in addressing a jury. But why would he resort to this tactic when communicating with his daughter unless he wasn't comfortable or familiar with any other means of human engagement?

If lawyers are deprived of the language and gestures of apologetic behavior, how can they possibly advise clients to seek any path other than what they know so well: the one that takes no prisoners and makes no apologies, for anything.

Lawyers reflexively resort to warfare, yet the best victory could avoid fighting altogether and has a chance of repairing relationships and preventing people from walking away as ticking bombs until their next encounter. A sincere, artful apology diffuses anger and creates opportunities for understanding, contrition, and forgiveness. An apology makes it possible to remove the hurt and indignity that underlies the insult of almost every lawsuit. And once the spiritual component is remedied, the law can then achieve the material objectives of justice: compensating for economic loss and punishing criminals for their crimes.

APOLOGIES IN PRACTICE

In the United States, when two people are involved in a car accident, most standard auto insurance policies prohibit the insured driver from getting out of the car and apologizing. Such a gesture, when reevaluated in an American courtroom, might be deemed as an admission of fault, or a statement against interest, and so insurance contracts are written so as to keep drivers who have been involved in car accidents away from each other. They exchange insurance information and wait for the police and ambulances to arrive, looking in opposite directions—arms crossed and faces fuming—formulating an excuse, getting their stories straight.

In Japan, however, the same scene is played out differently. After a car crash, provided that they are physically capable of doing so, both drivers rush to the aid of the other and immediately offer an apology, along with an expression of regret and concern for the other person's well-being. Indeed, Japan is a nation that virtually exists in a constant state of contrition and repentance. Criminal defendants are sometime released even if they would have otherwise been found guilty, because the prosecutor, or the court, became convinced that the accused displayed sufficient remorse, acknowledgment, and sympathy. Article 248 of the Japanese Penal Code, in fact, gives the prosecutor discretion not to institute formal criminal proceedings, or even file charges, if the accused has apologized in a way that is both meaningful and sincere.

Hiroshi Wagatsuma and Arthur Rosset wrote the seminal article on the varying cultural responses to apologies in both the United States and Japan. Published in 1986 in the *Law and Society Review*, it read, in part:

> Japanese apologize by acknowledging their fault, while Americans believe that a statement of explanation or justification of their behavior is an appropriate apology. Many Japanese seem to think it is better to apologize even when the other party is at fault, while Americans blame others even when they know they are at least partially at fault. Americans, as a group, seem more ready to deny wrongdoing, to demand proof of their delict, to challenge the officials' right to intervene, and to ask to speak to a lawyer. Japanese criminal offenders are said to be more ready than Americans to admit their guilt and throw themselves on the mercy of an offended authority. Only when an individual "sincerely" acknowledges his transgression against the standards of the community does the community take him back.

Of course, some Americans are capable of acting on conscience, even if it means ignoring the advice of counsel. Ironically, in one instance, the apology was actually offered to the Japanese by an American. In 2001, an American nuclear submarine, the USS *Greeneville*, sank a Japanese fishing vessel, the *Ahene Maru*. Commander Scott Waddle of the *Greeneville* asked to meet with the families of the *Ahene Maru* crewmen. The encounter was reported by one of the fathers of the lost Japanese crew members: "Commander Waddle bowed and they saw tears hit the floor. It had a profound effect. Kazuo Nakafa, the father of a fishing instructor whose son is missing at sea, did not understand much English, but he said . . . he understood two of Waddle's words very clearly: . . . 'very sorry.' . . . At that moment his anger suddenly dissipated."

Yet Commander Waddle undertook this moral gesture despite having been told by his attorneys that doing so might prejudice him in the event of a court-martial. Indeed, his first efforts at apologizing to the families of the fishermen were thwarted by his attorneys. He was advised to express remorse but not to admit fault. Commander Waddle issued what was a "partial apology," which I'll discuss shortly. It should not be surprising that the families of the Japanese fishermen rejected it. When Commander Waddle, unshackled from the advice of counsel, ultimately apologized without regard to liability or legal consequence, the apology was accepted and worked in a truly moral sense.

Another example where apologies would disarm the anger and take the steam out of a prospective lawsuit is in the area of medical malpractice. Jonathan R. Cohen, a law professor at the University of Florida, who has written extensively on the way in which apologies have only warmed the benches in the courthouses of America and are never actually deployed, estimates that 30 percent of all medical malpractice cases would never require legal intervention if doctors simply apologized for procedures that resulted in injury. Instead, most standard medical malpractice insurance contracts specifically instruct the doctor not to apologize, and, even more egregiously, to stay completely away from the injured party once it is clear that the procedure did not achieve a favorable result.

Taking its cue from the law, the medical profession inexplicably aggravates the injury that it was asked to remedy, or adds an entirely new one. It makes no sense that a doctor would ignore a patient, or the surviving relatives of a deceased patient, at the very time when these people are in need of a specialized kind of care called compassion—which only the doctor, the one whom they trusted and who performed the procedure, can provide. David Erickson, a senior attorney for a health-care company that owns two dozen hospitals in Utah, Wyoming, and Idaho was quoted in the *ABA Journal* as saying: "It's about empathy and compassion. It has nothing to do with admitting fault. . . . The thing to do is express your concern and empathy, then let the patient participate in what would make things right for him and her. If you refuse to acknowledge the suffering, you don't allow people to heal."

A basic moral principle, but infrequently applied in American medicine. The Veterans Affairs Medical Center in Lexington, Kentucky, is a notable exception. Specifically, it has a policy of admitting errors as soon as they occur, providing patients with information that a mistake had been made, even after they have been discharged. The hospital then apologizes for the error and encourages the patient to seek out a lawyer and accept financial compensation through a fair settlement. Connie Johnson, a nurse and clinical analyst at the hospital, was quoted in a law review article as saying: "Telling the truth is the right thing to do."

A very recent example of a doctor who ignored the standard legal advice of denial in favor of the moral path of acknowledgment and apology occurred in February 2003, with the tragic death of Jessica Santillan, a seventeen-year-old Mexican immigrant who died after receiving a heart-lung transplant with organs that were of the wrong blood type. The procedure was conducted at Duke University Hospital in Durham, North Carolina. Dr. James Jagger, the surgeon who performed the transplant, released the following statement, which was likely made against the advice of counsel, but was nonetheless morally commendable and unusual for an esteemed American physician:

"I am ultimately responsible for the team and for this error. I personally told the Santillan family about the errors that were made. . . . Everyone at Duke Hospital made great efforts to provide Jessica with a better life and we failed. We all join the family in their sense of devastation."

In England, medical malpractice cases are much rarer an occurrence. British doctors—stiff upper lip and all—presumably are better at saying they're sorry. Apologies in the United Kingdom are culturally built right into the crossroads where medical error meets human resentment.

Nothing is perhaps more spiritually injurious following a physical injury than to feel the chill of silence from those who have committed the wrong. It is exactly what is meant by adding insult to injury, even though doctors, ironically, are in the business of treating injuries. At the very moment when doctors, morally, should be at the patient's bedside, holding a hand and providing comfort, they are attending to other patients, keeping their personal and professional distance and surrendering the matter to the litigation department of their insurance carriers. And, very often, while the doctor is ducking his former patient, the hospital is preparing a bill for the very services that resulted in the harm. No wonder medical malpractice insurance rates have skyrocketed! The legal system becomes a sparring match between injured and ignored patients and faceless insurance companies. But the doctor in whom all that trust was initially placed is nowhere to be found. The courthouses, unwittingly, perhaps, have become the beneficiaries of bifurcated trials. One to determine the compensation for the physical injury; the other to assuage the betrayal and disrespect from a doctor who didn't even have the decency to come forward and express his regret and remorse.

Insurance companies have their own lawyers. They devise their own legal strategies. Doctors become merely witnesses to assist in the defense of the insurance policy, even though it is the doctor's reputation and humanity that are being called into question. Everyone is willing to invest so much time and money defending indefensible positions. But so few are prepared to take the simpler, moral high-ground approach of making human contact, looking people directly in the eye and expressing genuine sorrow for the loss and pain they may have caused.

In the American legal system, moral behavior automatically triggers exposure to liability. You do the right thing, and in the eyes of the law, you get punished. In the immediate aftermath of an accident, human beings shouldn't be thinking about how an act of human decency will later be perceived in a court of law. When a person is acting spontaneously, apologizes for his actions and shows concern, liability isn't, nor should it be, on his or her mind. The human element is furthered when attention is paid to humanity, not immunity. Yet the legal system robs this gesture of its moral force, and punishes those who bravely accept the legal pitfalls that arise from expressing remorse and regret. And insurance companies—the deep pockets in all of these actions, but not the entity that caused the actual harm—are focused entirely on presenting the best legal defense, which apparently is compromised if the insured says too much, or the wrong thing.

And when the law opens the window a crack to permit an apology, it does it in such a way as to defeat the purpose of the gesture, or deprive it of any chance at spiritual healing or moral rehabilitation. In order to encourage settlements, Rule 408 of the Federal Rules of Evidence—of which there is a similar provision in state courts—excludes statements made during the course of a settlement discussion from being introduced as evidence should the case fail to settle and proceed to trial. The rule essentially creates a prejudice-free talk zone, as long as these conversations are conducted in pursuit of a settlement. It is during these settlement talks that a party can apologize with impunity, although these discussions are not intended for this purpose, nor are apologies routinely offered at them. The whole idea is to motivate parties to have frank conversations about the nature of the injury and the scope of responsibility, the legal merits of each party's case, and the prospect of recovering or prevailing at trial. All this is done without fearing that something said during the settlement discussion will wind up being used against one of the parties should the lawsuit proceed rather than settle.

Unfortunately, settlement discussions generally occur long after the injury has taken place. And settlement talks imply that a formal legal proceeding has already begun. For the purpose of stripping some of the emotion out of the injury and neutralizing the anger, it does little good to keep the parties silent and unrepentant immediately following the harm only to open a window for apologies many months, if not years, later, when the resentment has hardened into an unappeasable grievance that transcends the lawsuit itself. The proper moment to apologize—morally, if not legally—is right after, or soon after, the damage is done. The legal system's preference for legal results over moral outcomes is manifested in this defensively minded practice of using apologies strategically, in the context of settling cases, rather than morally, for the purposes of repairing relationships and preventing the spread of spiritual indignity.

Similarly, courts sometimes coerce apologies, forcing those who have committed crimes to apologize publicly for their behavior. In such instances, the apology becomes part of the punishment. Some people have been ordered to take out advertisements in newspapers so as to formalize, and memorialize, the apology, or to make public appearances expressing remorse to those they have harmed. By doing so, the defendant can relieve himself of a portion of the penalty, or hope to have his sentence reduced. There are some states where apologies have been ordered as actual legal remedies—and not as bargaining chips for mitigation—in cases involving defamation, affirmative action, and employment discrimination.

The most common use of apologies heard inside courtrooms

are not ordered, but rather expected—a kind of show trial within the trial itself—as way of garnering more lenient treatment. This arises most often during the sentencing of criminal defendants. Federal guidelines permit judges to reduce prison sentences for a defendant who "clearly demonstrates acceptance of responsibility for his offense." Courts believe that the acknowledgment of guilt, coupled with an apology, somehow mitigates culpability. Showing proper remorse after receiving a guilty verdict may help in reducing the sentence. And even in prison, contrition is the kind of litmus test that demonstrates that the defendant has made progress toward rehabilitation.

Yet, what if the defendant who is found legally guilty is actually innocent? An interesting essay in the *New York Times* by Adam Liptak spoke directly to this issue. Liptak, a legal affairs correspondent, pointed out that the legal system has shown a willingness to grant early parole for those who admit guilt and express remorse. But what if the prisoner was innocent all along? Wrongly imprisoned, yet now being asked to apologize. Without an apology, the parole board will deem the criminal remorseless, unrepentant, and incapable of being rehabilitated. The law essentially prejudices defendants for telling the truth. In refusing to acknowledge guilt or apologize in situations where he was truly innocent, the wrongfully imprisoned criminal is punished for doing the right moral thing by not lying, even though lying would serve his long-term interest more.

Liptak's article discussed the case of Calvin C. Johnson Jr., who was sentenced to life imprisonment in Georgia for rape, a crime he did not commit. He served sixteen years in prison, and was finally released in 1999 on account of exculpatory DNA evidence. Throughout his time in prison, he attended a few therapy sessions for sex offenders, and was asked to admit his guilt, which, he was told, would make a difference when he came up for parole. In fact, one counselor told him that he would never get out without the apology. "A guilty person has a better chance of walking out and getting parole than an innocent person," Johnson said. "It's completely twisted."

For New Yorkers, there's a more recent example. Three of the five teenagers who had been convicted in 1989 for the rape of a female jogger in Central Park all maintained their innocence at parole-board hearings. In 1995, the parole board refused to release one of the three convicted defendants, Kevin Richardson, stating: "Subject continues to deny his guilt and does not demonstrate remorse for these brutal and senseless crimes." As many people now know, based on new DNA evidence and the confession of Matias Reyes, who had apparently committed the crime, those teenagers had, in fact, been innocent of the rape charge. Despite their earlier confessions, which no doubt helped put them in jail, once in prison, they refused to avail themselves of one of the great incentives of the legal system, which would have enabled them to perhaps receive an earlier release. Instead, they refused to acknowledge guilt and express remorse for a crime they had not committed. Had they shown contrition, they might have been set free, even though they would have had to lie in order for that to happen.

Given the way some apologies are coerced by courts while others are used as incentives to freedom, it's clear that the legal system regards an apology as a purely performative ritual. Courts like to see contrition, but they like to see it after a legal remedy has been imposed, and generally in connection with material, tangible injuries. But what exactly are they trying to accomplish here? Apologies are morally mandated, and they are legally most useful not at the end of a trial, or while a prisoner is in jail, but immediately after the injury or crime has taken place. Offering it after the law has entered a final judgment, as a performance piece or a mitigating gesture, calls into question the sincerity of the apology itself. Under the conventional legal paradigm, apologies are not given as expressions of remorse. Rather, they are cynically engineered, perfunctory, and spiritually meaningless, accomplished only through coercive or incentive-based means.

In all instances in which moral outcomes are desired, it's not enough that the offender merely extend an apology. The quality of the apology matters, as well. It has to stand the test of sincerity. Does the offender truly realize what he or she has done to the victim? Is there true remorse? And is there a genuine interest in making things right again?

There have been all kinds of "botched" or "bogus" apologies that the public has witnessed and that did nothing to revive the dignity of victims or restore moral balance to the community. Former president Richard Nixon apologized to the American people for Watergate, but he never told us specifically what he did, nor did he persuade us that he was aware of how harmful this presidential scandal was to our democracy. Even worse, he failed to take responsibility for his actions, and sought to justify them by saying that they were undertaken for the greater good of the nation. A far cry from how it was recently done in South Korea, with the resignation of President Kim Dae-jung and his expression of "agony" based on the shame that he had brought on his people and country. Former senator Robert Packwood apologized publicly to the roughly dozen women whom he had been accused of harassing sexually, by saying the following: "I'm apologizing for the conduct that it was alleged that I did." During the Nuremberg Tribunal, Hans Frank, the former Governor-General of German-occupied Poland, acknowledged the guilt of the German people, but refused to accept responsibility for his own murderous role in the Holocaust. Similarly, President Frederik W. de Klerk of South Africa offered a perfunctory apology for the crimes of apartheid, but denied having had any personal knowledge of some of the worst human rights abuses and indignities committed under his watch.

When former Boston Celtic guard Dee Brown, mistaken for a

robbery suspect, was wrongfully manhandled by Wellesley police officers, they finally said to him: "I'm sorry, but we were acting on information we received. . . . Sorry, you don't understand what happened." In bringing a lawsuit against the police department, Brown explained that these were not "apologies that you would accept." As a guard in the National Basketball Association, he was aware of personal fouls. But instead of sending him to the line to shoot foul shots, the police officers made excuses for themselves and offered nothing that resembled remorse. They acted as though they were entitled to treat him in this way. Long after Brown was assisted off the ground and escorted back into his car, the psychic scars remained and that's why he eventually sued.

Obviously, sincerity matters. Apologies, morally, are not to be tendered in a pro forma fashion. They must have meaning, and be done with feeling. That's what we expect from our children when they have done wrong. "Say you're sorry, but say it like you mean it." Why would the legal system believe that insincere, cynical gestures of feigned contrition have any value—or serve any spiritual, remedial purpose—to those who have been harmed? The person hearing the apology can often gauge whether it is being offered sincerely, in the true spirit of regret, as opposed to a scripted, halfhearted, soulless recital that may end up antagonizing the injured party even more. Words are empty without true acknowledgment and the moral acceptance of responsibility. Anything less does nothing to set things right—either for the individual or the community.

Paradoxically, some have suggested that we are experiencing a renaissance of public apologies. The United States apologized for conducting medical experiments on African-Americans in Tuskegee, and for the internment of Japanese-Americans during World War II. South Africa, as a nation, apologized for apartheid; the French apologized for deporting Jews to concentration camps. Southern Baptists apologized to African-Americans for endorsing slavery. A former college president at Rutgers University apologized for making a derogatory, racist remark. And, of course, daytime television shows are replete with bizarre acts of public confessions, people crying and seeking forgiveness in front of the entire nation. Given the increasing frequency of these episodes and the precedent they set as models of public contrition, why isn't it easier for most people to say they're sorry?

For one thing, many of these public apologies were made by governments or institutions that were not directly responsible for the original transgressions. They merely inherited the task of making things right. Knowledge of personal innocence makes it easier to take on the mantle of moral responsibility as a successor rather than as a guilty party. After all, the failings were committed by others—a prior error, based on mindsets that were misguided but seemingly justified by earlier times. There are other situations in which apologies are designed more for manipulation than moral repair. One example is when a government exploits a well-timed apology to win back popular support. This was the case in France, and even the United States. As for the public confession of individuals—sometimes graphically and pathetically displayed on television, or in the press—very often what's taking place is attention-getting remorse, contrition for effect alone. In our culture, people who gain access to the media become instant celebrities. Perhaps an apology is a small price to pay for the glory of ending up on the front page of a supermarket tabloid. All that contrived regret simply can't be taken too seriously.

This is precisely the problem with apologies in America. The culture, and the law, regard apologies only in exploitative terms—as way to score points, make the right impression, show the most sympathetic public face, reverse the stigma and recapture the sympathy. An apology has become more of a ritual than a morally rehabilitative act. When it's said pursuant to a script, when the tears are throwaways from a method acting class, the apology ceases to possess a moral component and becomes nothing but a joke.

Obviously, the legal system's penchant for immoral justice makes apologetic behavior much more difficult to emulate. There are so many barriers that the law erects to conceal the truth, to bottle up the emotions, to keep people apart for strategically legal purposes, instead of exhorting them to respond to one another humanely and morally. The law sets a precedent of defensiveness, a presumption of innocence that goes too far, which only reinforces the inclination toward blamelessness that exists naturally in our culture. Offenders invoke their Fifth Amendment constitutional rights, and thereby maintain their silence for fear of self-incrimination. But this silence not only thwarts truth, but deprives apologetic words from ever being uttered. Legal maneuvers that undercut story, truth, and apologies demonstrate how little moral duty is valued under the law.

The legal system treats an apology as a self-incriminating act, an admission of guilt rather than what it may in fact be—a spontaneous moral expression of sympathy. Sometimes attorneys advise their clients that if they feel the impulse to apologize, they must protect themselves legally by couching their language with words such as "without prejudice," meaning "I do so, but on the condition that I won't be prejudiced by this action, and that it will not foreclose me from exercising other rights." Such loophole language insulates the apology from being deemed as an admission of fault or liability, and, more important, disallows the statement from being used as evidence—essentially giving the apology and taking it back at the same time. Dickens has his lawyers in *Bleak House* rely on this legal technique, but in a way that shows them to be soulless and comical. Indeed, Mr. Guppy's marriage proposal to Esther Summerson was offered "without prejudice." It's true that Dickens hated London lawyers. But maybe he was on to something. What does it say about people who spend their days devising legal strategies for all manner of human interaction, robbing the moment of any spontaneity, conditioning their statements with precise limitation of liability language? And what kind of a person would say: "I'm sorry, but not if it means that there is any consequence to my saying it"?

Unfortunately, in our culture and legal system, far too many would. The fact is, if you're sorry, truly sorry, then the statement has to be *with* prejudice. There has to be an unequivocally stated, interior sense of wrongfulness, and also one of consequence. What's the point of saying you're sorry if the only reason you're doing it is so as to avoid responsibility for your actions?

At least three states—Massachusetts, Texas, and California—have passed what are sometimes known as "benevolent gesture," or "expression of sympathy," statutes. These are laws that are intended to make it easier to apologize without liability attaching itself to the statement. Case law in Georgia and Vermont have adopted similar legal principles without enacting corresponding legislation.

What these laws encourage are expressions of sympathy in the aftermath of an accident. They are what some have described as "partial apologies." The hope is that these statutes will precipitate benevolent gestures of the kind that can remove the rage and emotion from lawsuits and lead the parties to settle their differences out of court. It's a way to disarm the anger that follows when an offending party fails to come forward and say: "I'm sorry this happened. Is there anything I can do to help?" Under these statutes, such words of sympathy are not admissions of liability or self-incriminating statements. They are, instead, merely benevolent gestures. What is still left unprotected are true admissions of fault, even when spoken within the same breath of an apology. Therefore, what can't be used in court is the apology itself—"I'm sorry." What is still admissible are statements that extend beyond the mere apology to acknowledgments of fault, the awareness of the pain that was caused, and any expressions of regret for having caused it.

Many have rightfully criticized these statutes as not going far enough. After all, it's not just the apology as an expression of sympathy that matters. Any passerby to an accident can stop and say, "I'm sorry this has happened to you, and I'd like to lend a hand." When it comes to the party who is responsible for the damage, more is expected than mere sympathy. The injured party must also hear language that acknowledges the wrong-doing of the person who is extending the apology. Otherwise, all we are doing is encouraging Richard Nixon–styled apologies, which have no moral currency and are not calculated to bring about any meaningful repair.

What some scholars have proposed is a general blanket pro-tection for all apologies—and the ancillary language that accom-panies them—regardless of when the statements are uttered, and no matter how far they go in acknowledging fault. The point is to create incentives for the wrongdoer to accept as much responsibility for his actions as he is willing. These are what are known as "safe apologies," because they immunize apologies from giving rise to any future liability, and therefore render the making of them costless and safe. This would essentially do for apologies made at the scene of the accident what Rule 403 of the Federal Rules of Evidence does for apologies made at the confer-ence table during a settlement discussion. That way people can feel free to offer an apology, admit fault, and express regret and sympathy without fearing that the statement will later be made admissible at trial, with devastating legal consequences.

Lee Taft, an assistant dean at the Harvard Divinity School, has suggested, however, that these kinds of apologies are ulti-mately bereft of spiritual meaning. It is true that laws that ren-der apologies safe for evidentiary purposes will ultimately lead to apologies that would otherwise never get made. But at what moral cost? Safe apologies are no better than commodities, legal maneuvers intended to encourage the parties to settle, without regard to whether these settlements would result in moral heal-ing. What takes place is essentially a bargained-for exchange: responsibility gets traded for absolution; resentment is swapped for forgiveness. In citing the work of Nicholas Tavuchis, a sociologist who has written ably on the conciliatory power of apologies, Taft wrote in the *Yale Law Journal*: "The remorse and regret conveyed by the words 'I'm sorry' imply a willingness to change, a promise of forbearance, and an implicit agreement to accept all the consequences, social, legal, and otherwise, that flow from having committed the wrongful act."

This is what is demanded of an authentic apology, one that recognizes the moral dimensions of the gesture and not just the cynical, commodified exchange of empty recitals that induce settlements but thwart moral repair. Apologies are naturally weighted with moral imperatives. They can't be traded without corrupting the moral urgency of the reasons for making them. Apologies are tendered because they are morally necessary, and not so as to immunize the wrongdoer from liability. The whole point of a sincere apology is the acceptance of moral responsibility. But the law misapplies the essence of an apology, seeking instead to smooth the ground toward a legal settlement, without accomplishing more. In doing so, this kind of incentive-laden apology deprives the injured party of the very thing that is emotionally necessary to restore moral balance to the relationship. As Lee Taft pointed out in that same *Yale Law Journal* article: "When the performer of an apology is protected from the consequences of the performance through carefully crafted statements and legislative directives, the moral thrust of the apology is lost."

Moreover, as I pointed out in chapter 4, settlements, while efficient for judges who wish to clear their dockets and lucrative for lawyers who want to stuff their pockets, do not necessarily lead to the correct moral outcome. A settlement forecloses a public hearing and reduces the injury, and the remedy, to money alone. It also requires the confidentiality of the victim. So, to the extent to which the law is experimenting with apologies as a way of promoting and hastening settlements—either through benevolent gesture statutes or evidentiary rules that permit the making of safe apologies—this might once again lead to results that are legally correct but morally wrong. Creating incentives to apologize may be the right idea, but not if the purpose is solely to lead to settlements. That only substitutes one immoral outcome for another, perhaps lesser one, without necessarily healing the psychic, spiritual wounds that linger in the aftermath of an accident or injury. The apology never finds its public voice in the wider telling of the story. It becomes buried within settlement language that ultimately buys silence. And the apology itself becomes marred with questionable sincerity, since it may have been extracted and motivated simply by legal concerns rather than moral ones.

Sometimes the injured require a larger stage than a conference room. A face-to-face encounter without a public venue, or the creation of a public record, may fail to achieve a complete moral remedy. Even mediation, which I'll discuss in chapter 13, where apologies have proven most effective, is limited as a mechanism for creating moral repair, precisely because it ends in a hushed settlement agreement and not in a public ceremony that aspires to truth- and storytelling. Apologies may be the vastly underutilized secret weapon of dispute resolution—healing wounds before they spread into five-alarm fires, stoked by lawyers carrying a ready supply of tinder and lighter fluid. But in order to serve a greater vision of moral justice, apologies must not be perceived as calculated and wholly insincere.

The spiritual healing that apologetic behavior brings about works in both directions. The injured are treated with the respect owed to them given what they have lost and suffered; and those who have caused the harm achieve the possibility of self-renewal by owning rather than avoiding their blameworthiness. The American legal system promotes an atmosphere of misdirected hostility, with the focus always on defensiveness, revenge, and restitution. But apologies offer a natural remedy to all those underlying hurts and grievances. Apologies are the law's answer to holistic medicine. They don't require a prescription. They're much cheaper to obtain. And they're far less destructive than what happens when one must navigate through the landmines of law.

12

RESTORATION OR REVENGE

The moral force of an apology opens up a roadway to repair. Without it, and other human interactions and gestures that serve the purpose of healing rather than retribution, justice is reduced to mere vengeance, punishment, and self-help. Of course, in the conventional legal paradigm, the repair of relationships is not the centerpiece of dispute resolution. Resolution in the law is based on a punitive model. The dispensation and delivery of justice is retributive, not restorative. We resolve our problems by declaring one side the winner and punishing the loser, without regard to whether both sides—or society, for that matter—are made better off by that resolution. Criminals sit in jail. Tortfeasors pay money as compensation for causing injury and loss. Those who dishonor contracts are made responsible for their breach. Companies that violate regulatory laws are severely fined.

In fact, sometimes compensation itself isn't punishment enough. That's what punitive damages are for. Money on top of money. Money to compensate for loss; money to punish for past behavior. Sometimes this money is even trebled, to make sure that the offending action never happens again.

The law is interested in punishing, not mending. And there are many reasons why this is so. It's not very American to think in terms of healing the emotional scars and ills of society, or in terms of addressing all those disacknowledged hurts. We are, after all, a nation of quick fixes, and even faster turnarounds. We don't linger; that's what the remote-control switch is for—to change those channels on our languid attention spans. Move on to something else in between the commercial interruptions. Rely on the highlights rather than on the raw, live feed. The sound bite seems to communicate just enough of what we need to know. More thorough narrations are needless and dull. Hesitating is seen as lazy rather than reflective. Even in front of a judge, it's amazing how little time lawyers are given to make their case and explain the purpose for why they are there. Lawyering in America is not unlike making a pitch in front of a Hollywood producer. You have to be able to tell your story in twenty-five words or less. But what kind of a story is worth telling if it can be told in only three sentences? How can a client feel relieved if his or her grievance is robbed of all its subtext and nuance— backstory of a human story?

We are constantly being reminded that it is in our best interest to simply move forward and carry on. Whether it is the breakup of a marriage or a business, or after any abuse or indignity, we are told to: "forget about it," "put it behind you," "don't let it eat away at you," "come to terms with it," "start over." When we are injured or harmed, we are asked to accept our damages and move on rather than dwell on our misery and hurt. This is especially true when it comes to loss. Americans are not gifted when it comes to expressing grief.

"Mourning has become unfashionable in the United States," Margaret Mead, the sociologist, said. "The bereaved are supposed to pull themselves together as quickly as possible and to reweave the torn fabric of life. We do not allow for the weeks and months during which a loss is realized."

True mourning requires time. The healing process is always slow, but it must begin, otherwise the loss will always be front and center, thwarting and intruding on all future relationships and endeavors, never finding its proper, reconciling place. The same is true with mending and repair. It can't be done overnight, and it can't be bought off. There is no fast-acting remedy for an emotional wound. Most important, healing will not come about with silence, but healing always seems to accelerate when exposed to the open-air elements of truth.

But Americans have a hard time thinking of justice in terms of bringing about restoration and repair. It's not part of our cultural mindset. A people obsessed with personal autonomy and the pursuit of happiness is much more focused on scoring a decisive victory than on restoring moral balance to relationships and achieving repair. Indeed, victories are often gained by breaking things, and not by repairing them. The legal system doesn't mend what has been broken, it merely referees further breakage. If there is going to be repair, the injured are going to have to come to it on their own.

True moral justice, however, would not only render judgments on the nature of guilt, innocence, and liability, and whether or not to award damages. It would also seek to repair what has been damaged. Without repair, the original injury will never heal. Money and incarceration are not agents of repair, nor do they bring about healing. They are mere Band-Aids to the grief that accompanies violence and loss.

We take for granted that our "eye for an eye, tooth for a tooth" brand of justice is immutable. We assume that in order to be just, the law must always be prosecutorial and punitive, vengeful and retributive. But throughout history, other forms of justice, more restorative in nature, were practiced successfully and dominated the way cultures resolved matters between criminals and victims, while balancing the larger needs of society. Indeed, before the Middle Ages, kingdoms and governments had nothing at all to do with punishing wrongdoers. Such matters were generally handled among tribes and clansmen. The murderer's clan was responsible for carrying out whatever was the agreed-upon resolution. This could include the payment of a fine, or some modified future behavior. If the murderer didn't satisfy the debt, he might be killed by his own family for failing to keep the peace.

In Morocco, the Berbers banished murderers by sending them into exile. The Yurok Indians of California insisted on compensation to the victim's family. The payment could be anything from seashells to the relinquishing of the murderer's own daughter. A similar practice was required of certain indigenous Mexican communities, whereby the murderer was expected to care for the victim's widow and family for his entire lifetime. The Jolou of East Africa required the death of the murderer, along with impregnating a member of the victim's clan with the seed of the murderer's clan in order to ensure that the ghost of the victim would live on as if he still had a wife and child. In all instances, however, doing something to repair or satisfy the victim, or the victim's family, was at the center of the law's consciousness.

Ironically it took the Dark Ages to set back the clock on criminal justice. Under Anglo-Saxon law, a murderer paid a fine, called a "wergeld," to the victim's family, but he was also required to pay a similar fine, called a "wite," to the king. By the twelfth century, under English law, based on the decrees of Henry I, both payments were collapsed into one, which went directly to the king, leaving the victim's family with nothing. It was the Norman conquest that shifted the justice paradigm and created the fiction that crimes were committed against the crown, rather than the individuals who experienced them. Justice was served by keeping the streets of Medieval Europe free from mischievous men. The whole idea was to prevent future harm. Punishment took on a purely retributive atmosphere of deterrence. Justice was not served by repairing or making victims better, but rather by ensuring that such crimes would never be repeated.

Prior to this shift in thinking about crime, offenders were required to actually pay for the consequences of their behavior by compensating the victim's surviving family for their loss, or by performing other gestures or rituals that addressed the hurt that resided in the soul of the bereft spouse, or parentless child. But if the crime involves not a loss of life but the loss of some material possession, how can the criminal make the victim whole—restoring him to the position he would have been in had the crime not taken place—if he is in jail? Justice that is concerned with moral outcomes provides not only for punishment, but for restitution, as well. The true nature of reparation is ultimately to make repair. The burning down of a barn should be punishable as arson. But you still have a torched parcel of farmland on which there used to be a barn. The offender is at least one able-bodied person who should help rebuild it. But he can't if he's sitting behind bars. The new focus on incarceration and deterrence ended the presumptions of restitution and the making of reparation—whether in the aftermath of murder or property damage.

In literature, the architect of a restorative justice model for dispute resolution comes from Shakespeare, or, more explicitly, from his fictional Italian *consigliere,* Portia, the ingenious and disguised lawyer who outthinks all the men, and the merchants, in *The Merchant of Venice.* She offers an alternative vision of relief, one that is the spiritual opposite of retribution—the antidote to vengeance. In Act IV, Scene I, Portia, as lawyer and judge, pronounces:

PORTIA: Then must the Jew be merciful.
SHYLOCK: On what compulsion must I?
PORTIA: The quality of mercy is not strained; It droppeth as the
　　　gentle rain from heaven

Upon the place beneath. It is twice blest; It blesseth him
that gives and him that
takes. 'Tis mightiest in the mightiest; it becomes the
throned monarch
better than his crown. His sceptre shows the force of
temporal power,
The attribute to awe and majesty,
Wherein doth sit the dread and fear of kings;
But mercy is above the scept'red sway;
It is enthroned in the hearts of kings;
It is an attribute to God himself,
And earthly power doth then show likest God's
When mercy season justice. Therefore, Jew,
Though justice be thy plea, consider this:
That in the course of justice none of us
Should see salvation. We do pray for mercy,
And that same prayer doth teach us all to render
The deeds of mercy. I have spoke this much
To mitigate the justice of thy plea,
Which if thou follow, this strict court of Venice
Must needs give sentence 'gainst the merchant there.

This Shakespearean soliloquy is essentially a declaration on
behalf of restorative justice and a rejection of the kind that is
purely retributive. Portia is advising Shylock that there are two
paths to conflict resolution: one offered by the law and its provision of temporal justice; the other is granted as a divine act
of salvation and resides in the human impulse toward mercy
and forgiveness. Aside from the fact that these are Christian
virtues being dangled before and demanded of a Jew, Portia is
telling Shylock that he can argue strict breach of contract principles and insist on his pound of flesh if he wishes. But in the
end, even though he will have won, what will it get him? In
her vision of moral justice—ironically conceived by a judge—

looking to the law for relief always carries severe spiritual liabilities, because "in the course of justice none of us should see
salvation."

Salvation comes to those who are merciful, a virtue of God
that shows itself in man only when human beings "season justice
with mercy." Portia suggests a path other than the conventional
legal paradigm—a spiritual remedy to a legal dispute that results in neither punishment nor the payment of damages. Shylock is entitled to relief. But the principled and righteous path to
justice that he is seeking would produce an immoral outcome if
Antonio must surrender flesh and shed blood as satisfaction for
Shylock's bond. Neither the parties, nor Venice itself, would be
better off with such a result. Instead of cutting Antonio open,
Portia proposes a remedy of reconciliation and forgiveness, and a
new life of Christian salvation.

Of course, modern notions of restorative justice don't necessarily include religious elements. It's possible to achieve a moral
resolution without saving a Christian soul. But by deviating from
the literal and strict application of the law in favor of a moral
remedy, Shakespeare introduced the idea that punishment and
the payment of damages may not actually restore the injured
party—at least not spiritually.

From a modern Western perspective, the notion of looking
beyond pure retribution toward something that has restorative
possibilities began with the Nuremberg trials, an international
tribunal, the first of its kind, established to prosecute those who
had engaged in crimes against humanity during the Holocaust.
In the aftermath of World War II, the Allied powers, and the nations of the world, were faced with a monumental moral
dilemma. There were millions of civilians, most of whom were
Jews, who had been annihilated not as casualties of war, but
rather as part of a systematic plan of mass destruction. These
were not mere war crimes—actions associated in the context and
within the ground rules of war. These crimes existed apart from

the world war, where there were no rules. The Nazis brought perfection to murder, and a new originality to atrocity. There had been two theaters of war: the first bent on world conquest, the second directed against humanity itself. The question became: What to do about Nazis and Germans who participated in all this death and deprivation? It was one thing to carve up territories as spoils of war and bring about democratic reforms in newly conquered nations. It was quite another thing to know how to punish those who had committed acts of evil on a scale that no one before had ever imagined.

Prior to Nuremberg, nations essentially enjoyed sovereign immunity over their own citizens. The world had no legal right to intervene when it came to the sovereign acts of nations—even if it involved brutal crimes against civilians—provided that it took place within their sovereign territorial borders. Nuremberg changed all that. It created an international tribunal for the moral purpose of bringing justice and punishment for the crimes committed against the Jews, Gypsies, and homosexuals of Europe. No longer could nations claim sovereignty to justify barbarism. Justice was instituted from a moral perspective—a legal trial framed in moral terms. Judgment at Nuremberg was moral judgment even though it took a trial to bring it about.

Many people now know that Nuremberg wasn't the first and only option that was considered as a way to do justice in the aftermath of the Nazi genocide. There were those, most especially then U.S. Secretary of the Treasury Henry Morgenthau, who believed that given the enormity and sadistic nature of the crimes, justice would be more easily and naturally accomplished by way of summary executions. No trials. No showings of proof. No risk that the outcome of a trial might result in the acquittal of mass murderers. No reason to incur the expense and time that it would take to prosecute all those who had been directly responsible for the murders or morally complicit in them. The simplest path to justice would come from finding a Nazi, and then immediately killing a Nazi—right there, either with a bullet to the head, or a head hanging from a tree.

Of course, Secretary Morgenthau's eye-for-an-eye vision of justice was ultimately rejected in favor of an international tribunal. One of the reasons why a lengthy, costly trial was chosen over a far more expedient method of justice—one that most people would not have questioned given the gruesomeness of the underlying crimes—was that morally it wouldn't be enough simply to rid the world of such unmitigatingly guilty murderers. It was equally important that the entire world, and the Germans themselves, confront the magnitude of the evil and the loss that it produced.*

Only through a trial, on an international stage, located in the nation where the crimes were committed and among the citizens who had committed them, where witnesses could describe what had happened and where the most incriminating documents and film footage would be revealed, could there be some sense of justice that resonated beyond the purely retributive and punitive. Legally the murderers needed to be punished, and severely so. But not until the historically urgent purpose of true moral judgment had been achieved. There were no plea bargains, just truth—both emotional and historical. There was moral justice in having survivors and witnesses tell their stories in the most public of venues, graphically recounting the horrors they had witnessed and endured. Their testimonies were recorded by newsreels and transcribed by stenographers. And the offenders spoke as well, either proclaiming their innocence, claiming that

---

* More recently, the tribunal that has been established to prosecute those responsible for the Hutu genocide of Tutsis in Rwanda in 1994 was criticized precisely for failing to achieve the same moral goals as Nuremberg. This international tribunal has been convened not in Rwanda, but Tanzania, which makes it much more difficult for the Rwandans to feel a part of the process. Bongani C. Majola, a deputy prosecutor, was quoted in the *New York Times*, "Rwandans say, 'Listen, we are the victims, but we know nothing about what is happening there. We don't see it on the papers, we don't hear it on TV, we don't hear people in the bars talking about it. So to us, nothing is happening.'"

they were merely following orders, or apologizing, not individually, but on behalf of the entire nation—unredemptively arguing that they had personally done nothing wrong.

The Nuremberg Tribunal also ensured that there would be historical justice. Through the apparatus of the trial, a clearer picture of the Nazi murder machine unfolded, making it easier for historians to gather the evidence, assemble the records, and interpret the data in a way that served the inherently moral purpose of memorializing history. Justice requires truth as much as it requires punishment. Summary executions would have satisfied the understandable quest for vengeance, and, in the aftermath of the madness of World War II, such a response to the crimes of the Nazis would have been deemed justified and entirely appropriate. But it would have achieved only a punitive vision of justice, without the moral components of truth-telling and truth-seeking that this international tribunal ultimately provided.

Given the enormity of the crimes and the postwar retributive climate, Morgenthau's vision of vengeance was powerfully alluring. Why should the Nazis deserve to be treated justly, and receive the legal protection of a court of law—with American-styled constitutional safeguards—when they were merciless and morally lawless in their mass execution of Jews? Punishment is, after all, not without its own moral dimension. Punishment is often morally justified—the entirely right thing to do. Those who commit crimes and are guilty of wrongs should be held accountable, and punished accordingly. That's why one of Morgenthau's concerns—that some Nazis, given the imperfections of constitutional justice and the loopholes of due process, might end up being acquitted—never actually happened. All the original defendants were severely punished, and most received a capital sentence, allowing the world to feel a validated sense that justice had been served.

Yet, very often when people speak of justice, they are not referring to some abstract concept of law, or an ethereal vision of divine justice, but rather the more earthly idea of responding to a temporal wrong. They simply want to make sure that he who has caused suffering ends up suffering himself. The only way for the wrongdoer to know the pain that he has caused is by experiencing his own pain. That's why the seeking of revenge is an understandable human impulse, precisely because, to the revenge-seeker, the result feels like justice. It speaks to the underlying raw hurt, the primal sense that some life-altering event had taken place, and that the perpetrator must be made to feel the same sense of deprivation and loss.

"I want him to hurt."

"I want him to feel what I feel."

"I want him to know what he has done."

These are the words that animate and speak to revenge. It's not always so clear what form revenge must take—what exactly must happen for revenge to feel satisfying. While it is true that revenge can feel good, in many cases, no matter how gleefully devised and inflicted, it doesn't feel enough, or leaves the avenger feeling empty.

In *The Merchant of Venice*, Shylock admits that the pound of Antonio's flesh that he is seeking is truly valueless to him, other than that it will "feed my revenge." He is offered money—treble damages, in fact—and chooses the flesh instead. Obviously, revenge doesn't have to be satisfied in material terms. In fact, a civil remedy that results in a monetary judgment may not feel like the fulfillment of revenge at all. And having an offender languish in prison may not assuage the deep hunger for revenge, either.

Revenge has the unfortunate quality of feeling right to the victim, but only before ultimately taken. In theory it looks good, but might not sit so well later on. Violence and retaliation have a way of weighing on the conscience. Once revenge is completed, it's not clear whether the act of vengeance, and the altered landscape, live up to their promise. The idea of taking revenge is more alluring than the consequence of its aftermath. The prospect of revenge can sustain a life, but not without creating its own internal conflict.

One of the reasons why revenge is so appealing is that it contemplates some direct encounter between the victim and the offender. That in itself is an improvement over what the law provides. The legal system keeps victims and offenders apart. Step aside and the law will take over from here. But why should victims abandon the process so readily? In a civilized society, if you didn't have to surrender the job of justice to the government, and if instead you could either resolve or avenge the matter privately, would you? It's difficult to maintain trust in the law knowing what we know about its imperfections. And it's even more difficult entrusting it with something as important as bringing justice to a personal tragedy. The law isn't interested in tailoring, or personalizing, criminal remedies, or responding to our individual grief. Prosecutors don't ask victims what they would like to see happen to the offender, and then follow up on those wishes. At least with revenge, the victim is empowered by his own willingness to confront and punish on his own terms. There is no need to delegate the task to an emotionally detached assistant district attorney who shares none of the grief because he's merely doing his job, in most cases acting unilaterally, without regard to the victim's feelings.

Revenge grants the victim autonomy over the judgment. And in the absence of a moral legal system that seeks to heal wounds, air grievances, and restore moral balance to relationships and communities, revenge is a way to particularize the remedy, to make sure that the victim experiences his own personal satisfaction instead of being force-fed the retributive goals of the criminal justice system. This is particularly true when the law fails to do justice because of outright acquittals, procedural foul-ups, or trivializing plea agreements.

When artists look at revenge, for example in the classic French novel by Alexandre Dumas, *The Count of Monte Cristo*, the focus is always on its justification as an entirely moral and rational alternative to a nonexistent, futile, if not benighted legal system. The law itself is never shown as offering the kind of moral relief that would otherwise neutralize the need for revenge. Whenever loss is disacknowledged and the story is silenced, revenge becomes the only loud noise that the victim can control that speaks to his own individualized grief.

Perhaps most important, revenge contemplates some direct encounter. Revenge-seekers want to see the eyes of those upon whom they are taking vengeance. In every revenge drama, there is that moment—right before either the retaliatory death or the saving intervention of some third party—where former victims make clear why revenge was necessary, and how damaged and bereft the offender's actions have left them. The impulse for revenge itself is perhaps the best example of that damage. Without all that unremitting, implacable hurt, the victim would have been able to let it go, or resign himself to accepting that it was a matter best left handled by the police.

In 1986, a militant Palestinian shot and nearly killed a New York rabbi in Jerusalem's Old City. A dozen years later, the rabbi's daughter, Laura Blumenfeld, then a staff reporter for the *Washington Post*, decided to seek revenge against her father's assailant. Without letting him know her true motive or identity, she wrote him letters in prison and ultimately confronted him in an Israeli courtroom. Eventually she wrote a book called *Revenge: A Story of Hope*, about her personal experiences with vengeance, the way it changed her, and its effect on the assailant, as well.

"Revenge wasn't so much punishing the shooter for his deed as forcing him to confront his deeds," she said in an interview in the *New York Times*. "The only substitute for revenge is acknowledgment. Acknowledgment is more than regret; it's when you own your guilt, when you accept responsibility."

If Blumenfeld is correct, then revenge wouldn't be necessary if offenders acknowledged what they had done and accepted responsibility, which, as discussed in chapters 10 and 11, is one of the central elements of an apology. It's precisely the sense that an offender "had gotten away with it," walked away with a clean criminal record and a clear conscience, that makes revenge irresistible, and injustice so revolting. But by limiting remedies to cash and jail time, the conventional legal paradigm does nothing to defuse the desire for revenge. In fact, it has the potential to make revenge even more appealing. In removing emotion from the human drama of justice, in keeping victims and offenders apart, in providing no occasion for acknowledgments, apologies, and forgiveness, and in focusing entirely on punishment rather than on healing and restoration, the legal system ends up giving revenge a good name.

13

REPAIR IN PRACTICE

Historical and moral justice is served, and moral repair is made possible, only when the healing of wounds matters. Prosecutions and punishments silence stories, squash the truth, and hinder restoration. Individuals who have endured suffering and loss, and nations that have witnessed barbarism, eventually need to make the necessary transition away from grief and toward reconciliation—with themselves and with those who have caused harm. This forward movement cannot be accomplished merely by erasing the wounds of a nation's collective memory. Indeed, there is no moral future without a meaningful, public encounter with the past. Forgetfulness and cultural amnesia is not only a moral sin, but an ineffective method of erasure.

One distinctive vision of moral justice was firmly embodied in the spirit, and practice, of the South African Truth and Reconciliation Commission (TRC). Established in 1995 in the aftermath of apartheid, the commission heard over 2,000 accounts of victim suffering, and received submissions of 23,000 written testimonies, along with thousands of applications for amnesty from those who had committed crimes and heinous violations of human rights under the former regime. The idea was to create a living, testimonial record of the truth, and to force a cathartically public encounter with the evils of apartheid. All of this was done for the purpose of national healing and world reportage. The focus was on the victims and their families. Unlike the final judgment that arises out of a conventional trial, where true relief and finality are particularly elusive, a truth commission may actually be able to achieve closure, reconciliation, and perhaps even forgiveness.

"If it's important to a society to come to some kind of closure on what happened, you need a truth commission," Robert I. Rotberg, the president of the World Peace Foundation, was quoted in the *New York Times* as saying.

When one of the commissioners of the TRC asked Lucas Baba Sikwepere, a South African who had been blinded by a police officer, how he felt after giving his testimony, he stated: "I feel that what has been making me sick all the time is the fact that I couldn't tell my story. But now . . . it feels like I got my sight back by coming here."

The hearings were made public and they were widely publicized. Victims were given uninterrupted time in which to narrate the scope of their suffering. They told their stories and spoke freely until finished. The murderers and torturers spoke as well, also in front of live audiences and before television cameras. And when their testimony and disclosures were completed, those seeking amnesty were questioned not only by prosecutors, but also by victims and the surviving families of victims.

Amnesty was being granted to murderers. All the perpetrators had to do was tell the truth. The more truth they told, the more freedom they obtained. It wasn't even required that they feel or show remorse, or ask for forgiveness. Historical truth— the story of what happened, told in exacting detail—and the emotional repair that comes about from the telling of these stories and the pronouncement of grief, would serve as justice in South Africa rather than a more conventional, but politically destabilizing, retributive remedy.

"I'm very skeptical that we somehow learn lessons from history," Ian Buruma, the author of *The Wages of Guilt: Memories of War in Germany and Japan*, was quoted in the *New York Times* as saying. "But there is something very beneficial in having the truth publicly analyzed, researched as a public exercise. I think that for former victims, the fact that the truth is told is psychologically more important than financial compensation."

Full disclosure, in lieu of, and at the expense of, punishment. In fact, the TRC made no mention of legal justice, because justice—the kind that gets determined in a courtroom—is normally associated with punitive, retributive measures, whereas the TRC sought the moral justice that comes from social harmony and historical truth. With a truth commission, the gathering of information, the honoring of cultural memory, the compiling of a historical record, the acknowledgment of national and personal trauma, is all part of this intensely public enterprise. For this reason, a truth commission is not unlike Oedipus's truth-seeking prosecution of the unsolved murder in Thebes. It all takes place in an open amphitheater, in front of a Greek chorus, and the ultimate remedy, although disastrous for Oedipus, is restorative for his country.

Unlike a court of law, truth commissions assembled in Argentina, Chile, and Guatemala during the past two decades in response to other atrocious human-rights violations are focused entirely on truth, acknowledgment, and reconciliation. Punishment is seemingly beside the point. Justice is reframed in restorative, spiritual terms. Truth commissions essentially operate in contradistinction to tribunals and courts of law. One is a place of truth; the other is one of conventional legal justice. Truth commissions are reminders of the moral and spiritual limitations of courtrooms. Introducing some of the features of truth commissions into the practices of conventional trials would be a first step toward blending moral and legal justice.

With Nuremberg as precedent, the new democratic government of South Africa must have at least considered a tribunal as an option for bringing human-rights violators to justice. They could have chosen to prosecute and punish those members of the white-minority government and others who had so gruesomely violated standards of international law and human decency. But that would have led to unsettling consequences of civil unrest, since so many white South Africans had committed crimes, and the incarceration of all would have been politically unbearable. For this reason, a truth commission is generally motivated first by political necessity, and then, perhaps, by moral imperative. In order to make the necessary transition that would have allowed the new South African government to lead without animus or incapacitation, amnesty was granted in return for truth, and punishment was set aside in favor of reconciliation.

Trials or truth commissions? Two different concepts of justice, driven by entirely different objectives. And even though there are moral objections to amnesty, it is clear that truth commissions—and their insistence on hearing and learning the truth—accomplish a good deal of what should constitute moral justice.

Unlike a tribunal, truth commissions allow victims to tell their stories unconstrained by evidentiary and procedural rules. These rules, as discussed in chapter 6, narrow the scope of testimony and shut down the rhythm and flow of narrative. In a truth commission, victims are asked to tell their stories in a publicly acknowledged, free-flowing way, without outside shaping or interference. Similarly, unlike trials, truth commissions do not allow for the cross-examination of witnesses, further ensuring that testimony won't be reduced to passionless "yes" and "no" responses, nor will the witness be placed on the defensive and questioned in a hostile manner.

Moreover, in a truth commission, a great deal of deference and respect is shown to victims, whereas in trials, the focus is always on the rights of perpetrators, with victims consigned to the role of principal witnesses on behalf of the state. Indeed, in our legal system, the presumption of the defendant's innocence causes the testimony of the victim to be generally treated with skepticism or regarded with disbelief. The burden falls on the victim to rebut this presumption, and to convince the jury that the accusation against the defendant is true. No matter how harsh the level of suffering, the presumption favors the defendant's innocence over the victim's pain. But with a truth commission, the victim's pain is paramount. And truth commissions allow the pain to express itself, even if it rambles, even if it is emotionally unguarded, untempered, and unchecked. Trials, as we currently experience them, have little chance of producing closure. But with truth commissions, all is sacrificed—including punitive justice—for the very sake, and possibility, of closure.

What is restorative about truth commissions is not only the giving of testimony and the telling of stories, but the act of listening to them, as well. Listening not only by those who committed the crimes, but also by those who witnessed them in silence. Listening is part of the healing process—for everyone. It affirms the dignity of those who have suffered the harm, and it makes it possible for those who caused the harm—as well as those who stood by and said nothing—to contemplate their actions or inactions, and show proper remorse. Through acknowledgment also comes shame, and also the reintegration back into society of those who were both legally and morally culpable.

But is this alternative vision of justice a truly moral one? While its focus on the victimization of individuals, the telling of stories, the disclosures of truth, and the restoration of society, has strong moral components, is it moral not to prosecute and punish those who committed unspeakably horrifying crimes?

"The reality is that, when you trade amnesty for truth, murderers get away with murder," wrote Michael Ignatieff in the *New Yorker.* A noted black South African critic of the amnesty process was quoted in the *New York Times* and the *Boston Globe* as saying: "It stinks to high heaven. To imagine that after confessing, these people who committed the more horrendous crimes will then be patted on the shoulder by the TRC. The TRC is a denial of justice. Without justice, how can the victims feel healed?"

Punishment serves the ends not only of conventional legal justice. Punishment has a moral component, as well. One of the central arguments of this book is that moral considerations and private conscience should be integrated into legal decision-making. This does not mean, however, that doing the right thing must necessarily reject the retributive and compensatory objectives that are achieved through conventional legal remedies. The legal system should be capable of seeking truths and yet still impose punishments, to elicit acknowledgments and apologies, and yet also demand accountability and a public reckoning. It's immoral for a legal system to minimize the value of truth-telling and truth-seeking, and to ignore the healing possibilities that arise out of acknowledgments and apologies. But it is equally untenable and unjust to have criminals and tortfeasors end up paying no debt either to society or to the individuals they have harmed.

A moral justice-system requires that victims be treated with dignity, and that all efforts be made to restore whatever dignity has been lost and repair the necessary physical damage, as well. But an equally profound moral imperative is that individuals take moral responsibility for their actions. True reconciliation cannot occur if acknowledgment is unaccompanied by remorse and some form of penalty. That's why in the absence of punishment, the TRC recommended at least the payment of restitution to the victims. In April 2003, the government of South Africa granted reparations totaling $85 million to more than nineteen thousand victims of apartheid who testified before the TRC. This number was considerably less than the $360 million that the TRC had requested. Thado Mbeki, the president of South Africa, said in a speech before Parliament, "We hope that these disbursements will help acknowledge the suffering that these individuals experienced, and offer some relief." Yet for many black South Africans, the money—amounting to $3,900 per family—was too little, and the granting of general amnesty too hard to live with. After all, the payments, trifling as they were, came from the state, and not from the offending perpetrators.

While truth, story, and acknowledgment may have great restorative potential, as an alternative vision of justice, it is not enough. For a legal system to be just and not simply dispense justice, those who commit crimes or cause harm must take moral responsibility for their actions, and submit themselves to punishment or the assumption of liability. They must give something up, like their freedom, or make some contribution toward repairing the victim—not just spiritually, but materially, as well. The problem with the conventional legal paradigm is that justice feels just only to those who administer the system, and not to those who are thrust into the law as embattled victims. In a moral legal system, a remedy would provide not only healing and restorative capabilities, but also a sense that justice was served by attaching a consequence to an action that had caused harm.

One tortured ex-political prisoner of Argentina, a country that had undertaken its own truth and reconciliation process, was quoted by Alex Boraine in an article contained in the collection of essays, *Truth v. Justice: The Morality of Truth Commissions*: "How can I have peace when every day I risk meeting my unpunished torturer in the neighborhood?"

Forgiveness is yet another dimension of healing and repair. In addition to the initial harm, a victim can become a prisoner of the crime done to him, or of the injury that he had sustained. An entire life can become suspended while one is waiting for justice, which may take an entire lifetime and never arrive. Forgiveness puts an end to the wait. But forgiveness is the sole prerogative of individuals, not nations. A nation can punish and create conditions for reconciliation, but it cannot force individual victims to forgive, any more than it can force perpetrators to offer sincere apologies of remorse. The law can assign liability and find people guilty, but forgiveness requires an affirmative act—the relinquishing of the grievance—which can only be done by the person who has experienced the pain. Sometimes the impulse to forgive is initiated by the person who caused the harm, as when a perpetrator seeks forgiveness in an effort to restore moral harmony to the relationship. Asking for forgiveness is not the same thing as merely offering an apology. The former brings the injured party back into the relationship, making him part of the experience of reconciliation by asking something of him, as well.

Archbishop Desmond Tutu, Nobel laureate and chairman of the TRC, is also the author of *No Future Without Forgiveness*, a book that advocates for forgiveness as an essential, albeit an elusive part of the reconciliation process. While victims of apartheid were not required to forgive (nor were perpetrators required to apologize), for Tutu, reconciliation worked best when they did. But, as Tutu explained, forgiveness does not have to be given, or sought, for purely moral purposes. The act of forgiving can be pursued for selfish, self-interested motives, too. Forgiveness allows the hurt party to feel released from the bonds that tie him to the injury. Forgiveness is the act of surrendering the need for revenge. Doing so clears the path to moving forward. It serves the larger interest of repair in the same way that giving voice to the story, and recording the truth for posterity, is an act of moral justice—although an incomplete one—independent of whether there is punishment or the payment of reparations.

Truth without punishment can be healing yet still not feel entirely moral. The same is true of forgiveness, which loses its moral force, and, in fact, is more difficult if not impossible to give, when the perpetrator is unwilling to accept legal responsibility for his actions by either submitting to punishment or offering restitution. In the case of the TRC, the very fact that amnesty was traded for truth made it hard for the victims to forgive. The search for truth and the telling of stories may have offered, and in many cases succeeded in bringing about, emotional closure. But in the absence of punishment, the consequence of allowing murderers to escape justice simply because they were forthcoming with their testimony, can never feel right morally. Forgiveness can't come without the showing of remorse and the taking of moral responsibility. The act of forgiveness essentially wipes the moral ledger clean. But how can a victim cancel the spiritual debt owed to him if there has been no acceptance of responsibility and no surrendering to some form of retributive justice?

Another example of where restorative justice heals some wounds but reopens others has to do with the actual giving of testimony. Memory is not without consequence, because the act of recalling and retelling often resurrects the feelings and emotions of a painful past. To repeat the story can be tantamount to reliving it. This is why some believe that it is best to put the past behind, move forward and forge ahead, allow bygones to be bygones, and come to terms with the past rather than become stuck in it. Denial is not a restorative exercise, but rather a purely defensive and self-protective one. Furious remembrance and recollection is fraught with risk even as it offers the chance at repair. This is an aspect of storytelling that oftentimes gets overlooked. Giving voice to the hurt can be simultaneously cathartic and traumatic, moral and self-mutilating.

Rehashing all the harm—depending upon its degree of severity—has the potential to retraumatize victims. In some cases, truth commissions provided assistance to those who suffered psychologically from reanimating the past. But in other instances, those who told their stories were left with a new set of untreated spiritual injuries, all acquired in the service of acknowledgment and truth.

This can occur even when the testimony is not given in front of a commission, or for the purpose of national healing. In the case of Holocaust survivors who provided oral testimonies for archival purposes, some experienced the trauma of resurrected nightmares. Eva Fogelman, a New York–based psychologist, pointed out the psychological pitfalls inherent in oral-history projects.

"Unfortunately, the lingering psychological pain that survivors continue to experience more than fifty years after liberation is ongoing in their lives," Fogelman said. "And for some it has not gotten better after taping their testimonies. Oral histories, in themselves, could never have been expected to be the magic bullet that would heal the psychological wounds of the Holocaust, and we shouldn't delude ourselves into thinking that once the testimony is completed, there is closure for the survivor."

Reliving the past for acknowledgment and truth purposes can end up causing additional harm. This doesn't mean that the act of recalling is unjustified. Rather it suggests that truth commissions and tribunals, where appropriate, should take the necessary precautions to ensure that those who testify be properly cared for once they have exhausted their stories. This can come in the form of court-appointed mental health professionals and support networks that are brought in to intervene before the giving of testimony results in harm. After testifying, victims cannot always be expected to reintegrate back into society with seamless assurance. They are no longer the same people. In the telling has come transformation. Some of it is healing, and the rest may be in need of its own healing.

The TRC was generally referred to as the Third Way, a third option of what South Africa could do in the aftermath of apartheid and still make the transition to a democratic, majority-ruled society. One approach would have been to grant a blanket amnesty to all white South Africans, which would have ensured the most peaceful transfer of power. Another would have been to conduct a Nuremberg-style tribunal, which would have led to a largely retributive justice remedy of prosecutions and punishment. The third option, or the Third Way, was to establish a truth commission that permitted victims to reclaim their dignity by telling their stories, and granted amnesty to those who had committed political crimes, but only in exchange for truth-telling in a public forum. Whether this process resulted in the perfect symmetry of truth and justice, or repair and remedy, is still unknown.

The existence of the TRC raises the question of whether the American legal system is capable of embracing some of the moral values and restorative aspirations of truth commissions. Indeed, there is much to learn about alternative models of justice that go beyond the purely retributive and compensatory and seek instead to achieve healing and repair.

Other cultures—particularly ancient ones, from Arab, Greek, and Roman civilizations to Germanic tribes, Indian Hindus, and Buddhist, Taoist, and Confucian traditions—have long sought to restore the entire community, as well as the victims and the of-fenders, following a crime or injury. Some of the new reforms in criminal justice have been influenced by the experience of restorative justice programs that have succeeded elsewhere. For instance, in New Zealand, family group conferences were suc-cessfully instituted to help bring about both resolution and re-pair in criminal cases. And much has been learned from examining the traditional justice models adopted by Native Canadian Indians, with their healing and sentencing circles, along with similar practices found in Navajo Justice and Healing ceremonies and peacemaking courts. The Zapatistas tradition of community governance in Mexico, and the tribal practices of the Nanantes from Africa, are also helpful in introducing repair-minded reforms that would create a more morally centered jus-tice system.

For instance, the Hollow Water program in Manitoba, Canada, which is run by the Ojibway Native Canadians of northern Winnipeg, offers an example of restorative justice in action. Judges do not sit on elevated platforms, but rather they join a healing and sentencing circle, which includes the victim, the perpetrator, their respective families, and members of the community. All are treated equally in helping to find a resolution to the dispute. Everyone who is joined in the circle is permitted to speak, uninterrupted, which at times becomes very emotional. The goal, in all instances, is to reach some kind of community consensus. The circle might be convened for up to fourteen consecutive hours. Hundreds of community residents attend these sessions and witness the entire proceedings.

Currently, in Rwanda, in a national effort to bring some justice to the genocide of 500,000 ethnic Tutsi and moderate Hutu during a one hundred-day slaughter in 1994, a community-based system referred to as "*gacaca*" is being undertaken. The word means "grass," named for the thousands of people who gather on the grass to adjudicate some of the 100,000 cases against those who perpetrated the crimes. Because it is unable to prosecute all of these cases, the government has delegated many of them to community-based, cultural-dispute-resolution authorities. It all takes place out in the open, where anyone with an accusation against the prisoner is encouraged to speak without interference. If no one chooses to speak, the prisoner is set free.

The American legal system has experimented with several alternative dispute-resolution practices, some of which are guided by the principles of restoration and repair. Shaming penalties have gained a new following. California has considered forcing those with drunk-driving records to place license plates on their cars that read "DUI." Humiliation, and its severe spiritual price-tag, sends a stronger moral, expressive message than the relative anonymity of jail time or a fine.

Perhaps more successful have been Victim Offender Reconciliation or Mediation Programs (VORPs or VOMPs). First initiated in Ontario, Canada, in 1974, these programs have now grown to more than three hundred in North America, spread out in over forty-three states, and over five hundred in Europe, with two hundred more in Canada, Australia, New Zealand, and South Africa. During the 1990s, New Zealand and Australia significantly humanized their criminal-justice systems through these practices, and, in the process, repaired damaged individuals and restored broken communities. The concept of these programs is to truly resolve a conflict, and promote healing, rather than to merely punish wrongdoers.

Under these mediation and reconciliation programs, the victim—or the victim's family—as a way of healing, is given an opportunity, in a face-to-face encounter, to confront the offender and speak to the damage and loss. It is an entirely voluntary process; neither the victim nor the offender is ever forced to participate. They agree to these reconciliation sessions because they both believe that mediation will yield some moral or emotional benefit. These programs humanize the criminal-justice system and recognize the spiritual impact that crimes, and other traumatic experiences, have on victims. The effect is lasting and does not vanish with time.

Howard Zehr, who has written widely about the use of VORPs in America, wrote: "The central focus of the old paradigm (retribution) is on the past, on blame-fixing. While the new paradigm (restoration) would encourage responsibility for past behavior, its focus would be on the future, on problem-solving, on the obligation created by the offense. Restoration, making things right, would replace the imposition of pain as the expected outcome in the new paradigm. Restitution would be common, not exceptional. Instead of committing one social injury in response to another, a restorative paradigm would focus on healing."

In this kind of a repair-minded atmosphere, the victim, offender, and the community all have the burden to promote reconciliation and find ways to make things right.

But unlike a truth commission, which has no tribunal or retributive dimension, mediation or reconciliation programs occur after criminal sentencing and while the offender is serving time, whether it was for rape, murder, shoplifting, vandalism, arson, or armed robbery. Punishment has already taken place, and it is now time for repair. In most cases, the offender has no incentive to participate in a VORP or VOMP other than his own sense of private conscience. He must make a personal decision that meeting with the victim, or the surviving family, is simply the right thing to do. They deserve at least that much, and the offender may have something to say, as well. And since the court did not require a personal encounter, the perpetrator voluntarily consents to one, and, in doing so—spiritually at least—doubles his own punishment. The offender who once had invoked the Fifth, now willingly submits to the combined indignity of accusation and shame.

Not all victims wish to participate, however. Indeed, 25 percent of the victims who are approached about taking part in a VOMP or VORP flatly refuse. Yet the results of many of these sessions where victims and offenders confront one another are impressive, particularly from a restorative-justice perspective. Many have yielded apologies that were meaningful to victims. In other cases, there have been private arrangements where the offender agreed to make some form of restitution to victims and their families. Some examples of these arrangements include: the reimbursement for losses attributable to the crime; the repairing of property that had been damaged, such as from vandalism; or the performing of some service that is meaningful to the injured party.

An important distinction between truth commissions and reconciliation programs is that the latter are not in lieu of prison time. Truth, remorse, and contrition are not rewarded with amnesty. But as with a truth commission, forgiveness is not a primary goal of the process. What's important is the encounter itself, with the hope that it will help in healing. The victim doesn't have to forgive, but the offender does have to accept moral responsibility. One former director of a juvenile probation department from Idaho said about these programs: "The victim comes in angry, or hurt, or scared, and the offender comes in [acting] cocky. The goal, of course, is to get empathy on both sides. The offender [hears] how it is to be violated. It gives them a conscience."

To do so, the offender must engage in serious listening. The reconciliation between the victim and the offender, and between the offender and the community, can only come about if the offender hears the victim's pain and absorbs it into his own consciousness, which will ensure that his own conscience will never be clear.

Since most VORP and VOMP sessions take place after sentencing, there is no reason why this same process can't occur in the civil area, as well, either after trial and verdict, or after a settlement is reached. It is also possible to initiate these reconciliation sessions before legal proceedings commence. As a consequence of the rebuilding of damaged relationships, the acknowledgment of loss, the offering of apologies, and the voluntary decision to provide for restitution, some civil suits may never be filed, and prosecutors might decide, like they often do in Japan, not to bring criminal charges against a defendant. Indeed, even in cases of a gravely serious crime, such as rape and assault, victim-offender mediation has managed to produce apologies that took away much of the underlying grievance and gave rise to some meaningful healing of the emotional injury.

In a study of VOMPs and VORPs in Indiana, professors Robert Coates and John Gehm discovered that victims were satisfied with "the expression of remorse on the part of the offender," and offenders were "thankful for the chance to make things right." And Dr. Mark Umbreit, a professor of social work and a pioneer in this field of restorative justice, wrote in a 1994 study of four mediation programs: "[V]ictims who go through mediation were more likely to see their experience with the justice system as fair than those who went through the traditional court process."

Other programs that have similar restorative-justice features include Mothers Against Drunk Driving (MADD) and Parents of Murdered Children (POMC). In each instance, the voice of the victim, and of the surviving family, is paramount, and victims are able to have direct contact with the offender in order to communicate the impact that the crime has had on their lives. But not only do these programs empower victims and humanize justice, VOMPs and VORPs also seem to yield significantly lower recidivism rates for those offenders who participate in the program. A number of studies have been conducted, both in America and in other countries, which show that, particularly in the case of youth offenders, the return to a criminal life is diminished. One study reported that recidivism rates for those offenders, regardless of age, who participated in these programs is under 10 percent as compared to the customary recidivism rates, which range anywhere between 50 and 85 percent. In the conventional legal paradigm of criminal justice, the majority of offenders serve their time in jail only to repeat their crimes soon after gaining their freedom. Thus, these morally based programs can also serve the very conventional legal purpose of deterrence.

Another way of thinking about restorative justice is in the use of victim impact-statements. A creation of the victim's rights movement, and a feature of the 1982 Final Report of the President's Task Force on Victims of Crime, impact statements seek to expand the victim's participation in the criminal-justice process. It gives them a right to be heard and to present information about the impact that the crime has had—whether it be financial, emotional, familial, or societal—on their lives as well as on the lives of other survivors. In many state constitutions, this right extends "to all crucial stages of the criminal proceedings," meaning that victims are permitted to speak both during the trial and at sentencing.

In chapter 5, I discussed ways in which victims are reduced to mere witnesses for the prosecution in the criminal-justice system. Stories go unheard while the government prosecutes its case against the offender generally without consulting the victim, or accounting for the victim's wishes. Indeed, the offender is able to bring in as many character witnesses as possible to shape the jury's perception of his temperament and reputation, but the victim is bizarrely excluded from the process altogether. As an antidote to this moral imperfection of the legal system, victim impact-statements reintroduce the stories of victims back into the courtroom. While the victim does not become the center of the trial's attention, as he is with a truth commission, at least he is guaranteed some voice. The impact statement is more declaratory than remedial. The purpose is not to have the offender compensate the victim for the crime, but merely to advise the court of the extent of the harm the victim has suffered and the impact that it has had on him. In many unfortunate ways, impact statements have not sufficiently influenced prosecutorial decision-making. Prosecutors, for the most part, still have little obligation to consider the wishes of the victims in the strategies they choose and the deals they make with offenders.

In addition to victim impact-statements, there are other ways of incorporating restorative-justice principles within the conventional legal paradigm. Alternative dispute resolution, known as ADR, offers an alternative to traditional civil litigation that can bring about healing and repair. These practices include negotiation, mediation, and arbitration.

As I discussed in chapter 6, negotiation, which is the process that leads to settlements, is not entirely an effective tool for moral or restorative justice, since settlements virtually exclude the client from the proceedings, truth is ignored, and the eventual outcome is subjected to secrecy.

Mediation relies on a third party to help facilitate a resolution between the parties. The third party has no authority to render a decision or to make a ruling. The idea is to clear obstacles away so that the parties can reach an agreement on their own. And lawyers are usually not present to interfere with or zealously represent the client's interests. Mediation still involves a negotiation, but the parties are present and engaged, and they have the opportunity to speak to their grievance in a face-to-face encounter, confronting those who have caused them harm. It is a dialogue-centered process; the more the parties speak for themselves, and to each other, the more likely they will agree on some resolution. They may even reconcile, which seldom occurs in a pure, winner-take-all, adversarial process. Indeed, because it provides a human encounter and calls for accountability, mediation can result in achieving some of the goals of restorative justice, such as acknowledgments, apologies, healing, the repair of relationships, and perhaps even forgiveness. Mediation works to make peace rather than foment retaliation. And mediation, if done properly, resolves disputes by opening up the story rather than shutting it down. As Professor Carrie Menkel-Meadow has pointed out, "mediation should not be used to pacify legitimate grievances or conflicts that need to be expressed." Mediation should honor and recall the past as much as it should look toward the future, because memory is central to the healing process. However, given some of the themes of moral justice, mediation falls short, because it suffers from the lack of a public setting and the creation of a public record, and the absence of community involvement.

Arbitration is an adjudicatory process where a third party is empowered to rule in favor of one side or the other. The proceeding is conducted not in a governmental courthouse but rather is delegated to a private authority. For this reason, the decision is rendered more quickly, because there is less of a backlog of cases, and without many of the customary procedural or evidentiary rules. But for the most part, arbitration is not really that much different from litigation. The parties are represented by counsel who speak on their behalf instead of allowing the parties to speak for themselves. And arbitration, unlike a trial, does not have a public component, nor is the ruling made public, so it has no way of necessarily influencing future decisions or disciplining the bad behavior of those who might contemplate similar actions.

Recently there have been some new developments at finding ways to integrate the themes of restorative justice into the conventional legal paradigm. One is the concept of therapeutic justice, which originated in the area of mental disability law, but which has been applied to other areas, such as criminal, tort, labor, and domestic law, as well. Therapeutic justice, mostly advanced by legal scholars David Wexler and Bruce Winick, asks lawyers to consider the emotional impact that legal decisions will have on their clients and the communities in which they live. The goal is to create a jurisprudence of healing. Andrea Kupfer Schneider has written that "[u]nderstanding the emotional impact of the law could affect drafting documents and planning, could affect choices if there is a legal dispute, and affect the very design of rules and procedures to be applied in the future."

Another moral, spiritual approach would be to insert a second stage to trials. Following a final judgment in an American courtroom, no one should be permitted to leave. Instead, there should be an opportunity for all those who participated in the trial and its verdict—parties, jurors, witnesses—to discuss the experience. Let them speak to the injustice, and to the vindication, because in a winner-take-all contest, both of those feelings will exist in the same verdict. Parties invariably will harbor different perspectives. Essentially, in a second stage to trials, the doors to the courtroom remain closed, and everyone remains seated until all those who have something to say have said it. And if it takes too long, and there is simply too much to say, then they should all be required to return the next morning to resume the discussion. In light of the emotional insensitivity of the conventional legal paradigm, one thing at least is clear: The losing party is not ready to go home simply because the judge has pounded his gavel and entered a final judgment. In fact, we shouldn't allow the losing party to go home loaded up with all that rage, disappointment, and anguished sense of betrayal. The legal system is responsible for both ignoring and igniting the undischarged grief that arises out of irresolution. American courtrooms shamefully won't tolerate the showing of grief, or the release of anger and emotion. But those feelings, inevitably, must then spill out elsewhere—on the streets, in office buildings, schools, and in bedrooms. We are all vulnerable in the wake of that discharge, and we are also complicit in its occurrence when we pretend that the law has spoken and done its job, while it clearly has not.

THE NON-DUTY TO RESCUE
UNDER AMERICAN LAW

I n 1998, a television sitcom that proclaimed itself to be about nothing, fittingly completed its nine-year run by examining the moral and legal consequences of doing nothing while in the presence of something that otherwise required a moral response. The final episode of *Seinfeld*, which aired in May 1998, focused on the moral duty to rescue in the context of a legal system that generally imposes no such duty to take action on behalf of strangers.

The cynical, streetwise characters of the show crash-landed in a small Massachusetts town that had recently enacted a Good Samaritan law. The new statute required citizens to come to the aid of those in distress if at all reasonable to do so. Of course, as narcissistic, hard-bitten New Yorkers with no prior notice of the law and a habit of sitting back and making fun of others, the *Seinfeld* characters were surprised when a policeman arrested them for failing to aid an overweight person who, after struggling to get out of his car, was robbed at gunpoint. Instead of rescuing the stranger, they stood by, making jokes about his predicament, while he cried out desperately for help.

Upon being arrested, Elaine asked, "But why? We didn't do anything."

"Why would we want to help someone?" George wondered incredulously.

Not surprisingly, the *Seinfeld* crew retained a New York attorney to represent them at trial. As a lawyer locked into the conventional legal paradigm, he was stunned to hear that there was even such a law on the books, calling it "deplorable, unfathomable, and improbable." He then said, "You don't have to help anybody. That's what this country is all about." And later, in his argument before the jury, he said, "You cannot be a bystander and be guilty. Bystanders are, by definition, innocent. That's the nature of bystanding."

But are all innocent bystanders innocent, or is this idea simply an artifact of a legal system that has conditioned us to think of bystanders as witnesses who just happen to be standing around, minding their own business, with no liability or culpability attached to their inaction? From a moral perspective, there is nothing innocent about simply standing by and doing nothing. Morally, doing nothing when doing something could avert or minimize harm should arouse feelings of guilt, and invoke the legal consequences of that guilt. A moral legal system would make no distinction between the body in motion and the body engaged in neglect. Just because the body refuses to move doesn't mean that it is doing nothing. Standing by in silence is often an independent choice. It is an act—the act of indifference.

Perhaps nothing in the law reveals such a gross violation of moral failure as the absence of a duty to rescue. Students hear about this non-duty in law school, and many of them are either too cowed to question their professors, or are silently, morally revolted—bystanders themselves in the presence of an immoral rule. Yet the non-rule remains, unchallenged, almost as a barometer of the American legal system's moral deficiencies. While negligence law is activated by the breach of a duty of care, and contracting parties are required not to breach their agreements, and there is an implied duty of good faith in all transactions, when it comes to situations of human distress, there is no general duty to rescue that would require people to act on the behalf of others. You can breach human decency all day and rarely become answerable in a court of law.

The duty to rescue does exist in certain limited situations of emergency, usually in cases where there is a special relationship between the victim and the rescuer. For instance, in all jurisdictions, a parent has a duty to rescue a child, and one spouse owes the same duty to the other. Certain contractual situations give rise to rescue obligations, such as a doctor's duty to a patient, and a police- or fireman's duty to the community. Eight states have passed Good Samaritan, or duty to rescue, laws, similar to the one satirized on the final *Seinfeld* episode. These laws, in many ways, are improperly named, because they don't really apply to good Samaritans, but rather bad ones, by criminally punishing those who fail to assist a stranger in peril. The states that have passed such legislation are Florida, Massachusetts, Minnesota, Ohio, Rhode Island, Vermont, Washington, and Wisconsin. Few of these states, however, have actually tested these laws by enforcing them, nor have the laws been subjected to much, if any, judicial review. The citizens of these states mostly ignore this affirmative statutory duty. The law exists on the books but lies dormant in the heart, a symbol of forsaken civic responsibility. Neither citizens, nor lawmakers take it seriously. In contrast, various European nations, including Portugal, the Netherlands, Finland, Italy, Norway, Russia, Turkey, Denmark, Poland, Germany, Romania, France, Hungary, Greece, the Czech Republic, Bulgaria, Yugoslavia, Albania, Switzerland, Spain, and Belgium all recognize and enforce a general duty to rescue. A citizen of these countries can be fined, and in some cases imprisoned, for failing to honor it.

Unlike the cynical characters on *Seinfeld*, for whom human vulnerability is always meant to be observed and mocked rather than assisted, most people are surprised to learn that there is no actual duty to aid a stranger. A drowning man can scream for hours in front of a crowd of Olympic swimmers and no one would have a legal obligation to dive in and attempt to save his life. You don't have to take any action at all—even actions that are benign and require little effort. There is no requirement to make a cellphone call to an experienced lifeguard or to the Coast Guard. Standing by and watching the victim drown is completely legal. But is it moral? And if it's not moral, then why would the legal system hold itself to a lower standard so inconsistent with doing the right thing?

Even worse, not only is there no legal duty to rescue, but the law generally provides disincentives to even try. If one should impulsively go beyond the mandates of the law and attempt to save someone in distress, and should that person cause additional harm (say, breaking a rib while administering CPR), the rescuer is responsible for whatever excess damage he causes in the service of acting as a good Samaritan. Many states have attempted to modify this general rule by enacting a different kind of Good Samaritan statute, one that doesn't impose a duty to rescue but rather creates a limited tort immunity for rescues gone bad. The idea is to protect rescuers—true good Samaritans—from civil liability.

There is no legal duty to act, yet there is a clear legal consequence to acting in ways that bring about unexpected harm. The unsuccessful rescue results in civil liability partly because the duty to rescue itself is nonexistent. Under the law, a rescue is deemed an independent voluntary act—with all assumptions of liability—rather than as a compulsory moral response to someone in danger. In attempting a rescue, the rescuer is acting beyond the call of duty, therefore, he is held responsible for any damage traceable to his improvised efforts. Paradoxically, the punishment falls not on the person who fails to act, but rather on the one who acts with only qualified success. The law makes a distinction between misfeasance, or active misconduct, in which a victim is made worse off because of someone else's action or intervention, and nonfeasance, or passive misconduct, in which the bystander, in doing nothing, neither benefits nor harms the victim. Acts and omissions are accorded a different status under the law, and standing by and doing nothing falls moderately into the category of nonfeasance. But it's not as if omissions, generally, carry no consequences. The nonpayment of taxes, for instance, results in penalties, sometimes even imprisonment. The failure to register a motor vehicle is an omission that may not require a lot of action, but it is certainly not risk-free. And avoiding the draft can't be defended by pacifism alone.

Without a legal duty, the rescuer's choice is purely a moral one. By doing the right thing, he's taking a chance, because liability can attach to his chivalry. The burden is placed on the rescuer to be perfect in his execution. This is true despite the fact that rescues are normally performed in the heat of the moment and without time for rehearsal—the exercise of caution balanced by the urgency of the situation. At the end of a failed rescue, they may not pin any medals on the rescuer, but they may slap him with a lawsuit.

Such a result is clearly unjust and immoral. Under our legal system, rescue amounts to an unrequited, one-sided risk: The rescuer puts his body and his life on the line, and, at the same time, exposes himself to possible liability. The law essentially says: "Be careful when you take your first step toward rescuing a fellow human being, because you're not required to do so, and the choice is not without consequence." Once the rescuer announces his intentions, his conduct comes under close scrutiny. The law will be checking for flaws. So why would anyone aspire to become a good Samaritan? The innocent bystander is ultimately better off; morally questionable, but at least safe from the law's harsh judgment.

Few would question whether responding to someone in distress is a morally virtuous act. But the law doesn't require that we model ourselves on being moral. Instead of encouraging humanitarian interventions, the legal system sends an implicit message that rescue is risky and indifference is safe. It isn't rational for citizens to come to each other's aid when the law doesn't require it and penalizes those who try but in some manner fail. If nothing else, we can safely say that our rescuers are drawn from the pool of irrational men. This is where the decent people are found wading through life.

The reasonable men, by contrast, are playing it safe, acting cool, hugging the sidelines, simply standing by. As I discussed in chapter 1, the reasonable man test, which sets the standard for applying most legal rules, is generally determined by looking at what most people would do in a given circumstance. When it comes to matters of rescue, we know what most people do. Situations that present risk cause people to flee, withdraw, or simply watch. Such responses are deemed reasonable, and therefore lawful. Rescues are irrational, and therefore fall outside the law. But this rule produces immoral outcomes. How can it be that the cowards are considered law-abiding while rescuers, legally speaking, are flying without a parachute? The reasonable person is acting lawfully, and yet his indifference may be morally reprehensible. He is overly reasoned, and yet severely lacking in humanity. Given such low moral standards, we should all hope to be surrounded by a few good irrational men if we ever find ourselves in mortal trouble.

Reasonable though they may be, bystanders are not exemplary. As children we are taught not to follow the crowd, to think independently, and to aid those in distress. But under the law, the reasonable man is someone who is without any of these virtues. Indeed, in some cases, the actions of a reasonable man are immoral. During times of crisis and upheaval, the man who follows orders, folds himself into the crowd, never voices any protest or dissent, may indeed be acting reasonably. After all, no one wishes to be placed in harm's way, or to attract unnecessary attention. But the reasonable man, while reasonable, is also a moral coward. He will close the blinds on the windows of his house—and of his conscience—when a neighbor is taken away at night. Shouldn't the law require more than he is willing to give?

A moral legal system would honor the rescuer, not punish him. And a moral legal system would create and enforce duties that would bring out the rescuer in all of us. Rather than legitimizing indifference, the law should influence our quiet actions and legalize rescue. The indifferent should not be reassured that all that comes from their neglect is shame—if that. Sometimes we simply need to be less reasonable. Some risks are important to take. Other risks we simply must undertake.

We all know examples of crimes or injuries that could have been averted if bystanders had instead acted in some way. Perhaps the most famous is the tragic tale of Kitty Genovese. Approximately forty years ago, Genovese, a young woman from Queens, New York, cried out for help for more than half an hour outside her apartment building while she was attacked by an assailant who eventually returned to kill her. As many as thirty-eight people, tucked away safely in their own apartments, heard her pleas but did nothing to lend assistance. Perhaps some believed that others were calling the police, or were about to come to the screaming woman's rescue. But no one did anything to help, or even call for help.

The nature of the bystander is the impulse to remain unaware. The bystander operates under the assumption that he or she is ultimately powerless, impotent in the face of any danger. Intervention will simply do no good. And worse, it could backfire. The failed rescuer could become a victim. It is an instinct of self-preservation, selfishness, and fear that influences him to stand still. "Who am I to help out?" "I'm only one person, after all." "What business is it of mine?" "There is no way I could prevent anything from happening." "If I act, or say something, then something bad could happen to me." "All I want to do is look out for number one."

This is the language of indifference, the vocabulary of neglect. They are the very words that bystanders use to justify and rationalize their silence. But the bystander is always naive, and his assumptions false. Far from being impotent, those standing by and watching have all the power in the world. Most people are neither in harm's way nor are causing the harm. The majority of people are simply an audience of immobilized, untapped strength. In their witnessing lies the potential for rescue, but they refuse to acknowledge it, or they are simply too afraid. Warehoused heroism, locked away like a winning lottery ticket that never sees the light of day.

There are all kinds of bystanders, and there is an equally diverse range of rescue narratives. Many speculate about how they might respond to a situation that requires rescuing someone. Would they try to protect their neighbors, or would they avert their eyes? Are you the kind of person who would hide Anne Frank, or would you turn her in? We all like to think of ourselves as heroic, our valor instantly accessible and dramatically displayed. But why are those the only images of heroism that we allow for ourselves? Some rescues can be accomplished without great fanfare—without heroic war songs or daring acts of self-assertion. The rescuer can bring about tremendous change, sometimes done silently, almost imperceptibly. She can go behind the lines, moving underground, organizing others, calling attention to other values, spurring on protest and dissent.

We live in a culture that glorifies the action hero. But some heroes travel without guns and have no martial-arts training. Moral courage doesn't have to require the breaking of a sweat. Hollywood and other venues of popular culture show only one dimension of heroism. Whether it is Rambo, Indiana Jones, Buffy the Vampire Slayer, or the firemen who ascended the stairwells of the World Trade Center not knowing where they would lead, we are taught that rescue requires strength and must always be accompanied by risk. And this is one of the reasons why heroism resides only in our fantasies rather than in our daily lives. We can't imagine making it real, because our models are essentially super-heroes. These images of rescue are given to defy our imaginations and the limits of our capacity for courage. We end up believing that rescue is not a task for ordinary men and women, and the law warns us not even to consider it. But how can we tolerate not requiring even riskless interventions—boring, undramatic, but certain to save lives?

During the late spring of 1997, a seven-year-old girl, Sherrice Iverson, was sexually assaulted, strangled, and tossed into a toilet in a Nevada casino, near Las Vegas. A nineteen-year-old from California, Jeremy Strohmeyer, confessed to the crime, but his best friend of the same age, David Cash, a college sophomore, was with Strohmeyer in the women's bathroom, watching him struggle with the child. Cash finally left and waited outside. He neither intervened to save the girl, nor did he go for help, nor did he even report the crime after his friend emerged and revealed what he had just done.

Since there was no legal duty to rescue in Nevada, and Cash neither touched the girl nor assisted in the crime, the State couldn't charge him with anything. He was only an accomplice in his neglect, and not in his actions. In the eyes of the law, what he had done was nothing, and in Nevada doing nothing was not a crime. Nor was it unlawful to fail to report the crime that had taken place. Cash simply stood by, and then went home. The legal system remained slack-jawed with futility in the face of such heinous disregard for human life. Cash eventually told the *Los Angeles Times*, "I'm not going to get upset over somebody else's life. I just worry about myself first." And the *Boston Globe* reported him saying, "It's a very tragic event, okay? But the simple fact remains I do not know this little girl. . . . The only person I knew in this event was Jeremy Strohmeyer, and I know as his best friend that he had potential. . . . I'm sad that I lost a best friend. . . . I'm not going to lose sleep over somebody else's problems."

In response to Sherrice Iverson's murder, and in her name, Congress proposed legislation that would require states to enact laws compelling third-party witnesses to report sexual crimes against children. The failure to do so would result in criminal penalties. Under the proposed law, states that choose not to enact such legislation would no longer be eligible to receive federal funds for child abuse prevention, neglect and treatment programs. The status of this federal legislation, and the response to it by state legislatures, is still very much undecided (although even in California, where the movement began, the bill was vetoed, and its passage elsewhere remains doubtful), but had such legislation existed in Nevada, David Cash might have been sent to jail alongside his best friend. The passage of such legislation might have the effect of transforming the moral landscape from one of indifference with respect to rescue to one of accepted practice. Courts that had once refused to impose such a duty would now require its enforcement. Yet, the only way to implement this moral rule, apparently, is by withholding federal funds. Somehow states can't achieve this moral outcome without significant financial incentives to do so. And why should the rule only apply in cases of child abuse? Aren't other rescue scenarios equally deserving of being mandated under the law, and shouldn't they also be subject to legal duty?

In the aftermath of so many school shootings during the late 1990s—whether in Pearl, Mississippi; West Paducah, Kentucky; Jonesboro, Arkansas; and, most memorably, Columbine High School in Littleton, Colorado—the parents of some of these slain students brought lawsuits against the parents of the children who did the shootings, as well as the grandparents, school districts, and gun manufacturers. There was also some consideration about whether to include in these lawsuits students who were aware of the plans for the shootings but failed to report them. The idea was to hold liable individuals who could have taken measures to prevent the deaths, but didn't. Naturally positioned to become rescuers, they instead chose to look away and take no action at all. Such lawsuits against third parties, however, rarely succeed.

"There's a tremendous desire to find someone besides the child responsible, but our legal system is built around responsibility for one's own actions," Professor Naomi Cahn of George Washington University Law School was quoted in an article in the *New York Times* as saying. "As a general rule, there is no duty to control the conduct of a third person." And Martin Guggenheim, a law professor at New York University Law School, added, "This is a society which generally does not impose duties on people to go out and intervene in other people's behavior."

But why not? There are so many tragic examples of interventions that would have required very little effort but would have changed the outcome enormously. So, why doesn't the law at least insist that these benign, easy acts of rescue be undertaken on behalf of those in peril? In the case of Sherrice Iverson, the law perhaps shouldn't have required Cash to beat up his friend. But Cash should have been obligated to call for help. And individuals who might have known about the plans for a school shooting didn't have to throw themselves in front of a bullet, but they should have done something, anything, to thwart the plans.

One of the cases that I assign to my students is *Osterlind v. Hill*, which is a 1928 state supreme court decision from Massachusetts. I call it the "canoe case." In it, a man who was somewhat inebriated rented a canoe and paddled out onto a lake. While he was out there, the canoe overturned and the man hung on for his life perilously, screaming for thirty minutes. The person who rented the canoe watched the scene and did nothing. The man finally drowned, and his family brought a survivor action on his behalf. The issue was whether it was negligent to have rented the canoe to this particular individual, given his drunken condition. The court concluded that there was no negligence, because even though the man may have been drunk, he wasn't actually helpless. The best evidence of that was that he managed to cling to the canoe and scream for help for half an hour. "On the facts stated in the declaration the intestate was not in a helpless condition," the court ruled. "He was able to take steps to protect himself. The defendant violated no legal duty in renting the canoe to a man in the condition of the intestate."

Emotionally detached, and immorally unjust to the core. Not only does the court ignore the duty-to-rescue issue entirely (perhaps because there was none), but it uses the decedent's cries for help—the very pleas that should have created the legal duty to intervene—as evidence that the drowning man was not, in fact, helpless, despite his precarious condition. For this reason, the bystander had not been negligent in renting out the canoe in the first instance. The very unanswered plea for help was exploited as evidence to defeat the dead man's claim, rather than as evidence of the bystander's immoral indifference and legal culpability in the death. Perhaps the law shouldn't necessarily have required the bystander to swim out and rescue his customer. But to do absolutely nothing, to be able to so callously witness a death—without such inaction carrying any consequence—once more demonstrates the way in which legal results are split from moral outcomes in American law.

RESCUE AS MORAL
IMPERATIVE

T he underlying thinking that supports such gross passivity and indifference in the law can be traced, unintentionally, to the philosophy of Immanuel Kant. Indeed, the influence of Kant can help explain a good deal of what passes for immoral justice in America. For Kant, the moral and legal are naturally and inexorably separate. He would be pleased and it would have come to him as no surprise that the American legal system focuses on one and ignores the other. From a Kantian perspective, moral duties do not possess a legal counterpart. We should simply resign ourselves to the fact that people who do the right moral thing are simply better than the rest of us. They have more virtue, and therefore conduct themselves more virtuously. Their motivation comes from within; it is part of their spiritual and personal makeup that makes them act in the way that they do.

According to Kant, the law has no application in the spiritual sphere of human existence. The law is about regulating external conduct, looking at what people have actually done, and judging the lawfulness of those actions. The law, however, should not be involved in forcing people to do what they otherwise would not do on their own. The law simply can't compel citizens to be virtuous. We are all better off when virtue exists in the general population, and we are worse off when it is absent. Yet in Kant's view, you can reward people for being better human beings, and you can subject those who are not to moral censure, but you can't legally require them to act against their nature.

In *Making Men Moral: Civil Liberties and Public Morality*, Robert P. George echoes Kant's philosophy when he states, "Laws cannot make men moral. Only men can do that; and they can do it only by freely choosing to do the morally right thing for the right reason." According to his thinking, the law should take an interest in you only once you decide to act, and it should vigorously scrutinize those actions. The law, however, can't force you to act against your will, even if your will is otherwise morally deficient and depraved.

A moral legal system would make no distinctions between moral and legal duties. But freedom from legally mandated moral obligation is one of the many liberties that Americans possess. In some ways it is the guiding ethos of what it means to be an American: our national obsession with freedom and autonomy. These All-American principles make imposing a duty to rescue nearly impossible within our legal system. Requiring such a duty would impinge severely on one's overall liberty. It would force one to act, even minimally, in a situation where he may not wish to.

As far as the law is concerned, legal accountability is directly related to causation. The court needs to know not just that an injury occurred, but who or what caused it. Generally there is no duty to prevent a harm that one did not cause. Not having caused the injury, the bystander has no responsibility for its abatement. He has the legal right to watch. For this reason, an act of rescue— no matter how heroic or simple to execute—is beyond the call of duty, because there is no such duty. Or, if it exists, it is entirely a moral one, and not one that is mandated under the law.

But why should this Kantian perspective dictate the duties of moral agency in American law? Presumably we hail our rescuers as moral men and women, but legally we don't model ourselves on the example they set. We neither aspire to be like them, nor are we legally required to do so. Our moral failures are given a free pass, and therefore we are not encouraged to improve on them. Instead, we refuse to sacrifice the freedom that we have to be left alone and to ignore our neighbors in distress if we so wish.

Like the *Seinfeld* characters, judges and law professors take the position that doing nothing is not an action and therefore not answerable under the law. The legal system is only interested in the body in motion, the body that causes something to happen, the action that results in some reaction or altered circumstance. The body at rest, loitering in its own indifference, is paradoxically beyond the law's reach, outside the range of its radar. Negligence and neglect are treated differently under the law, yet the impact on the injured party might be exactly the same. The former is a legal concept, the latter a moral one, which essentially means that one will carry a legal consequence, while the other is only a matter of private conscience.

But is doing nothing really without action? The bystander is not without choice or agency. There is, indeed, action in the bystander's decision to stand by. It is the act of not acting, of choosing to distance oneself from his or her surroundings, of not taking part in what is so obviously happening before one's eyes.

Yet what about the person who wishes to do the right thing, wants to assist and aid but freezes from fear or doubt and ultimately plays no rescue role? Unlike Cash, who unapologetically tells us not to trust him in a crisis, there are those who have the souls of the good Samaritan but also have the courage of

Barney Fife, the hapless, stumbling sheriff's deputy on the old *Andy Griffith Show*. In a legal system that imposed an unequivocal duty to rescue, it wouldn't just be virtue that the law monitored. Courage would be expected, as well. Would cowards be indiscriminately punished for their moral weakness in not being able to act? Not necessarily. Nothing would prevent those who failed to rescue from explaining to a jury how they were overcome by fear, how they wanted to do the right thing and regret the result of not doing so, and why the outcome should be attributed to incapacity and not moral indifference. The breach of such a duty—whether in criminal or civil law—would not foreclose the raising of mitigating and extenuating circumstances in defense, not unlike other legal actions in which the defendant is accused of causing harm rather than not acting at all.

In a seminal article that appeared in the *Yale Law Journal* over twenty years ago, Ernest J. Weinrib argued that even if moral virtue cannot be legally mandated, we could at least impose a duty on citizens to undertake easy, minimal rescues— those that don't endanger life and limb, the kinds of actions that aren't extraordinarily heroic or virtuous but might ultimately save a life. Placing a 911 call is a good example of such an easy rescue. So, too, is racing to get help, or reporting a crime or injury either while it is occurring, or soon thereafter.

In 1997, the actress Halle Berry pleaded no contest to a misdemeanor charge of leaving the scene of a traffic accident. Apparently she had hit a motorist and then, rather than stopping to lend assistance, continued on her way. For all of the negative press that she received, no one questioned the behavior of all those other motorists who drove by the scene of the accident and didn't bother to stop, or use their cellphones to alert the police. We wouldn't think to take down the license plates of these motorists. Yet they, too, were fleeing the scene of an accident. They were drive-by bystanders. But since they have not acted to bring about the injury, there was a complete absence of causation, and therefore it was perfectly lawful for them to either rubberneck or accelerate without regard to the way in which their neglect might have actually aggravated the harm.

This incident is not unique. Every day people witness injuries and acts of cruelty and feel no obligation to intervene, and are under no duty to even try. Rescue is deemed a completely voluntary, ill-advised enterprise. But as Professor Weinrib suggests, what of the easy rescue? Is that also a moral urgency unsupported by a legal imperative, something that you should do but are unbound legally from doing so? It seems strange that calling the police when someone else is in trouble should be considered above and beyond the call of duty, as if it was a supreme sacrifice instead of what it is—the right thing to do, which the law should require of us, at all times.

In the film *The Accused*, the prosecutor who negotiates the plea reduction with the gang-rapists comes to realize that this arrangement—although perfectly legal and accepted by district attorneys all over the country—failed to provide any meaningful sense of moral justice. In order to do the right thing and give the victim the chance at some moral victory—one that arises out of the law itself—the prosecutor decides to bring a new set of charges, not against the rapists, but against those who witnessed the crime and cheered it on. These were the men who entreated, encouraged, and applauded what the rapists were doing. The prosecutor's case hinges on a novel legal theory, and she ultimately succeeds in convincing a jury that the bystanding witnesses were guilty as accessories to the rape.

The movie was loosely based on an actual trial held outside of Boston, which produced a similar result. Of course, in both the fictional and real-life context, the focus was not on the failure of these men to rescue the victim, but rather on their participation in the crime by rooting it on. The bystanders don't actually move, but what they say by way of encouragement is deemed an action, and that action makes them complicit in the crime.* Indeed, it is the words and shouts of the bystanders—unaccompanied by any physical movement—that are ultimately deemed tantamount to an action, and indispensable to the rape. The witnessing and failing to rescue is not what triggers their culpability. As usual, given the conventional legal paradigm, the court requires that there be some action, and the entreating words stand in for what would otherwise be more blatant, physical gestures of assistance. The bystanders are not punished for failing to act. They are punished precisely because they did act: not as true silent bystanders, but as a cheering audience. But what if they had said nothing? What if they had merely watched from the perimeter of the room, nursing their beers while a woman was raped on top of a pinball machine? Would they then have been accomplices or accessories? Despite its otherwise moral tone, the film does suggest that witnessing the commission of a rape is neither an indictable offense nor a plausible crime. And the filmmaker would be right in this presumption.

The law simply does not have a sufficiently long moral reach to embrace these circumstances. Indeed, the law's intention is never to reach this far. *The Accused* makes a case for a step in the right moral direction, but it is ultimately a short step, and one that most prosecutors wouldn't even contemplate taking. A truly moral legal system would prosecute the bystanders for saying nothing. Simply by being in the room, at that time, without doing a thing, is sufficient for them to surrender any claim to their innocence. What kind of person would witness such cruelty and humiliation—luridly and without conscience—and not in-

---

* Similarly, at Nuremberg, Julius Streicher, a newspaper publisher, was hanged for the propaganda he disseminated against Jews. He carried no gun and wore no uniform, but in the end his malignant words and racist images made him as murderous and culpable as the Nazis. More recently, in December 2003, an international tribunal convicted three Rwandans who owned a newspaper and controlled a radio station for publishing and broadcasting reports that fomented hatred, poisoned minds, and lured Tutsis to killing grounds. An action that otherwise may have resembled free speech was examined morally, and punished legally, as if it were no different from physical violence or cold-blooded murder.

tervene? And shouldn't the law take an interest in such a person, someone who enjoys the privileges of citizenship but refuses to undertake even a minimal reciprocal duty in defense of another?

Moses Maimonides, the medieval Jewish philosopher, physician, and rabbi, wrote the following in his *Code*, otherwise known as the *Mishnah Torah*:

> If one person is able to save another and does not save him, he transgresses the commandment. *Neither shall thou stand idly by the blood of thy neighbor* (Leviticus 19:16). Similarly, if one person sees another drowning in the sea, or being attacked by bandits, or being attacked by wild animals, and, although able to rescue him either alone or by hiring others, does not rescue him; or if one hears heathens or informers plotting evil against another to laying a trap for him and does not call it to the other's attention and let him know; or if one knows that a heathen or a violent person is going to attack another and although able to appease him on behalf of the other and make him change his mind, he does not do so; or if one acts in any similar way— he transgresses in each case the injunction, *Neither shalt thou stand idly by the blood of thy neighbor…*
>
> Although there is no flogging for these prohibitions, because breach of them involves no action, the offense is most serious, for if one destroys the life of a single Israelite, it is regarded as though he destroyed the whole world, and if one preserves the life of a single Israelite, it is regarded as though he preserved the whole world.

This passage essentially sums up Jewish law on the question of the duty to rescue. Interestingly, the Jewish perspective on this matter does not seem all that much different from Kant's separation between the moral and legal. Maimonides writes that failing to rescue results in no "flogging . . . because breach of them involves no action." Again, similar to the general legal rule, without action the moral duty does not apply to impose a legal consequence. Yet unlike the conventional legal paradigm, where rescue scenarios are discouraged because the law creates disincentives to even trying, under Talmudic law, the duty is not merely a moral one, but also has clear legal implications. For instance, the rescuer can recover any financial losses that he incurred as result of his efforts to rescue another. Also, while engaged in an act of rescue, the rescuer is exempt from performing other duties and rituals of a political, civil, and religious nature. And finally, and perhaps most important, in the event that the rescuer should fail to achieve a successful rescue, he cannot be found liable in tort for causing or worsening the injury. Under Jewish law, everything is done to maximize rescue scenarios. Far from deterring good Samaritans, the rule presumes that a moral person will undertake the task of aiding a stranger and should not be penalized for his efforts. Without such legal protections, the fear of exposing themselves to liability might dissuade morally righteous people from acting on their private conscience.

In contrast, under American law, when it comes to rescue, the incentives and guidance lead in only one direction: self-preservation and moral irresponsibility.

In the Broadway musical *Beauty and the Beast,* Cogsworth and Lummiere, household servants of the once prince, now beast, contemplate their fate of having been transformed into a clock and a candelabra. They, too, have been punished by the curse that was placed on the castle. But what did they do to deserve it? The prince, after all, had been selfish, shallow, and vain, and had spurned an old woman who was seeking charity. Perhaps there was moral justice in the curse that turned the prince into the beast. And perhaps there was still time for the beast to perform the necessary acts of repair that would restore everyone to their human form. But Lummiere still wants to know why the household servants—mere innocent bystanders—should have been consigned to the same fate as the prince?

Cogsworth, the keeper of both time and moral virtue, knows the answer when he reminds his friend that it happened under their watch.

THE LAW'S PREFERENCE FOR
THE BODY OVER THE SOUL

In late 1946, the legendary conductor of the Berlin Philharmonic Orchestra, Wilhelm Furtwängler, found himself the subject of a de-Nazification investigation in which he had to defend himself against charges that he was complicit in the crimes of the Nazis. No one claimed that Furtwängler was a member of the Nazi Party, because he was not. Nor was there any proof that he was in any way sympathetic to Hitler. In fact, there was evidence that he had assisted many of his Jewish musicians in fleeing Germany for safer musical havens. Furtwängler considered himself merely an artist living in a time of madness, and during times of madness—especially in times of madness—the world still needs its music. And it was music that was his domain and responsibility to provide—for both the world and the continuation and enrichment of German high culture.

Yet Furtwängler was exposed to a very protracted, humiliating, and contentious de-Nazification process. Indeed, other musicians who had collaborated more directly with the Nazis and whose sympathies were less in doubt were, curiously, treated less harshly. Furtwängler was eventually exonerated of all charges, but not without great personal cost to his reputation, which was severely and irreparably undermined. Two American orchestras, in response to widespread criticism and protest, rescinded offers made to him in the postwar era.

Why should Furtwängler have been treated in this way? After all, he carried only a baton, and not a gun. His forte was not in gas, smoke, and fire, but rather the music of Beethoven, Bruckner, and other lush orchestrations of German Romanticism. Perhaps what inspired the investigation was not conventional notions of guilt and innocence, complicity and collaboration. It seems that in so many external ways, Furtwängler was innocent. But the same cannot necessarily be said about his spiritual and moral conduct, which requires a deeper investigation and where the accusations are much more damning.

Music offers spiritual uplift, and during a time of murder, Furtwängler provided the music to murder by. His concerts and recordings were the primary means by which both mass murderers and ordinary Germans were able to engage themselves with the nobler aspirations of high musical culture, and Germany's unparalleled contribution to it. He made it possible for people to commit unspeakable acts during the day and unwind at night, without conflict or discomfort, simply by listening to the spiritual sustenance of his music. And even bystanders who were indifferent remained even more so because they were able to lose themselves within Furtwängler's conscience-numbing symphonies. He was the antidote to their suppressed guilt. His music enabled people to surrender their moral convictions, and, paradoxically, at the same time, reaffirm the justness of their cause.

And for this reason, the propaganda and spiritual resilience that his presence in Germany represented eventually subjected him to legal prosecution and moral censure. The issue is not that he should have left Germany in protest as so many other artists had done. And it's not that he didn't physically come to the rescue of his musicians, because in some cases he did and he certainly shouldn't have been expected or required to stand up to Hitler. But a more complex appreciation of his actions also revealed that he had provided spiritual comfort to murderers during a time when they should have been made to feel profoundly uncomfortable. They should have returned home at night with blood on their hands and with no way to wash it off. Instead of music, it would have been better to have them rendered deaf by silence, forced to sit alone and contemplate what they had done rather than become anesthetized by the miasmic haze of Furtwängler's music.

The story of Furtwängler's postwar difficulties is reminiscent of yet another immoral feature of the legal system: its obsessive focus on the body and neglect of the soul. The body in movement, and the body that has been bruised, is the foundation of legal causation and consequence. Under the law, the body is sacred and inviolable. The spirit, however, receives no protection, as if the interior life of human beings has no independent existence or significance. In the religious spheres of life, there are distinctions made between the body and the soul. Sometimes even the religious among us regard these distinctions with ambivalence. But there is at least the recognition that human beings are not only comprised of flesh, blood, and bones. Those are the material, tangible parts of the anatomy, which can be seen and described. Yet what of the soul? It has no physical or material dimension, yet we know that it is there. And we don't have to be presented with a Faustian bargain in order to prove it. Soul is the nerve center of our emotions and private conscience. It is the operating system of the human heart. It makes us cry with the recall of a sudden memory. It is responsible for our charity and benevolence. It is the place where we are at our most tender and vulnerable. It makes us appreciate people and things we might otherwise forget. It's what makes us good friends and even better lovers. It keeps us up at night. It is the engine of our guilt. Sometimes it is the choreography of our best dance moves. And sometimes, even though we can't see it, the soul is what stares back at us in the mirror, making it hard to look at ourselves when we wake up in the morning.

Lawyers and judges get squeamish with this kind of talk. Their eyes glaze over; their minds wander. It is a conversation steeped in too much abstraction, and the law tolerates little in the way of ambiguity. Extolled by the religious and romanticized in art, the soul is unsung and unappreciated in law. What is actionable instead is the body in motion—physical, aggressive, and ultimately liable for any damage it leaves in its wake. And in order to qualify for the law's paternalism, the body must show itself to be scarred and bruised. Courts need to see a neck brace, a wheelchair, a bullet hole, some incontestable proof that the body has been materially altered. Broken spirits don't count, because they leave no such obvious clues. And those who have eyes for such injuries sadly are not employed in the legal profession.

But there are ways to inflict pain without the necessity of any physical movement. Human beings know this, and feel it in their bones, and yet only broken bones are what light up the law. A soul that has suffered indignity has no recourse, no place to turn, other than yet another dive inward. The killing of the spirit has never been recognized as a common-law crime, and yet soul murder is as common as any physical death.

Overly body-conscious and with no regard for the human spirit, the American legal system routinely falls into action whenever conduct results in external scarring: the wrongful amputation of a limb, a head injury, damaged property, a breached contract. But internal wounds, felt deeply but invisible to the legal eye, have no place in the courthouse. Spiritual damage goes unremedied and uncompensated. Does anyone doubt that evil Iago, who exhales spiritual poison throughout Shakespeare's *Othello*, had committed a grievous injury, one that was far more murderous than any physical bruise? Indeed, morally he is responsible for two murders. Yet the American legal system would have had no answer to Iago's crime, because he never lifted a finger against Othello, causing him no physical injury—only spiritual violence and self-inflicted pain.*

The legal system, whether in criminal law or in tort, has no concept of spiritual harms, and its worst manifestation—the murder of the soul. In situations of domestic violence, the 911 call gets answered for black eyes on battered spouses. But the police would not respond to a call in which the husband is merely heaping unremitting insults in the direction of his wife. Those who work with victims of domestic violence will generally tell you that battered women often admit that the hitting is not nearly as bad as the parade of humiliations that precede the punch.

And it's not only vitriolic speech that can be abusive. Spousal withdrawal—when a husband or wife refuses to speak with or acknowledge a partner for weeks on end—can be extremely damaging to the soul. But what police dispatcher would send out a patrol car to answer a 911 call that came in with these words: "She hasn't spoken to me in over a week!"

Why the distinction between the body and spirit, and why so guardedly vigilant with one and neglectful of the other?

The law operates in a rarefied world where ambiguity and nuance, which are eternally present in the human condition, are nearly always sacrificed to the predictable and concrete. And because the law requires physical proof, it is naturally oblivious to

---

*A similar point can be made about the distinction between murder and attempted murder. Why should the law punish more harshly those who actually succeed in killing their victims, and reduce the punishment for those who fail to accomplish what they had set out to do? The answer is again somewhat related to the law's extreme focus on the body to the exclusion of spiritual issues, such as, in this instance, the intent and malevolence of the perpetrator, and the spiritual damage done to the victim. If the body is left unmurdered and untouched by the perpetrator's crime, then, under the law, the perpetrator can't be punished as if he had actually succeeded. But why not if that's what he had intended to do? After all, he had performed the acts necessary to do murder, and but for his own error or some other intervening circumstance, the body would have been dead. And there is murder in attempted murder, even if the body lives. The spirit of the victim will never be the same again.

spiritual pain. The spiritual sphere of human existence is too mysterious and elliptical to have any place in the courtroom. And as Kant might remind us, morally we shouldn't subject our spouses to the deep freeze of silence, but legally we can't be forced to speak to them if we choose not to.

The law hides behind the body—the law's shield, the aim of all its attention. Curiously enough, the governing principle of the law seems to be based on the children's rhyme: "Sticks and stones can break my bones but names can never hurt me." Yet what brings many people to the courthouse are precisely these unacknowledged grievances, the hurt behind the external flesh wounds, the spiritual injuries that have little in common with bodily harm.

Bruises are bad, but so is spiritual violence, and a moral legal system would make no distinction between internal and external injury. Both would be worthy of protection. But since the material, quantifiable, and concrete is the squeaky wheel in the engine of law, without tangible harm, the law finds itself at a loss for what to do. There is simplicity behind its focus on the physical. The body never lies; the soul just might. The legal system fears that spiritual injuries can be feigned. Absent verifiable, objective proof, we have no way of knowing the sincerity of the claimed injury. Since we can't see it, how can we tell if the soul has truly been damaged? We don't even know what it looks like when it is well. A fair point, but how do we then explain allowances made for the body that are unreciprocated for the soul?

People show up to court all the time with fake physical injuries. Their neck is wrapped in a brace, but when they get home, the brace comes off as they dash away to get in a few games of tennis before dinner. People who can otherwise walk require the assistance of a cane in a courtroom. It's all a charade, yet with the body we tolerate this uncertainty. Experts testify, eyewitnesses come forward, we observe the tentative, halting movements of the plaintiff, and yet we can't be sure whether he is actually damaged, or whether we should hand him an

Academy Award for Most Convincing Performance of Chicanery and Manipulation in a Court of Law. For some reason, when it comes to the body, we trust our instincts that we can sort out the charlatans from the truly impaired. Yet we know that we make mistakes and award damages to those who have successfully fooled us with their bandages, people who were all along undeserving of legal relief.

With spiritual injuries, however, we regard ourselves as being helpless in the face of deception, impotent in the presence of con men, oblivious to snow jobs. We have no confidence in our ability to sniff out the hypochondriacs, and the confidence men. We have such fear of the unknowable—and the mystery of the soul—that we place no trust in our ability to recognize a wounded spirit when we see one.

Do we actually doubt that the spiritual machinations Iago inflicted against Othello were not at least equally destructive to anything that he could have done to his body? Given a choice, would Othello have not preferred Iago to take a baseball bat to his head rather than the poisonous head games that he played with Othello's heart? Similarly, if the Nazis had killed no one but had merely humiliated, dehumanized, branded, interned, and force-separated six million Jews and five million others, would they have not equally been guilty of genocide? Must the body go up in smoke for there to be a crime, or is the suffocation of the soul no less an annihilating event?

The genius that the Nazis had for genocide was that they knew what American judges fail to recognize every time: Sometimes the body is beside the point. Kill the spirit and the body will follow. The death of the body, in fact, is not all that difficult to bring about. Anybody can do it. But the death of the soul requires more nuanced bludgeoning. And the soul dies slowly. It doesn't succumb to seizures and attacks, but rather, like a wilting flower, the layers of the spirit peel off until there is nothing left but a black hole. Vital signs lose their vitality and simply sign off. There is no chance of life support. All sorts of people walk among us with perfectly functioning pulse rates and heartbeats. Yet they are spiritually dead, their inner lives gone while their external selves mask the funeral within. They are engaged in the world, but only for show—punching clocks, cashing checks, making meetings, yet all the while dead inside. Paradoxically, soul murder can take place right in front of our eyes without the law paying any attention. But merely scratch the body, and watch the legal system shift into the high gear of screaming bloody murder.

Sometimes the legal system appears to be protecting the spirit, but what it's really trying to do is safeguard the body. The soul is then the beneficiary of the law's unintended largesse. This is particularly true in the case of free speech. The First Amendment of the United States Constitution guarantees free speech. But the right is not limitless. There are certain proscribable categories of speech that receive no such protection, because they are considered something other than speech—words without any ideas or content attached to them. Some examples of these categories include libel and slander, obscenity, the incitement of imminent lawlessness, and "fighting words." In 1942, in *Chaplinsky v. New Hampshire*, the Supreme Court established the fighting-words doctrine, which essentially provides no First Amendment protection for speech that can be deemed "fighting words"—words or conduct that are likely to provoke a violent retaliation and a breach of the peace.

The fighting-words doctrine has been severely eroded over the years in favor of allowing more speech with fewer restrictions. Indeed, it's no longer clear whether the doctrine even represents the law of the land. But regardless of its present relevance, philosophically it's interesting to consider what motivated the Supreme Court in deciding *Chaplinsky*. The decision appears to be concerned with the spiritual violence that arises from harmful speech. Did the Supreme Court have a moral, spiritual agenda in mind? The answer is no. The fighting-words doctrine is yet another example of the law's favoritism toward the body. The reason fighting words fall outside the contours of the First Amendment is not because insults, slurs, and indignities are capable of inflicting harm to the spirit and psyche, but rather because they are likely to result in retaliatory acts of physical violence and breaches of the peace. Even in the recent decision of *Virginia v. Black*, the cross-burning case discussed in chapter 9, the Supreme Court was transparent as to where its loyalties lie in a contest between body and soul. In allowing a state to outlaw cross-burning provided that the act was sufficiently threatening, the Court wrote that a state may "choose to prohibit only those forms of intimidation that are most likely to inspire fear of *bodily* harm" (emphasis supplied).

The fighting-words doctrine was never intended to protect feelings. Its purpose was to make a pre-emptive strike against foreseeably damaged property and retaliatory punches that bruise the body. The soul was only an accidental beneficiary of this rule. The main focus was all on the necessary cleanup that fighting words can provoke: the black eyes, busted noses, and broken glass.

In 1978, when a group of neo-Nazis decided to march in Skokie, Illinois, a village that not only had a considerably large Jewish population, but also an unusually high presence of Holocaust survivors, the Court of Appeals for the Seventh Circuit allowed the demonstration to proceed. No one doubted that the sight of the marchers in their uniforms would trample on the profound sensitivities of these resident Holocaust survivors. But the free-speech interests of the neo-Nazis prevailed and superseded the pain and disgust of the survivors of Jewish genocide. The court, in *Collin v. Smith*, invalidated on constitutional grounds three village ordinances that would have prohibited this public demonstration. These ordinances were precursors to today's hate-speech laws, outlawing actions that were calculated to "incite violence, hatred, abuse, and hostility toward a person or a group of persons by reasons of reference to religious, racial, ethnic, national or regional affiliation."

The lawyer for the Village of Skokie conceded that he didn't believe that the presence of the neo-Nazis in Skokie would have resulted in retaliatory violence. For this reason, the court rejected the application of the fighting-words doctrine. This in itself was a preposterous conclusion. Simply because Holocaust survivors were of the age or disposition where they weren't likely to fight back, the law wouldn't protect them from an aggressive act of spiritual violence. As long as the streets of Skokie were going to be free from retaliatory violence, the injury to the psyche of Holocaust survivors would not be prevented.

The lawyer for the village further argued that the march by the neo-Nazis, in this particular town, was clearly a provocative gesture that presented no ideas and only promoted racial and religious hatred. The animus and harm that the march would have engendered should have negated any free-speech interests of the neo-Nazis. Skokie's lawyer invoked a novel theory, maintaining that the march would have inflicted psychic trauma on the survivors and therefore amounted to the intentional infliction of emotional distress. At the time, emotional distress was a relatively new theory of tort. The court, however, rejected the argument, ruling that emotional distress has no relevance in a matter involving a criminal ordinance. As for the special emotional sensitivities of the survivors, the court suggested that they stay home on that day and not attend the march altogether. The duty was essentially placed on the survivors to avert their eyes. The traumatic pain to the survivors was less significant to the court than the rights of the neo-Nazis to personally deliver their message, regardless of how spiritually damaging that message may be. Even the town's law-and-order interests and desire for social peace carried little weight when it came to thwarting the symbolic speech aspirations of the neo-Nazis. In completely ignoring the spiritual damage that this march would undoubtedly inflict, and the emotional significance that uniforms and swastikas would have on this already vulnerable group of residents, the court ruled that the neo-Nazis merely intended "a silent march, attended only by symbols and not by extrinsic conduct offensive in itself." The court was persuaded that neo-Nazis wielding words and marching silently are not harmful, unlike their bat-toting, glass-breaking predecessors.

A decade later, in *Texas v. Johnson*, which involved the burn-ing of the American flag, the Supreme Court summed up the rule in this way: "If there is a bedrock principle underlying the First Amendment, it is that the government may not prohibit the expression of an idea simply because society finds the idea it-self offensive or disagreeable." The Court ruled that Johnson's expressive conduct was protected by the First Amendment. His-torically, the Supreme Court has minimized the hurt and dam-age that certain words, speech, or conduct can inflict. As long as they express a shred of an idea, the First Amendment can be in-voked as a defense against any government action to censor it.

But speech has the potential of communicating more than an idea. It can also be used to deliver a blow—an act of spiritual vi-olence that is no less lethal merely because it is not physical. In a moral legal system, what should be unlawful about certain words in certain contexts is not that they will induce a retaliatory fight, but that they are injurious in themselves. After all, there is a rea-son why a person might retaliate against fighting words—it hurts that much to hear them, that they cannot go ignored, and all efforts at composure are rendered futile once the words have been launched. It is a primal response to a damaging assault, in some ways an act of self-defense. The words, delivered alone, are tantamount to a physical fight.

Today this argument sometimes finds itself expressed in the form of hate-speech codes on college campuses, or hate-speech statutes in towns and cities across America. There have been some academics, such as professors Richard Delgado and Mari J. Matsuda, who have argued forcefully that in addition to criminal hate-speech laws, the legal system should also create an independent tort action for racist speech. The reason this is necessary is because the law minimizes spiritual injury and instead heaps all sorts of protection on the body, and on those who, through their words, would do spiritual violence. A civil action in tort for hurtful speech would serve the moral purpose of acknowledging that words can, and often do, cause harm. Professor Delgado believes that racist speech, in particular, deserves a special category of civil liability because of this nation's traumatic legacy of racism.

There is violence in words, and this violence has the potential to inflict tremendous wounds. Those who hold absolutist positions with regard to the First Amendment—believing in its sanctity and inviolability, asserting that it is the most fundamental of constitutional rights—are grossly unmindful of the harms that insults and slurs can cause, or perhaps they simply believe that the body is more precious and fragile. The burden is always placed on the victim to show restraint, to turn the other cheek, to remember from childhood that words will never have the same force as a stick, that bones will remain unbroken even as the spirit shatters. In order to promote free speech, we place the duty on the insulted listener to either walk away or acquit himself with the stiffest of upper lips. Meanwhile, we unleash the speaker, letting him mouth off with virtual impunity. Words are not actionable when they are merely hurtful and offensive. This is the bizarre litmus test of the conventional legal paradigm, as seen in the Skokie case, that permits spiritual injury to flourish in the good graces, and trumped-up blessings of free speech.

When the law does protect the spirit, it always seems to be doing it more by accident than design. In the 1967 Texas case of *Fisher v. Carrousel Motor Hotel, Inc.*, an African-American sued for assault and battery when a white cafeteria worker snatched a plate away from the plaintiff and yelled that because the patron was a Negro, he couldn't eat in the cafeteria. Other than taking away the plate, the employee never touched the patron, although the patron alleged to having been left feeling "very embarrassed and hurt." A Texas appellate court ruled that mental anguish without physical injury cannot give rise to a battery, but the Supreme Court of Texas reversed this holding, ruling instead that the seizure of the plate itself constituted the necessary battery.

This was a bit of clever lawyering on the court's part, finding a battery in the snatched plate itself, and not in the true source of the harm: the racial insult. A battery requires an intentional, unauthorized physical touching, and while insults may land severely and cause great harm, they penetrate the soul without a forced, physical entry. The court also stated that battery is a tort designed to protect human dignity as well as physical security. So why go to such pains to identify the actionable physical touching when the assault on human dignity should have been enough on its own? In some ways, the mere mention of human dignity was an unusually spiritual ruling coming from an American court. Yet the fact is that without the snatched plate, the court would not have assigned liability, even though the words themselves—in a moral legal system—should have sufficed to prove that something offensive had taken place, and a tort had been committed.

Similarly, the intentional infliction of emotional distress does not sufficiently address injuries to the spirit. Emotional distress is generally applied only as an add-on to a physical injury, and it rarely exists as an independent tort without there being some physical harm and some other tortuous conduct. In the aftermath of a car accident where there have been significant physical injuries, the jury might award damages for emotional distress. But it's rare to find a case in which damages for emotional distress are awarded on their own terms, without a body having undergone some physical, material, objective pain and trauma. The reason why emotional distress is not taken as seriously as a physical tort is similar to why spiritual harms receive no protection under the law: the fear of fraudulent claims, and the nonquantifiable nature of the suffering. As professors Wagatsuma and Rosset pointed out in their seminal article on the different reactions to apologetic behavior in the United States and

Japan, "The legal system tends to reduce disputes to the types it is comfortable handling. Claims for personal injury are treated as if the issue is how to put a dollar price on pain and suffering, while claims essentially based on insult and psychic hurt are not dealt with well, if they are recognized at all."

The burden of establishing a claim for intentional infliction of emotional distress is virtually impossible in the absence of physical harm. The emotional distress must be "severe," and caused by "extreme and outrageous conduct." What is outrageous is generally understood to be beyond the bounds of human decency. Name-calling, regardless of how abusive or damaging, is not deemed sufficient to constitute a tort for emotional distress. Yet the same obstacles to recovery would never be thrown in the path of the body. A broken arm doesn't have to be severely broken for damages to be recoverable, and the manner of its breaking would not have had to be extreme and dangerous. Why make it that much harder to recover for spiritual injuries when the damages they cause might be more lasting and severe than what the human body ever experiences?

Words alone are rarely if ever deemed sufficient to warrant recovery for emotional distress. Some cases allow relief when an employee severely insults a patron. But why make an exception only in contexts in which the insult materially and tangibly harms a business relationship? Why shouldn't the same indignity be actionable if delivered from one patron to another, or in any encounter where the hurt would nonetheless be palpable and real? Instances of sexual harassment generally are not considered sufficiently outrageous and extreme unless the emotional distress arising from words, insults, and indignities is accompanied by physical touching. Such a simplified prescription completely ignores the pain brought about by indignity itself, and the way the law takes no account of it, unless there had been a tangible, measurable effect on the body.

In a 1999 article that appeared in the *New York Times Magazine*, titled "What's So Bad About Hate?," Andrew Sullivan challenged the entire notion of hate crimes, arguing that all crimes essentially have hateful elements to them, and therefore no special distinction should be made for attacks made against a person's spiritual integrity. "[V]iolence can and should be stopped by the government. In a free society, hate can't and shouldn't be. . . . For hate is only foiled not when the haters are punished but when the hated are immune to the bigot's power. A hater cannot psychologically wound if a victim cannot psychologically be wounded. And that immunity to hurt can never be given; it can merely be achieved. The racial epithet only strikes at someone's core if he lets it. . . . The only final answer to this form of racism, then, is not majority persecution of it, but minority indifference to it. . . . For all our rhetoric, hate will never be destroyed. Hate, as our predecessors knew better, can merely be overcome."

While I applaud Sullivan's relativistic perspective on the complexities of hate, he is largely making a sticks-and-stones argument, and, in doing so, grossly underestimates the violence that is done to the spirit—whether through the expression of prejudice, or other, more nuanced acts of spiritual violence.

The fact is, the legal system is kryptonite to the human soul. And it shows no interest in the soul. And sometimes, as Franz Kafka has reminded us, the law seems to be in the business of crushing souls.

The spiritual and physical spheres of life intersect daily, except in the courtroom. The law focuses on the material world without acknowledging that spirits live within that world, as well. The rock group The Police seemed to know what judges, lawyers, and law professors never imagine: that there are indeed "Spirits in the Material World." According to Kant, the law must only concern itself with regulating external conduct. But why should the interior lives of human beings be so unnaturally, immorally insulated from legal protection and punishment? And there are spiritual prisons that have many of us in lock-up, even though we are, by all other accounts, essentially and physically free.

And because the law underrates the damage done by way of spiritual injuries, it also fails to appreciate the values that might be achieved from spiritual penalties. If the victim's spirit is capable of being damaged, why not consider tailoring punishments for perpetrators that are equally spiritual in their impact? Pillories once served this purpose, as well as the wearing of a scarlet letter. Such punishments leverage shame in lieu of jail time. What's the point of incarceration if it neither reforms future behavior, nor makes the victim whole, nor teaches the community a lesson? Today shaming penalties, such as requiring an offender to perform a public act of contrition and repair, or to wear a sign indicating the nature of the crime that they committed, is implemented only infrequently. But when employed, it is done not only to register the moral disgust and outrage of the community, but also to punish the offender in a manner that is certain to hurt and leave an impression—the spiritual indignity that comes with humiliation, exile, and shame. And perhaps through this process of spiritual reflection, true reform might take place, which seemingly does not occur when punishment is limited only to the denial of personal liberty.

The murder trial of Dr. Clara Harris presented several examples of the ways in which the conventional legal paradigm obsesses over the human body and ignores the soul. Dr. Harris's husband, David, had been having an affair with the receptionist who was working in their office. When Clara Harris made this discovery, she confronted him and he promised to end the adulterous relationship. But he didn't. Instead he continued to see the woman and humiliated his wife by comparing her unfavorably to his mistress.

Dr. Harris's defense lawyer, George Parnham, essentially argued that his client was a victim of severe spiritual abuse that should have mitigated her crime. He asked the jury: "How can you subject the person you profess to love, the mother of your kids, to that kind of humiliation? . . . It just absolutely devastated her."

In an effort to win her husband back, Clara Harris, a former beauty queen, scheduled breast-enhancement and liposuction surgeries, hired a fitness trainer, dyed her hair chestnut-blond, went to a tanning salon, bought new clothes, stopped coming in to work, cooked her husband his favorite meals, and had sex with him three times a night the week prior to his murder. Yet when she discovered him coming out of a hotel with his mistress, she used her Mercedes-Benz as an instrument of revenge and death.

In making her summation to the jury, Assistant District Attorney Mia Magness said: "You can't help but feel sympathy [for her], but you know, the solution is to get a divorce. For heaven's sake, if a man is cheating on you, you do what every other woman in the county does: Take him to the cleaners. Take his house, take his car, take his kids, take his respect in the community, and you can make him wish he were dead, but you don't get to kill him."

The government's lawyer could not have stated this strange discontinuity in the American legal system between the legal and the moral, and between the body and the spirit, any better. The prosecution's assessment of this tragic domestic situation was essentially the following: No matter what David Harris did to his wife, his body can't be touched. She can't harm him physically. Nevertheless, it would be legally permissible for her to deprive her husband of virtually everything else that was important to him—his money, house, car, reputation, even his children. For this, the law would look away, or even assist in the reallocation or his assets, and the deprivation of everything that he owns. Indeed, the prosecutor suggested that any of these remedies would be the proper solution to compensating her for his betrayal. And every other woman in Houston, the prosecutor argued, would have done the same thing. In the prosecutor's view, these deprivations are acceptably retaliatory. They, after all, are mere possessions and can be taken away without bruising the body. But, in fact, they constituted everything that was David Harris's life—except his body.

The prosecutor was equally dismissive of whether there were mitigating circumstances that should have reduced the nature of Dr. Harris's crime, given the fact that she was a suffering wife exposed to an insensitive and unfaithful husband. The prosecutor told the jury: "Suffering is lying on the asphalt like some kind of wounded animal, drowning in your own blood while your teenage daughter watches. . . . There is a level of desperation there that I know touches you and you feel sorry for her because of it. But you cannot excuse what she did intentionally and knowingly because she was hurt."

Not surprisingly, the prosecutor minimized the hurt that was of a spiritual nature, and accentuated the physical dimension of the crime. A wife suffering from humiliation and the betrayal of her husband is not equivalent to a husband lying in his own blood. She loses our sympathy once she actualized her rage by violently killing her husband. But the violence of his crime against his wife is not considered at all, because it is not violent in a conventional sense. He never harmed her body, and so the criminal justice system has no mechanism or impulse to remedy the hurt—other than to grant her a divorce and divest her adulterous husband of his material possessions and his children.

The adultery may not have justified what Dr. Harris did. But it was a mitigating circumstance. The husband's actions were not irrelevant in understanding this murder. Indeed, short of dismissing it, the court should have factored in the husband's continuous and pervasive acts of humiliation against his wife in deciding how to morally deal with Dr. Harris under the law. Instead, the prosecutor smugly concluded that what Dr. Harris endured—the unfaithfulness of her husband; the way he flaunted his mistress's good looks in front of her—was of a much lesser form of suffering than "lying on the asphalt like some kind of wounded animal." And in making that value judgment, the prosecutor reaffirmed the law's prejudice that spiritual harms in no way compare to physical injury. But those who have experienced indignity know that this form of suffering can be its own private torture chamber, incomparable in its own way, and deserving of profound sympathy, respect, and relief.

The law looks to the frontage, the purely external and explicit, the most obvious of exhibits, the body that bleeds. The police refuse to draw a chalk outline of a dead soul on a street sidewalk. Clearly what Clara Harris did was a crime, and she should have been punished for it and severely so. But what's also clear is that her husband had committed crimes, as well, against his wife, perhaps even murdering her soul. Before she had pressed down on the accelerator, he had already run over her repeatedly—not with his car, but with the humiliation and betrayal that was a necessary consequence of his affair. Other than filing for divorce and "taking him to the cleaners," what recourse did the law allow Dr. Harris for the damage that she had suffered? What she was feeling, the story that she would have wanted a court to hear, was not legally relevant to the dissolution of marital assets. But it had everything to do with marital emotions, and the impermanence of eternal bonds.

How can we be so sure that "cleaning" him out of his material possessions, personal reputation, and children would have been a satisfactory remedy for her pain? Street justice is a natural outgrowth of buried hurts and grievances. In a legal system that knows no rescue and owes no duty to the spirit, vendettas and self-help remedies become highly attractive options, precisely because they speak to the moral and spiritual void that the law ignores and deepens by its own complicit neglect.

There is vast complexity in the layers that dominate the interior world of the spirit. And those human experiences should have a place in the courtroom, as well. What it means to be fully human is not only our physical qualities and our external actions, but also our interior lives, aspirations, and dignity. And both of those dimensions of the full human experience should be subject to legal scrutiny and protection.

FRUSTRATED LAWYERS AND THE PUBLIC'S DISCONTENT

W hen I was a practicing lawyer at a large, prestigious New York corporate-law firm, a few of my friends and I would get together almost every day and tape a fictional cable television program that we called *The Disaffected Lawyer Show*. We didn't actually videotape it; the cameras were rolling only in our heads. It sounds pathetic, but under circumstances in which our days were increasingly making less sense to us, this fictional program proved to be a life-saving act of imagination.

The show took place in my office, usually in the afternoon, as if it was no less subversive than a dead poets' society among aspiring but spiritually dead poets. And while there was no camera, sometimes we had actual guests. Real people. Other associates from the firm. Someone who worked in the mailroom; a working actor who earned extra money as a proofreader. It was an informal but intellectually rigorous and sometimes hilarious talk show. A *Wayne's World* for overly educated, handsomely compensated, but spiritually depleted lawyers.

The conversations ranged from literature to movies, from *The Godfather* to Milan Kundera's *The Book of Laughter and*

Forgetting. We'd discuss the most recent books we had read, or lamented about the ones that we would never have time to begin because our time had already been claimed elsewhere, recorded on time sheets, where the reading of novels and the watching of movies were not acceptable entries. We were forever stuck inside the cubicles and conference rooms of the law firm, producing documents, doing due diligence, working as low men on tall totem poles, writing pleadings on behalf of others rather than pleading for ourselves. We were losing our vision, and not all of it was related to eye strain.

When we became overly frustrated, we'd talk about sports. We discussed how the dreams that we once had for ourselves somehow lost all connection to the treadmills on which we were now sprinting. We were on a partnership track, but this track offered no detours, only tunnel vision. On one program we focused on the absurdity of having to wear business suits each day when we never left the office to go to court, and our clients never came to visit us because they were institutionally based and we dealt with them only over the phone. (With respect to this issue, we ended up being prescient, because, ten years later, law firms began to phase in casual workdays, allowing a considerable dress-down in workday attire.)

Our show proved to be so popular, and necessary, that it got to the point where I made sure to tell my secretary to hold all my calls while we were "taping." I don't think she ever knew what was going on in there. Better that she didn't.

Trapped in a skyscraper, we felt somewhat removed and distant from the world. Yet the life that mingled on the ground floor without us somehow opened up during these discussions, whereas at the firm, virtually everything felt as though the world was actually closing in on us, or was it that despite the elevation, we were actually shrinking.

The lawyer's life, particularly at large corporate law firms, is an endlessly bureaucratic, narrowing existence, ineluctably divisible, like the division of cells or the splitting of an atom or carrying out the decimals of pi to infinity. Boxes within boxes, with human beings filed inside.* The way lawyers analyze a legal issue, dispose of a problem, or delegate and carry out tasks, is with laser-beam precision, breaking it down to its smallest, constituent parts, splitting hairs to the point where conditioner would no longer do any good. The routine is numbing. The thinking process is rigid and implacably hostile. There are simply too many boilerplates and cookie-cutter forms from which to choose. The law is soul-crushing to those who enter it, from almost any direction. Lawyers apply the lessons they have learned in practice, radiating them out to those who come before the law, a blanketing humidity of airlessness and annihilation.

For so many lawyers, there can be no personal meaning in a day spent filling out time sheets. Real life, after all, isn't so easily reducible to fractions of an hour. And it's not just the sheets, but the manner in which the time is being occupied—what is described within those boxes. So many tasks that lawyers perform are highly compensated wastes of time. And the result has produced a legion of spiritually empty practitioners. Lawyers experience a great deal of professional boredom and frustration, and live with the deep sense that somehow they have lost their way, that no amount of salary can possibly compensate for the deterioration of the soul. Lawyer unhappiness and the overall dissatisfaction with their jobs is the dirty little secret of the profession.

It is the underlying message in Herman Melville's *Bartleby, the Scrivener.* The young copyist is a dead ringer for an associate in an early incarnation of a New York law firm. It's amazing how clairvoyant Melville was about the actual practice of law, how its future adaptation would worsen by becoming even more machine-like, bureaucratic, and deadly. The brick wall has now

---

*I must mention here that I was employed at what was considered, and indeed was, the most civilized and humane law firm in town, and despite my fictional talk show dalliances, I was very grateful for the years that I spent there.

been replaced by the windowless office or the retractable conference room. Poor Bartleby's firm was a precursor to today's New York behemoths. And Melville was so right in anticipating the effects that such mechanical rigidity would have on future Bartlebys, and on those of us who might depend on their services. Today young associates at large law firms are not mere scriveners, but many spend their days standing in front of copying machines, or staring at the paper trail that comes out of such machines, examining it carefully for error and precision. In Melville's story, the airlessness of the office, and the routine of the work, reduces Bartleby to a lifeless, cadaverous spirit. His day is described as one that Byron, the poet, would never tolerate. But somehow, 150 years later, in this same city, young lawyers sacrifice their inner lives for superficial, external goals without having the courage of a Bartleby to proclaim the possibility of choice, stating, in quiet defiance: "I prefer not to."

It is the hardened reality of the profession, but this truth is virtually verboten in law school. Law schools teach students how to think like lawyers, but they spend little time advising them about the kind of lawyers they should want to be, or warning them about the lawyers they might become. The fact is, for a profession that is largely paper-pushing, the lawyer's job always looks better on paper. And it's always presented as being far more interesting and dramatic on television. In *The Practice*, cases move quickly, and lawyers spend their days in the courtroom, dazzling the jury and their adversaries. And when not in court, they're engaged in meaningful pursuits. It's difficult to bring drama to drudgery, however, and so you never see lawyers on television sitting at a desk for hours on end drafting agreements for some corporate transaction. The actual practice of law often doesn't feel so purposeful. And lawyers wonder all the time why they ever went to law school. A number of books have captured the sheer breathlessness and mindlessness of it all, such as Scott Turow's *One L*, John J. Osborn's *Paper Chase*, and, more recently,

Cameron Stracher's *Double Billing: A Young Lawyer's Tale of Greed, Sex, Lies, and the Pursuit of a Swivel Chair.*

Most students attend law school for the wrong reason. I see this all the time. In a culture that defines people by what they do, being a lawyer produces a satisfyingly external self-definition, even though, internally, most law students would be much better off doing something else. Somehow, over the past twenty-five years, law and business degrees have achieved unparalleled, and perhaps undeserved, cachet. There was a time when teaching primary and high schools offered both job security and great spiritual reward. Today, few college students believe such jobs are dignified or lucrative enough even to be called professions, though many of those students would make terrific teachers. Obviously, the significance of what it means to be a professional in our culture has undermined and diminished the public perception of many worthy, although perhaps also underpaid, livelihoods. So these misguided seekers of American happiness apply to law schools, not sure why they would even want to be lawyers, not sure what a lawyer even does. Many have told me that a decision not to attend law school would disappoint parents, spouses, neighbors, and friends, those who are impressed with the law degree but privileged not to have to do any of this kind of work.

Lawyers themselves know better. The fancy business card tells you only so much of the story. The job is a facade. So much of what gets done doesn't even require a legal education. Why then have law schools become so popular over the past two decades, with an unprecedented number of college students eager to join a profession of which they know very little and which is generally detested by the public at large?

The answer is somewhat related to America's obsession with the pursuit of happiness, and the way this concept is tied more to the pursuit than to the achievement of any actual happiness.

In America, Thomas Jefferson's guiding ethos, the pursuit of happiness, has led to two morally destructive impulses. First, pursuit is purely a competitive endeavor. In order to be happy, one has to chase after happiness, or, better yet, chase it down and pin it to the ground. Happiness has to be conquered before it can be enjoyed. And in order to sufficiently conquer, one must show no compassion for those who falter in their own pursuits or get in the way. They are to be vanquished, because they either are, or may be, pursuing the same thing. Happiness in America has been reduced to a zero-sum affair. My happiness somehow depends on your defeat and eventual unhappiness. All this pursuit is an end game, where citizens seek to claim victory in a primal, often unintelligible, but relentlessly competitive chase after the illusion of happiness, often at the expense of others. The last one left standing wins, a reality game show where all Americans are automatically entered as contestants. This irrepressible impulse toward competition carries over to the legal system, which is understood as a contest of skills, resources, and luck. The law, in fact, is the perfect embodiment of this madness because it is one big unnavigable obstacle course with lawyers as tour guides and clients usually getting knocked down in their pursuit of both justice and, even more important, money. Because money is yet another moral deficiency of the happiness pursuit. Happiness, in America, is appreciated and understood almost exclusively in the material realm.

Professor Richard Easterlin, of the University of Pennsylvania, in a paper that he wrote in 1974, took a critical look at the paradox of rising incomes and deflated happiness. He concluded that human beings routinely travel on a "hedonic treadmill." Once they acquire something, their expectations and interests change, and they set upon the task of pursuing something else. Not surprisingly, chasing down the next aspiration on the checklist of desired targets yields no greater happiness. Richard Ryan, a professor of psychology at the University of Rochester, and Tim Kasser, a professor of psychology at Knox College in Illinois, have published a number of studies that reveal "the dark side of the

American dream" for those who pursue money over more spiritual values, such as mutual caring and connection, and emotional fulfillment.

In some instances, of course, those who enter law school are self-selected toward aggressiveness, competitiveness, and a desire for wealth over spiritual reward—personality traits and attributes that will serve them well in the legal profession. Many have good social skills but little interest in emotions or the feelings of others. Most lawyers are quite capable of narrowing their vision well past the point of myopia, and have scant appreciation for creativity. But most of all, lawyers tend to prefer thinking over feeling. Lawrence R. Richard, who conducted a study on how dissatisfied lawyers are with their jobs, explained this distinction between thinking and feeling, which appeared in an article written by Susan Daicoff in *The American University Law Review*:

> Those who prefer to make decisions on the basis of Thinking prefer to come to closure in a logical, orderly manner. They can readily discern inaccuracies and are often critical. They can easily hurt others' feelings without knowing it. They are excellent problem solvers. . . . Thinkers are often accused of being cold and somewhat calculating because their decisions do not reflect their own personal values. . . . Those who prefer to make decisions on the basis of Feeling apply their own personal values to make choices. They see harmony and, therefore, are sensitive to the effect of their decisions on others. They need, and are adept at giving, praise. They are interested in the person behind the idea or the job. They seek to do what is right for themselves and other people and are interested in mercy.

Perhaps the legal system would be better served if we could bring in more feelers and either root out or reform all those otherwise stoic, lifeless thinkers. And it may be that feelers would not only make for better, more compassionate and moral lawyers, but that these qualities, adopted within the profession, would make these practitioners spiritually happier and self-fulfilled, as well. And it is not necessarily true that these qualities can only exist among attorneys who practice public-interest law, or commit themselves to doing pro bono work. Lawyers who do such work may be more naturally gifted feelers, but it is not the case that the moral and humane attorney has no role to play in private commercial settings or in criminal practice.

Of course, sometimes these traits are not simply a matter of predisposition and self-selection. Sometimes law school itself is responsible for encouraging and developing these lawyerly characteristics. In a review of the existing empirical research on attorney attributes, Susan Daicoff noted the effect that law school has in changing the preexisting attitudes of students. She observed that those who are in law school are less altruistic, show a decreased interest in public service, and an increase in cynicism as compared with students attending other professional schools. Law students also become less intellectually curious, and less interested in philosophical, introspective, and abstract ideas. Worst of all, they end up becoming more aggressive, competitive, and focused on academic achievement, while becoming less enamored of emotional and moral development. They also report unusually high levels of stress, anxiety, depression, substance abuse, and psychiatric problems. Similarly, in a 1998 article titled "The Moral Failure of Law Schools," published in the journal *Law & Politics*, Alan Hirsch blamed the use of the Socratic method, otherwise known as the case method of teaching, for desensitizing law students and transforming them into moral relativists. This, in turn, has resulted in their becoming less idealistic and altruistic, more selfish and cynical, with no strong convictions about anything. Law students are taught that there are no right answers, no objective truths. The law is a purely abstract, intellectual exercise with no real-world applications or consequences.

As Hirsch wrote, "The goal is not to determine whether the case was decided correctly or incorrectly, but to show that it easily could have been decided either way.... [T]hinking like a lawyer means feeling comfortable arguing for anything." Indeed, law students are taught to begin their discussion of cases with the following refrain: "I would make an argument," or "I would argue." (Lawyers end up speaking like this all the time, even when they are not lawyering, which makes them particularly unpleasant to be around sometimes.) The stance is always one of confrontation—sometimes for the mere sake of confrontation—without regard to whether an embattled position is necessary or best. Lawyers don't say: "The right result in such a situation should be the following, so how can we find a way to apply the law, or reach some conciliation or agreement, so that we can achieve the correct moral outcome." Instead, given the argumentative, relativistic nature of their jobs, there is no room for ethical or moral considerations, or the views of private conviction. They are not supposed to think like people with feelings, but rather as lawyers whose emotions are always held in reserve. In an adversarial system, the idea is to advance the client's cause, and not to consider right and wrong. That's the jury's job. The point is: Relativistic, unprincipled thinking is devoid of the fire that comes with truly believing in, and ardently feeling for, your cause. And without such passion and emotion, who wouldn't be cynical and unhappy about their future line of work.

Of course, all this carries over into the profession. Attorneys, when honest about their lives, express a great deal of self-hatred. The American Bar Association, along with independent lawyers and social scientists, have conducted several important surveys determining that 20 percent of lawyers are "extremely dissatisfied" with their jobs, 19 percent experience high levels of depression, and 15–18 percent engage in substance abuse in order to cope with these stresses and disappointments. And these statistics are higher than they are for other professions. Some of the reasons cited for this "emerging crisis" in the profession include: too much work, lack of communication and contact between attorneys and their clients, isolation in the firm, and lack of mentoring and training. What this really says is that lawyers need human contact, too, and a more meaningful sense of caring, connection, and purpose about their day. Not surprisingly, those lawyers who do public interest or pro bono work, neither of which is performed with the expectation of financial reward, do seem to have greater job satisfaction and feel a deeper sense of meaning in their lives.

These laments speak to a spiritual void more than anything else. The law focuses on values that are externally directed, and fails to address the intrinsic needs of human fulfillment—not just for clients, but for lawyers themselves. Attorneys are not trained to seek out spiritual rewards or remedies, and therefore they don't receive them, or advocate for them on behalf of their clients. The result is that they externalize their frustrations back at us—the lessons that they learned in law school, and the spiritual purposelessness that they experience each day at work. Unhappy and resentful people are giving us legal advice, and charging us for it, too. These are the people—suffering from the loud internal noise of an empty soul—whom we listen to for sound counsel. Is there any wonder why the law is so easily disposed to ignore spiritual injury, and yet, at the same time, so often responsible for its creation? Lawyers and judges dish out what they know—the interior damage that comes from jobs that are deliberately divorced from emotional and moral development—and reject the rest.

And this has led to our own sense of cynicism, discontent, and dissatisfaction about the law as it intercedes in our own lives. The public image of lawyers continues to decline each year. This low opinion gets played out in various ways, from lawyer bashing to anti-lawyer jokes to the general mistrust and suspicion that most people have about attorneys. The American Bar Association has commissioned a number of surveys and polls that have confirmed the animus underneath these stereotypes. As Andrea Kupfer Schneider wrote, "Lawyers are too often today seen as sharks, feeding on society, rather than as responsible and dedicated practitioners carrying out socially important and highly respected work."

Stereotypes sometimes stick, and for good reason.

Much of this disrespect is no doubt related to the fact that lawyers are perceived, rightly perhaps, as sharing values and exhibiting qualities that are not consistent with the concerns of the general population. Lawyers have a way of seeing that sets them apart from the rest of us. In some way this special vision makes them invaluable, and in other ways, repulsive. Lawyers are much more focused on rational, logical, and objective criteria to the exclusion of the emotional, subjective, and sometimes irrational responses to the world. Moreover, lawyers like to show no emotion, and possess a particular disdain for the emotions that are found in others, which has the quality of making them seem inhuman. Added to this is the sense that lawyers are uncaring, dispassionate, and overly competitive. Lawyers are perceived as being purely rule-oriented, and driven by cold, lifeless facts. They are taught that their personal views are unimportant, and so they appear as passionless, unprincipled people, mercenaries of a rampant, unyielding advocacy. Subjective feelings are equally irrelevant, because lawyers aren't supposed to have any. As Professor Daicoff points out, since lawyers are thinkers and not feelers, and their moral development is locked into the rigidity of maintaining law and order, they often come across as impersonal, insensitive, amoral, and not particularly human to the clients they serve. In fact, this absence of emotional sensitivity and moral accountability is precisely what infuriates many people about lawyers. And, perhaps not coincidentally, these deficiencies are found not just in lawyers but, even worse, in the administration of the law itself.

THE ARTIST AND THE LAW

B eyond lawyer jokes and bashing, what's even more prevalent in our society are artistic representations of lawyers
struggling through legal and moral quandaries. Artists find
lawyers and legal systems fascinating. It's not simply the human
drama that reveals itself on the legal stage—a ready mix of plot,
atmosphere, and emotion. Artists sense our collective longing for
justice, for the law to do what's just and right. And yet artists also
see the way in which we end up feeling disappointed and resentful, precisely because the law—administered by lawyers—has
such difficulty making good on those desires. Artists know what
happens to people who stand before the law: the spiritual devastation from its blindness to the inner lives of human beings. The
result is an almost inexplicable discontinuity. We despise our
lawyers and hold them in low esteem, yet we can't seem to get
enough of them in our cultural and artistic landscapes. We read
about them, and watch them on celluloid. They have become our
favorite fictionalized entertainment. Yet the true lawyers in our
lives provide none of the mix of emotional complexity and moral
integrity that we see in art. We want more from our actual
lawyers, but we continue to get less in return. It's as if attorneys

have no respect for our needs, or gratitude for our devotion. The artist delivers the message of this longing and lament, but the law is never listening.

In *The Trial*, Joseph K.'s lawyer, Huld, has done nothing for his client other than boast about his personal connections with influential judges. Finally, sensing K.'s frustration, he tells his client that sometimes having a lawyer builds expectations that something is getting done, when in fact nothing is happening, making it no different than not having a lawyer at all. Retaining a lawyer does offer psychological comfort, the belief that an advocate is on the case, watching your back, guarding your interests, holding your hand. But this feeling of relief is not long-lasting. So much of the law is about waiting—for court dates, discovery and briefing schedules, filing deadlines, adjournments, and final dispositions—and there is a great deal of aggravation that comes from this waiting. We are ready to tell our story, but the law is busy with other matters. And then there are all those unreturned phone calls. The client places them, and the lawyer ignores them. The client has but the one case, while the lawyer is managing many. The lawyer aggressively campaigns to be retained by the client, and then passively attends to the management of the case. Thereafter, lawyers often fail to explain the tedious process of the law, while clients remain anxiously awaiting a resolution that takes an eternity to come.

Clients can't move forward until something affirmative happens. But the law is not guided by the emotional needs of those waiting for relief. It operates according to its own time clock, and its own urgencies. And most lawyers, being mostly thinkers rather than feelers, are not particularly good hand-holders. They lack the empathy, or the necessary self-awareness that working the case and attending to the client are two separate matters entirely.

While he is waiting, the client's inner peace is destroyed, and what's left of it dies shortly after the court's verdict. Charles Dickens assigns this predicament to Richard Carstone, who feverishly awaits the fateful, though prolonged outcome in *Jarndyce v. Jarndyce*. And there are peripheral characters, such as Miss Flite, who waste away, as well. Regarding this interminable, nonsensical delay of resolution, Miss Flite says that the entire experience draws "peace out of them. Sense out of them. Good looks out of them. Good qualities out of them. I have felt them even drawing my rest away in the night."

Lawyers and novelists perceive the world differently. As a lawyer and an artist, living within the margins of two professions ultimately inimical to one another, I know what the artist sees, and what interests him about the law, and why. And yet I also recognize the moral deficiencies, the lapses that get overlooked, and even celebrated, as loopholes. The lawyer and the novelist both rely on language and stories, but how they use language, and the way in which they tell stories, is what largely sets them apart. Lawyers deploy lawyer-speak as a way to obscure and distort, to make their knowledge inaccessible and unintelligible, to keep everyone else out. It is their own trade secret, an incomprehensible code, virtually unrelated to plain speech that creates an unnecessary distance between their clients and themselves.

This is one of the reasons why online legal services have simplified and democratized the legal profession, making it easier, cheaper, and more user-friendly to obtain, although not without the self-interested objections of the bar. Isn't it possible to draft a simple agreement that doesn't rely on language such as "pass the said salt." The novelist, however, unlike the lawyer, is truly seeking to communicate with the world, one reader at a time, not just through words but also with emotions, in language that is meant to convey a moment, rather than to cloud over it.

Yet, despite all that they do to bastardize the language and complicate the tale, lawyers are in the story-telling business. They have to consider how to tell the story, and from what point of view. They also have to account for time frames, create a narrative rhythm, and describe exactly what took place. Although dark, what was it that could be seen within the shadows, and what noises pierced through the silence?

But in many ways, that's where the similarity ends. Because while both the lawyer and the novelist tell stories, what makes a literary novel great has more to do with backstory: How did the characters get in this situation? What made them the way they are? What grievances have festered and what abuses had been inflicted that caused them? For the novelist, the question is not so much what the characters are doing but what they are feeling while they are doing it. The lawyer seeks a final resolution, while the artist operates in a world of messy irresolution, where emotional complexity tells the reader everything that he or she needs to know. The lawyer lives for the open-and-shut case, while the novelist doesn't believe in final chapters, even in his own books. With lawyers, focused purely on the frontage and the cold facts, with no regard for the interplay of emotion or the injuries of the past, stories are much easier to tell. And that makes their stories far less interesting and sometimes disconnected from the varied and harried entanglements of human beings.

A novel is a work of imagination. What lawyers do is often a failure of imagination.

The lawyer is focused on the law, while the novelist is stuck on life. That's why the artist sees the spiritual injury and the moral neglect of the law. The artist allows himself a much grander canvas of the world. Artists more naturally look beyond the external and are more comfortable with that which can't be seen, explained, or even described. Lawyers, by contrast, are always looking for answers, and they are certain that there are answers. They also have a particular contempt for ambiguity. Artists, by contrast, sit comfortably with questions and make no demands on certainty. They assume that everything they see will be refracted and reinvented, not unlike the uncertainties of life. The artist is interested in complicated characters, while lawyers go about their business as if no one else is in the room. The law is mostly interested in the reasonable man, while the novelist is far more intrigued by what the irrational man has to say.

While the artist peers at the law through a lens that is unfamiliar to lawyers, the rest of us can't seem to get enough of these particular images of attorneys and how they spend their day. Whether they are in the form of legal thrillers, or daytime simulated courtroom dramas, or feature films projecting on a legal case or trial scene, the cultural interest in law borders almost on obsession. In addition to *Court TV* and *Judge Judy*, so much law is repackaged as entertainment. But why would we find any of this entertaining, given that, for many people, real-life lawyers evoke mostly feelings of disgust, not amusement?

Perhaps the answer lies in the fact that the lawyers that exist in art have very little in common with the lawyers whom we end up having to retain as our counsel. In our imagination, we adore a particular kind of attorney, the one who is unretainable because he isn't real. And because of this idealized lawyer's personal values and private conscience, and his own emotional struggles, his day job seems much more interesting to us, as well. The artist inserts diverting plot devices that compensate for the inherent bloodlessness of the law. This is why, for instance, *L.A. Law* showcased a good deal of lurid sexual politics within the law firm, which had as much to do with the appeal of the show as did its morally challenging cases. The lawyers of our imagination are flawed, regular people, desperate for a second chance— those with drinking problems; or emerging, haltingly, from a busted marriage; or grieving from the death of someone that they had once loved. In fiction and in film, art provides lawyers with an opportunity to confess, to struggle with their own interior selves, to express regret, to make amends. These are lawyers who have embattled, difficult lives but seek redemption through advancing the hopeless cause of another. Lawyers who don't sleep so well at night because they can't put their consciences to rest. And through their fretful sleep, we receive a glimpse of the moral and virtuous lawyers we long to encounter, real people who show emotion and want to make things right.

Sometimes, while doing the right thing, they end up forsaking the law altogether. The conventional legal paradigm becomes too oppressive and therefore too much, and they must leave. Once the practice of law was all that they wanted out of life, and their days produced no internal conflict. But these fictional lawyers eventually undergo a change of heart, which is when we meet them, and begin rooting for them. They can no longer soldier on within such a soulless legal system. A change in scenery becomes necessary.

In Francis Ford Coppola's *Rainmaker*, based on the John Grisham novel, Rudy Baylor, played by Matt Damon, ends up leaving the law after his first case. He simply won't continue to do what the law requires of its lawyers in order to be successful. The same result occurs with the lawyer Ben Affleck portrays in the film *Changing Lanes* (2002). In the film *Sleepers,* a district attorney does the right thing even though it requires him to breach his ethical duties as a prosecutor. He is a moral prosecutor with compromised motives. But after this last case, he will no longer practice again. In *The Devil's Advocate* (1997), based on the novel of the same title by Andrew Neiderman, Keanu Reeves plays defense counsel Kevin Lomax, who, after years of engaging in aggressive tactics on behalf of clients whose actions were morally indefensible, nearly loses his soul to the devil. Indeed, the message of the film is that such lawyers essentially have the duplicity, if not the DNA, of the devil himself. Soon after a blistering cross-examination of a young girl, he looks at himself in the mirror and unethically withdraws from the case.

A reporter says: "A lawyer with a crisis of conscience. This is huge."

His wife says: "What are you doing, baby?"

Lomax replies: "The right thing. The right thing."

When it comes to the fictional treatment of attorneys,

Harper Lee's small-town Alabama defense counsel, Atticus Finch, in *To Kill a Mockingbird*, is the model of moral rectitude. Throughout the novel he repeatedly says that, despite everyone's objections, if he didn't represent the falsely accused Tom Robinson, he wouldn't be able to parent his children, or represent the town in the legislature, or feel at peace with himself. He is the compassionate, moral attorney who seeks to do what is just and bring about necessary change, even if it comes about only incrementally and at great personal sacrifice. In doing so, he recognizes great human and emotional qualities even in those who otherwise appear filled with nothing but hate and malice. Atticus tells his daughter, Scout: "You never really understand a person until you consider things from his point of view . . . until you climb into his skin and walk around in it."

We see similar fictional portraits of lawyers with uncompromised principles to match their faith in the virtue and rightness of law. There is Jacob Ascher in E. L. Doctorow's *The Book of Daniel*, a man of integrity and an almost naive sense of morality who defends the doomed Isaacsons even at the cost of his own health. And Boris Max, the lawyer who defends Bigger Thomas in Richard Wright's *Native Son*, who calls attention to the backstory of racism in Chicago at a time when no such self-awareness, or mitigation to the crime, is possible. And finally, there is Portia, in Shakespeare's *The Merchant of Venice*, and her plea to temper and season justice with mercy.

It is, in fact, these fictional characters that draw public approval of lawyers in unaccustomed ways. But this paradox, this discontinuity between cultural obsession and popular discontent, has much to do with the fact that in art, lawyers are moral men. In the actual practice of law, moral considerations play no part in a lawyer's workweek. In fiction, we see lawyers as heroic and virtuous. And what makes them so compelling is our own collective longing for these characters to hang up actual shingles and represent us faithfully—with all the emotion, heart, and self-sacrifice of those we read about in novels, or watch on big and small screens.

There are, of course, some lawyers who already have the Atticus Finch in them. And sometimes, though rarely, judges do, as well. Benjamin N. Cardozo, a former United States Supreme Court Justice, and, even more famously, the chief judge on the New York Court of Appeals, was in many ways the model of a moral judge, a man capable of integrating moral consciousness into his legal decision-making. He often suggested that a judge is like the "wise pharmacist" who balances and combines a number of ingredients, such as logic, history, custom, and a sense of rightness in arriving at a just decision. The case of *Hynes v. New York Central Railroad Company*, a 1921 New York Court of Appeals decision written by Judge Cardozo, is an example of how a moral judge would analyze a tragic circumstance in which a death occurred on account of someone else's failure to act.

In *Hynes*, a sixteen-year-old, "a lad of 16," as Cardozo affectionately refers to the boy whose estate he is about to reward, died when he went swimming in the Harlem River during a hot summer day. Hynes and his friends were diving into the water from a springboard, a man-made abutment. This springboard, however, was located on the right of way where the railroad company operated its trains. For a number of years, swimmers had been using this plank as a diving board, without the railroad company's objection. On this unfortunate day, however, an electric wire dangled above the springboard and, when Hynes readied himself to dive, the wire fell from a cross-arm and he became entangled, electrocuted, and tossed into the river, where he died instantly. Prior courts determined that Hynes was a trespasser, because he was standing on the board when the wires hit him. These courts ruled that had he already been in the water, or had he simply been standing beside the springboard, the railroad company would have been liable for his death. For Judge Cardozo, this reasoning, that "[i]n climbing upon the board, . . . [Hynes and his two friends] became trespassers and outlaws," although reasonable and overly legalistic, is also absurd. Lawyers love to make distinctions, but this distinction, as to where Hynes was standing at the time the electric wires might have hit him, is one that a moral judge cannot tolerate. Cardozo writes, "[W]e are persuaded that the rights of bathers do not depend on such nice distinctions. . . . Rights and duties in systems of living law are not built upon such quicksands."

This is a typical Cardozo opinion, often mocking lower courts that luxuriate in overly narrow, highly technical, soulless applications of the law. Cardozo was guided by the "living law"—what makes sense in a particular situation. In this case, the death happened during a hot summer month, in New York City, at a time when there were no public swimming pools. Hynes was a teenager trying to find a place to cool off. These bathers, according to Cardozo, were merely enjoying the public waters. Regardless of where Hynes was standing at the time, the wires shouldn't have been dangling, nor hot with electricity. If the railroad would have been liable if Hynes had been standing near the board or jumping off it, then they should be equally liable even though he was standing upon it.

Technically, legally, Hynes may have been trespassing. But morally, Cardozo wouldn't have been able to live with such a result. For him, in this case and in others, it's important for a judge to exercise both legal reasoning and moral judgment. Legally, Cardozo may have been wrong. Hynes was standing in a place where he wasn't supposed to be, and the springboard was on the railroad's right of way. Morally, however, the abutment made for an attractive diving board, the wires were dangerously out of place and negligently hot. *Hynes v. New York Central Railroad* is a perfect illustration of a moral judge rejecting the formulaic, technical, and mechanical application of law in favor of a result that feels more just, compassionate, soulful, and humane.

This moral approach to legal decision-making contrasts sharply with the one often taken by Judge Richard A. Posner, who sits on the United States Court of Appeals for the Seventh

Circuit. Judge Posner, a legal theorist, widely published author, and a pioneer in the area of law and economics, has steadfastly dismissed moral and emotional reasoning as a way to decide cases. With respect to empathic or emotional considerations, Judge Posner writes: "The internal perspective—the putting oneself in the other's shoes—that is achieved by the exercise of empathetic imagination lacks normative significance." And with regard to moral thinking, Posner wrote: "[M]oral theory has nothing for law . . . even if moral theorizing can provide a usable basis for some moral judgments, it . . . is not something judges are or can be made comfortable with or good at; it is socially divisive; and it does not mesh with the issues in legal cases. . . . If I am right that there is no necessary or organic connection between law and morality, then judges need not take sides on moral questions. . . ."

Two contrasting views and philosophies of judicial activism and restraint. Judge Cardozo's decisions always contain some detectable moral stance. In Judge Posner's views, judges should not allow their legal reasoning—otherwise infused with all that nuanced logic and fidelity to narrow rules—to be contaminated by emotional and moral considerations. Judge Posner believes that judges are ill equipped to adopt these impulses, and that, moreover, there are no standards for applying them, whereas, according to Cardozo, the moral judge has no choice but to survey more than just the law, which also includes the human dynamic and urgencies of the lives that come before it.

One of the reasons why some legal results produce immoral outcomes can be attributed to the legal system's emphasis on precedent and *stare decisis*. Lawyers are taught to analogize their cases to other, earlier cases that address the same or a similar issue, to rely on preceding cases as legal authority for all future ones. Stare decisis is what stops most lawyers from taking moral stands. The law is forever subject to precedential authority. It is bound by it. Prior cases are what lawyers and judges look to in deciding on the cases before them. Old law is unmercifully controlling, which is why it is so difficult to make new law. Throughout law school, students are taught to avoid cases of first impression, those that have never been considered before. These cases are nakedly without precedent, and therefore stand alone, without any legal authority as support. Law students are cautioned that the worst possible scenario is to come before a judge without any preceding, controlling law backing the attorney up.

But why is this so bad? In a moral legal system, lawyers would be able to invoke not just legal authority, but moral authority, as well. Doing the right thing should have some bearing on the law, and lawyers should be encouraged to take virtuous positions on what is right, independent of whether these arguments have already been tested in earlier cases and anchored in precedent. Precedent, after all, locks lawyers into one possible, although contested, outcome, while the exercise of independent moral judgment, unbound as it is by precedent, does not. The unprecedented path may not be predictable, but that in itself is no reason not to walk upon it. It is precisely on these roads of conscience and valor where moral men travel.

Hewing to the letter of the law often leads to an unimaginative dead end, while seeking out the spirit of the law might actually produce a moral outcome. If nothing else, in some cases, flying solo, without any precedential parachute, is at least the righteous thing to do—a responsibility that moral lawyers should undertake even if they don't prevail.

Most lawyers, however, would regard this advice as treasonous. But what I'm saying is not without precedent, either. The Nuremberg Tribunal, for instance, was an example of laws created to address a situation that had never been contemplated or imagined before. The spirit of Nuremberg is based on the idea that when the enormity of a crime is so great, an alternative path to justice is sometimes required, even if it otherwise undermines and contradicts the Constitution. As Supreme Court Justices Arthur Goldberg and Robert Jackson, on separate occasions, once remarked, "the Constitution is not a suicide pact," meaning that occasionally the strict application of constitutional protections would, during certain threatening times, produce a dangerous result. There are times when there are two paths to justice—a moral and a strictly legal one, operating simultaneously to correct for the imperfections of the conventional legal paradigm.

The judgments made at Nuremberg represented a tacit recognition that our justice system, and the Constitution, is often flawed. Procedural errors routinely take place. Evidence is hard to come by or is tainted. Proof is ultimately not beyond a reasonable doubt. Criminals sometimes are set free. This, however, could not be tolerated with the Nazis. And, more recently, this is what Attorney General John Ashcroft neglected to mention in justifying his post–September 11th initiatives in dealing with terrorism pursuant to the Patriot Act. Had we prosecuted the Nazis—or some of the collaborators of Al Qaeda—according to our own constitutional standards, many would have gone unpunished. We couldn't play it straight, because the acquittal of mass murderers would have been morally unbearable.

The Constitution works best in more tranquil times, with more mundane crimes. During times of emergency or when no other controlling precedent exists, a moral, parallel path to justice opens up, and lawyers must be attentive enough—and intellectually honest enough—to look out for these detours and know which direction to take.

We have seen activist attorney generals before, those who sometimes go it alone, bucking the same system of which they are in charge, acting without precedent in pursuit of a more moral outcome. Robert F. Kennedy, the attorney general under his brother, President John F. Kennedy, combated racism in the South in the years before there was any civil rights legislation, or any federal commitment to protect Southern blacks not only from the Ku Klux Klan, but also from state law-enforcement officers, prosecutors, and juries who neglected to punish those who were responsible for committing crimes against the descendants of former slaves. With the assistance of the FBI, Kennedy instructed his local United States attorneys to prosecute Klansmen and others—not under state criminal laws, over which the federal government had no jurisdiction, and because state prosecutors were failing to either bring these cases or follow through on them—but sometimes under obscure, post-Reconstruction laws, or anything else they could find that would work. The point was to send the moral if not legal message that Southern blacks were indeed protected under the laws of this country. Many of these cases were without precedent, but Kennedy empowered and instructed his United States attorneys to bring them anyway. He also took a similar position of aggressive activism with respect to organized crime.

Ironically, Attorney General John Ashcroft, as a political conservative, is somewhat in a philosophical bind. After all, the instincts of his personal politics would usually require him to believe in states' rights, the autonomy of local law-enforcement bureaus, and a strict adherence to the text and original intent of the Constitution—all of which calls for restraint, not activism. Yet Ashcroft recently began to invoke the spirit of Robert Kennedy when he told the Council of Foreign Relations, "In order to fight and defeat terrorism, the Department of Justice has added a new paradigm to that of prosecution—a paradigm of prevention," which is just another way of saying that terrorism is going to require a new manner of doing things, which may be the right thing to do even if it's not entirely legal. Such actions are tantamount to the government's own version of self-help.

In art, we tend to root for those who resort to self-help, even when we know that what they have done is wrong. It gives us a secure sense of biblical, eye-for-an-eye justice, even if it feels more like vengeance. This comes about largely because the law, in providing justice, sometimes fails to do the right moral thing. Emotionally, self-help feels moral, particularly when the law accomplishes the opposite—a result that feels immoral and unjust. In *A Time to Kill* (1996), a film based on a John Grisham novel of the same title, a black man in the Deep South during the 1960s kills one of the men who brutally assaulted, raped, and urinated on his young daughter, leaving her for dead. There is no question that a murder had been committed. The only issue is whether there is any mitigation to this otherwise capital crime, or whether the jury will determine that the killing—under these racially motivated and grotesque circumstances—was morally justified. Surprisingly, the father is ultimately acquitted of all charges.

Is this a fictional example of legal justice being served through the law, or moral justice being imposed on the law? Movie audiences walk away feeling good about the outcome. The murder victim, who was himself a murderer, had it coming. Emotionally and morally, it is possible to witness this trial and feel vindicated about the justice system. Yet, at the same time, legally we know that a murder was committed and did not receive a corresponding punishment.

The moral attorney always tries to seek the moral path, because there is virtue in doing the right thing. Marc Shiner, a former prosecutor in West Palm Beach, Florida, eventually became a defense attorney after struggling internally with a case in which he had to prosecute a child for murder as if the child was an adult. "My personal opinions [as a prosecutor] don't matter," he said in an article in the *New York Times*. "I never voiced them anywhere. I felt it wasn't appropriate to do that because I took an oath to uphold the law. . . . I had a role to fill and I took my role seriously." This crisis of conscience, however, eventually led him to switch sides and defend children who were being prosecuted as adults.

It would be better for everyone, including attorneys, if lawyers thought of themselves as healers rather than as mere advocates. Doctors are relearning these lessons, as well, particularly in the

area of bereavement, where after years of abandoning the aggrieved, many doctors are comforting the surviving family members of deceased patients. Now if only lawyers could feel the same
sense of responsibility to their clients, treating them with both
human touch and legal skill. Lawyers are trained to think like
lasers and to bill their time in fractions of an hour, but such precision and divisions serve to cut them off from the life source of
humanity, which knows of no such narrowings and constrictions.

There is simply not enough caring and connection in the law
to match the abundance of self-importance and elitism. The
moral lawyer is capable of showing compassion, empathy, and
emotion; of trying, like Atticus Finch, to imagine himself in situations of vulnerability and desperation. The moral attorney has a
bit of the psychologist in him. "Although lawyers should not
hold themselves out to be psychologists," Professor Andrea
Kupfer Schneider has written, "it is clear that many clients
would benefit from some insight into their non-legal concerns as
well as into their legal ones." And it would be equally helpful if
judges could surrender their imperious tone and officious routine. The wearing of the robe should be enough; maybe it's time
to lose the attitude.

This is the only way that lawyers and judges can earn back
the respect and esteem of their profession that has been lost in
life, and now only exists, if at all, in art. They need to become
better at listening to the expressions of human grief, to expand
the idea of what a remedy actually means, and what some harms
look like underneath the surface of the skin. Most of all, lawyers
need to embrace a moral consciousness and integrate their private lives with their professional responsibilities, rather than
split these values, keeping them distant and unrelated to their
jobs. There is indeed a great difference between legal ethics and
private morality. A high score on the bar's ethics exam scores no
points in proving the worth of an attorney's soul. It should matter to lawyer's what they look like when they stare into the mir-

ror, not because of their vanity, but because of the condition of the conscience that reflects back at them.

Professor Carrie Menkel-Meadow has argued for the introduction of spiritual values in the various practices of alternative dispute resolution, such as mediation. She writes: "As long as the practice of law continues to reward 'hired guns,' bottom lines, or simply people who prefer a good fight or a good argument, the healing values of lawyering must be transmitted not only to the mediators, but to the lawyers who appear in mediation and their clients. . . . [B]ut instead of our law schools teaching the 'healing arts,' or problem solving, I see courses on 'mediation advocacy,' an oxymoron that promises to continue [the] traditional adversarial combat values. . . ."

In the Justice Department's antitrust case against Microsoft, one of the lawyers representing the company said, perhaps for the wrong reason, "Litigation is not good for the soul of an individual, or a company." Yet if some lawyers—even those who represent faceless institutions rather than real people—actually believe that the warlike atmosphere of the legal system is bad for the soul, then why is it that a spiritual, moral reform of the legal system is so resisted and unlikely? As Franz Kafka pointed out in *The Trial*, "[I]t never occurred to the lawyers that they should suggest or insist on any improvements in the system."

The best and simplest means of reform would be to introduce moral thinking into the consciousness of all lawyers and judges. And perhaps some guidance here can come from religious thinkers, and the healing possibilities of forgiveness, mercy, the restoration of relationships, and the bringing about of communal peace. In St. Paul's First Letter to the Corinthians, he says, "In fact, to have lawsuits at all with one another is already a defeat for you. Why not rather be wronged? Why not rather be defeated?" And in the writings of St. Francis of Assisi, there is a strong undercurrent of moral repair between the parties to a dispute, and on restoring some sense of human harmony and moral balance to the relationship so that the parties can transcend the incident rather than self-destruct. St. Francis, like Atticus Finch, also believed in trying to see the world from the perspective of others. The persecutor, after all, may properly regard himself as once having been persecuted.

Maimonides, in his introduction to the Talmud, expressed a clear preference for compromise over adjudication, knowing that the declaring of one side as the winner will not result in a true final judgment, but rather will foster future unrest and no reconciliation. It is much better to allow both parties to feel some sense of satisfaction than to leave one vanquished and the other ambivalently vindicated. "[The judge] must strive in all his cases to formulate a [compromise] settlement, and if he can refrain from passing a verdict his entire life, constantly [facilitating] a fair settlement between the litigants—how wonderfully pleasant that is." And in the *Mishnah Torah*, Maimonides lamented the consequences of a legal judgment: "The loser leaves angry and without accepting the result." Jews are believed to be the people of the law. There are those, like Shylock, who insist on the strict and principled application of rules. Yet perhaps, in the soul of Jews, there is a deeper moral sense that a compromised peace is valued more highly than a rigid and potentially hostile adjudication. In a winner-take-all contest, there may be no actual winners, only refurbished grievances and new occasions for resentment.

Whether it is in the Christian spirit of transformation—seeking to create a better, more humane world—or in the Jewish concept of *tikkun olam*—the repair and healing of the world—what is certain is that the legal system would serve us all much better if it embraced these moral, repair-minded perspectives rather than encouraged everyone to lace up their gloves and commence with war. Instead of being perceived only as immoral gladiators, perhaps lawyers can develop an equally vigorous persona as relentless peacemakers.

CONCLUSION

I know there are many well-meaning attorneys who went to law school for noble, arguably heroic reasons, and who are engaged in a practice of law that is both spiritually fulfilling and morally redeeming. They struggle internally with many of the issues I discuss in this book. They are neither unaware nor unmindful of what I am saying here. It's just that they don't feel that any other alternative is either possible or necessary. The fact that there are imperfections in the legal system doesn't deprive them of their faith in it. Instead, they spend countless, sometimes uncompensated hours with their clients, showing them true compassion and concern. For these lawyers, the conventional legal paradigm, with its sporting theory of justice and all those competitive thrusts and parries, brings about a resolution that could never have been achieved through quieter means. And these legally correct results make them feel purposeful, and good.

I also know that some clients, in visiting with an attorney, are never seeking spiritual or moral relief. Even if such remedies were presented to them, they would still choose a cash or retributive solution to their problem. For them, the law is not an appropriate place to bring their grief, and justice doesn't have to be just—it merely has to pronounce some judgment so they can get on with their lives.

Yet, there is still everyone else to worry about—the majority of lawyers, who are unhappy with their careers precisely because of the perceived moral failings of their profession, and the vast masses of citizens who are disenchanted with their justice system. There is little question that all of us would be infinitely better off if there was a symmetry and alignment between legal results and moral outcomes. The moral and legal should not be so irredeemably and irreversibly split. Preserving our social order is one thing; abandoning other communal values and losing our souls is quite another. In a new paradigm of moral justice, courthouses would provide us with a forum in which to express our stories of hurts and grievances—uninterrupted, unredacted, indulging whatever emotional releases and excesses accompany our words. The acknowledgment of our harms and the way we have been injured or victimized would become paramount. And every striving would be made to allow us to confront those who have wronged us, making them aware of the lasting damage they have caused. Perhaps they, in turn, will speak sincere words of regret and accept responsibility for their actions. The breaking of our spirits—whether by way of humiliation, disrespect, or indignity—will find redress equal to the remedies the legal system provides for broken body parts. Lawyers would become less interested in winning than in truth, and less inured to the pain of their clients. Judges would deflate some of their self-importance, and recognize that their courtrooms are indeed emotional cauldrons that cannot be so easily simmered or tamed.

Yet I know that lawyers—some, not all—will find this call for reform ludicrous. In their mind, the basic working machinery of the legal system doesn't require any tinkering, and there is certainly no need for an overhaul. Money damages and imprisonment are the bread and butter of the law. There are no other values or remedies that the law can reasonably be expected to achieve. Besides, few lawyers ever admit to having dissatisfied clients, and judges are notoriously disdainful of being overruled. No one is prepared to admit that there is widespread discontent—even though it is so easily verified in our culture, and in our art. For these people, lawyer jokes are never funny, or simply inapplicable to their practice.

A true vision of moral justice cannot readily be integrated into the legal establishment. The bar is far too powerful, and it has been raised too high in its rigidness and conformity. Lawyers are too defensive and too set in their ways. Empathy and communal values that are manifested in the spirit of repair will never compete successfully with the warlike atmosphere that is the ground zero of a lawyer's day. Client confidences will always be closely guarded, because they are the trade secrets of this profession. Most lawyers don't wish to be healers and hand-holders. Many went to law school not to save the world, but to lock in a lucrative livelihood. The moral, spiritual remedies that I am proposing are, regrettably, cheaply administered. Peace is invariably easier to sustain than costly, protracted, violent conflict.

A dramatic transformation of the legal system will come only if there is a groundswell of public sentiment, combined with the aspirations of some lawyers and judges, to invigorate the law with a renewed moral consciousness and spiritual awareness. An army of frustrated attorneys want to do the right thing, marching beside morally indignant citizens who wish for their attorneys to resemble Atticus Finch rather than the slick talking heads who hold press conferences on courthouse steps.

How can we possibly move the law in such a way that moral considerations would begin to influence and inform legal decision-making? If the legal system is indeed the grinding, bureaucratic machine that Kafka foresaw in his nightmares and transformed into art, then how can such an apparatus be swayed—regardless of the public will or the conscience of lawyers themselves? Isn't it, by definition, immune to humanity?

It would help if moral education was more highly valued in our schools, in our churches, synagogues, and mosques, in our government, and in our society. The right way can be contagious, but somebody has to catch it first, and then pass it on. The legal system—so far behind—can't remain invulnerable forever.

Public schools around the country have recently introduced moral issues into their curricula, from discussions about the Holocaust, apartheid, and American slavery, to the relative merits of punishment and reconciliation, to understanding the consequences of moral indifference. Why are our schoolchildren being taught to take account of the moral universe while our judges continue to render decisions without the benefit of these emotional and spiritual spheres of human existence?

Tort reform has recently garnered national attention, whether in capping medical malpractice damage awards, or in limiting the contingency fees that lawyers are permitted to receive in cases that settle quickly, and where the work they have performed was only minimal.

But these reforms are still administrative and, essentially, legal. What I'm speaking of is moral reform—not mechanical changes from within, but human values that can be implanted in the law, virtues that derive from the very best of humanity. What's necessary is not a complete overhaul, but an appeasement, a joining of the legal and the moral, a consolidation between legal precedent and private conscience, between the reasoned reliability of law and the subjective leaps of moral conviction. It's not a matter of scrapping, but rather of modifying the mindsets and procedures that have long since sedimented in our judicial system. We need a massive attitude adjustment—among citizens and practitioners—a legal-renewal movement that seeks a change in what we expect from the law and in what lawyers and judges expect from themselves as servants of the law. If the law could provide us with moral lessons in addition to legal precedents, there would be less reason to seek an appeal. Private conscience should not answer only to abstract moral standards without the force of law equally and solidly behind it.

Some entities and organizations have offered serious suggestions for reform, but have thus far gained little attention. The International Alliance of Holistic Lawyers, the International Center for Healing and the Law, and the Project for Integrating Spirituality, Law, and Politics, through their conferences and newsletters, have raised awareness of the spiritual consequences of the conventional legal paradigm. So, too, has *Tikkun* magazine and its vision of a politics of meaning and how it applies to the legal system. The law-and-literature movement in law schools across America has elevated many of these themes by teaching novels, plays, and films, and the intersections between morality and justice, to future lawyers. It is amazing how Kafka, Dickens, Sophocles, Shakespeare, Camus, Dostoevsky, and Melville, among so many other artists, each writing from different time periods and geographic distances, managed to charge the same indictments and draw the same conclusions about the law. All of their work constitutes a manifesto of reform, a literary rebellion against the soullessness and spiritual violence of the law.

One of the most highly praised and successful recent off-Broadway productions has been *The Exonerated.* It is essentially the written words, taken from actual interviews, of death-row inmates who eventually escaped the death penalty by way of DNA evidence. There is much to learn in this play about illegal justice, coerced convictions, false identifications, perjured testimony, racial prejudices—a panoply of miscarriage, of the law grinning with sharpened, ferocious, unmerciful teeth. But it also contains an even deeper message.

Before becoming exonerated, each of these inmates had to adapt and learn to survive spiritually, knowing that they had been wrongly accused and would die cruelly and unjustly. Without the spirit, they would have succumbed long before the evidence that would free them had emerged. And, once they are exonerated, we are reminded how damaged spiritually they had become, and how difficult would be their reentry into a world where electricity is used to light homes and not extinguish lives. Yet this spiritual dimension of resilience and decline is always lost in the law—as both injury and remedy. None of us will ever be exonerated from indignity and injustice until the law takes notice of the humanity that transcends any judgment of mere guilt and innocence.

ACKNOWLEDGMENTS

With tremendous gratitude to the following individuals who both assisted and inspired this author to do the right thing when it came to this book, and lessened, somewhat, the burdens of writing it:

Dan Arshack, Paul and Judy Berkman, Sandee Brawarsky, Heather Case, Joe Feshbach, Keni Fine, Eva Fogelman, Danny Goldhagen, Vered Hankin, Andrew Hartzell, Marcie Hershman, Tracey Hughes, Annette Insdorf, Carolyn Jackson, Myrna Kirkpatrick, Andy Kovler, Stephanie Martini, Alex Mauskop, Ellen Pall, Brett Paul, Jim Papoulis, Paula Rackoff, Solenne Rose, Gerald Rosen, Stuart Sarnoff, Brenda Segel, James Sexton, Nina Solomon, David Stern, Ivan Strausz, John Thomas, William Treanor, Robert Weil, and Susan Wolfson.

My editor, Julia Serebrinsky, for her devotion to me, and Gheña Glijansky, for her special attention and assistance. Lydia Weaver, from HarperCollins, for her dedicated and skilled handling of the production of this book. Jennifer Swihart, from HarperCollins, for faithfully publicizing this book and its author. The Harry Walker Agency and the Ellen Levine Literary Agency-Trident Media Group, for their continued promotional activities on my behalf.

I would very much like to acknowledge all of my former students, who respectfully listened to me, and from whom I have learned so much, which no doubt both influenced and informed the development of my thinking and the writing of this book. A special mention to Michael Morrison, who helped me gather some of the necessary research.

I would also like to acknowledge both the human rights, and the law and literature movements, and all the faculty around the country who teach these courses and write law review articles in this regard. I am honored to be in your company. I would particularly like to single out Richard Weisberg, a pioneer in the field of law and literature, among other endeavors, whose work as a lawyer and writer is truly exceptional, and to Susan Tiefenbrun, whose syllabus helped get me started.

And finally, with enormous gratitude to Razi Myers, whose unwavering commitment and expressions of affection truly created the space that made this book possible.

NOTES

INTRODUCTION

Articles

Thane Rosenbaum, "Where Lawyers with a Conscience Get to Win Cases," *New York Times*, May 12, 2002, Arts & Leisure, p. 23.

Thane Rosenbaum, "The Writer's Story, and the Lawyer's," *New York Times Book Review*, August 20, 2000, p. 27.

CHAPTER 1

Films

The Verdict. Directed by Sidney Lumet. Produced by Richard D. Zanuck and David Brown. 2 hr. 9 min. Fox. 1982.

12 Angry Men. Directed by Sidney Lumet. Produced by Henry Fonda. 1 hr. 36 min. MGM. 1957.

A Civil Action. Directed by Steven Zaillian. Produced by Robert Redford, Scott Rudin, and Rachel Pfeffer. 1 hr. 53 min. Touchstone Pictures. 1999.

Novels and Short Stories

Albert Camus, *The Stranger* (New York: Vintage Books, 1954).

Charles Dickens, *Bleak House* (New York: Bantam, 1992).

Franz Kafka, *The Trial* (New York: Schocken, 1977).

Harper Lee, *To Kill a Mockingbird* (New York: Warner Books, 1982).

Herman Melville, "Billy Budd, Sailor," in *Billy Budd And Other Stories* (New York: Penguin, 1986).

Books

Jerome Frank, *Courts on Trial: Myth and Reality in American Justice* (New Jersey: Princeton University Press, 1973).

Articles

Marvin E. Frankel, "The Search for Truth: An Umpireal View," 123 *University of Pennsylvania Law Review* 1031 (1975).

CHAPTER 2

Films, Plays, and Dramatic Television

Sophocles, *Oedipus the King* (New York: Washington Square Press, Pocket Books, 1994).

In the Bedroom. Directed by Todd Field. Produced by Graham Leader. 2 hr. 18 min. Miramax. 1997.

The Practice. Created and produced by David E. Kelley. ABC Network.

Erin Brockovich. Directed by Steven Soderbergh. Produced by Danny DeVito, Michael Shamberg, and Stacey Sher. 2 hr. 11 min. Universal/MCA. 2000.

The Sopranos. Created and produced by David Chase. HBO.

Books

Nina Jaffe (and illustrated by Louise August), *In the Month of Kislev: A Story for Hanukkah* (New York: Viking 1992).

Articles

Steven Erlanger, "Vienna Skewered as a Nazi-Era Pillager of Its Jews," *New York Times*, March 7, 2002, Section A, p. 3.

CHAPTER 3

Novels and Plays

William Shakespeare, *The Merchant of Venice,* Act IV, Scene 1 (New York: Penguin Books, 1970).

Franz Kafka, *The Trial,* p. 42–43 (New York: Schocken, 1977).

Articles

Lee Taft, "Apology Subverted: The Commodification of Apology," 109 *Yale Law Journal* 1135, 1136 (March 2000).

John Langone, "Medical Schools Discover Value in Dispensing Compassion," *New York Times,* August 22, 2000, Section F, p. 7.

Adam Liptak, "U.S. Suits Multiply, But Fewer Ever Get to Trial, Study Says," *New York Times,* December 14, 2003, Section A, p. 1.

CHAPTER 4

Articles

Thane Rosenbaum, "The Writer's Story, and the Lawyer's," *New York Times Book Review,* August 20, 2000, p. 27.

Elizabeth Kolbert, "The Calculator: How Kenneth Feinberg Determines the Value of Three Thousand Lives," *New Yorker,* November 25, 2002, p. 42, 45–46.

Lisa Belkin, "Just Money: It's not about the money, say the families of 9/11 victims. But it's all they have. And it has prompted some people to accuse them of greed—and the government of making arbitrary and God-like distinctions among disasters," *New York Times Magazine,* December 8, 2002, p. 92.

David W. Chen, "A Slow, Deliberate Process of Judging 9/11 Victim Awards," *New York Times,* February 18, 2003, Section B, p. 1.

David W. Chen, "Beyond Numbers, 9/11 Panel Hears Families' Anguish," *New York Times,* April 1, 2003, Section A, p. 1.

Diana B. Henriques, "Concern Growing as Families Bypass 9/11 Victims' Fund: Deadline Is in December: Some Preserving Right to Sue—Officials Plan Campaign to Increase Awareness," *New York Times,* August 31, 2003, Section A, p. 1.

Desmond Butler, "Threats and Responses: Trial in Hamburg; Relatives of Sept. 11 Victims Face a Suspect in Germany," *New York Times,* January 21, 2003, Section A, p. 12.

Lynette Clemetson, "Lockerbie Victims' Relatives See Glimmer of Hope," *New York Times*, August 16, 2003, Section A, p. 6.

Daniel Cohen and Susan Cohen, "Libya Can't Buy Us Off," *Wall Street Journal*, May 30, 2002.

Case Law

Predmore v. Consumers' Light & Power Co., 91 N.Y.S. 118, 120 (N.Y. App. 2d Dep't.1904).

Films

In the Bedroom. Directed by Todd Field. Produced by Graham Leader. 2 hr. 18 min. Miramax. 1997.

Books

Stuart Eizenstat, *Imperfect Justice: Looted Assets, Slave Labor, and the Unfinished Business of World War II* (New York: Public Affairs, 2003).

Michael J. Bazyler, *Holocaust Justice: The Battle for Restitution in America's Courts* (New York: New York University Press, 2003).

CHAPTER 5

Articles

Steven Greenhouse, "Transit Workers 'Stop The Clock' on Strike Threat, Talks Go Past Deadline: Union Announces Progress on Noneconomic Issues, but a Deal Still Uncertain," *New York Times*, December 16, 2002, Section A, p. 1.

Jon Pareles, "Stop! In the Name of Nostalgia," *New York Times*, April 5, 2000, Section E, p. 3.

Jim Rutenberg, "Before Going, Van Susteren Told CNN of Hurt Feelings," *New York Times*, January 28, 2002, Section C, p. 8.

Lynda Hurst, "Belgium reins in war-crime law," *Toronto Star*, June 29, 2003, Section F, p. 4.

Craig S. Smith, "Belgium Resists Pressure from U.S. to Repeal War Crimes Law," *New York Times*, June 14, 2003, Section A, p. 5.

Richard Bernstein, "Belgium Rethinks Its Prosecutorial Zeal," *New York Times*, April 1, 2003, Section A, p. 6.

Dale Fuchs, "Spanish Judge Is Charging Bin Laden and 9 in 9/11 Plot," *New York Times*, September 18, 2003, Section A, p. 6.

Novels, Films, and Plays

The Verdict. Directed by Sidney Lumet. Produced by Richard D. Zanuck and David Brown. 2 hr. 9 min. Fox. 1982.

The Accused. Directed by Jonathan Kaplan. Produced by Stanley R. Jaffe and Sherry Lansing. 1 hr. 50 min. Paramount. 1988.

Sleepers. Directed by Barry Levinson. Produced by Steve Golin. 2 hr. 20 min. Warner. 1996.

Sophocles, *Oedipus the King* (New York: Washington Square Press, Pocket Books, 1994).

Harper Lee, *To Kill a Mockingbird,* p. 205 (New York: Warner Books, 1982).

E.L. Doctorow, *The Book of Daniel,* p. 179 (New York: Plume 1996).

CHAPTER 6
Articles

Stacy Caplow, "What If There Is No Client?: Prosecutors as 'Counselors' of Crime Victims," 5 *Clinical Law Review* 1 (Fall 1998).

Stephen Gillers, "Why Judges Should Make Court Documents Public," *New York Times*, November 30, 2002, Section A, p. 17.

Mark Curridan, "The Lies Have It," *ABA Journal*, May 1995, Volume 81, p. 68.

Lisa C. Harris, "Perjury Defeats Justice," 42 *Wayne Law Review* 1755, 1769 n.61 (Spring 1996).

Richard H. Underwood, "Perjury! The Charges and the Defenses," 36 *Duquesne Law Review* 715 (Summer 1998).

Andy Newman, "Hollywood Accounting Cost Him $12 Million, Allen Hints," *New York Times*, June 4, 2002, Section B, p. 2.

Akhil Reed Amar, "Foreword: Sixth Amendment First Principles," 84 *Georgetown Law Journal* 641, 644–45 (1996).

Novels and Films

The Rainmaker. Directed by Francis Ford Coppola. Produced by Michael Douglas. 2 hr. 11 min. Paramount. 1997.

A Civil Action. Directed by Steven Zaillian. Produced by Robert Redford, Scott Rudin, and Rachel Pfeffer. 1 hr. 53 min. Touchstone Pictures. 1999.

Erin Brockovich. Directed by Steven Soderbergh. Produced by Danny DeVito, Michael Shamberg, and Stacey Sher. 2 hr. 11 min. Universal/MCA. 2000.

Russell Banks, *The Sweet Hereafter* pp. 97–98 (New York: HarperCollins Publishers, 1991).

Case Law

Briscoe v. LaHue, 460 U.S. 325 (1983).

CHAPTER 7

Novels and Films

Franz Kafka, *The Trial*, p. 186 (New York: Schocken, 1977).

Charles Dickens, *Bleak House*, p. 806–07 (New York: Bantam, 1992).

One Day in September. Directed by Kevin MacDonald. Produced by Arthur Cohn and John Battsek. 1 hr. 32 min. Sony Pictures Classics. 2000.

Articles

Sarah Boxer, "Lawyers Are Asking How Secret Is a Secret?" *New York Times*, August 11, 2001, Section B, p. 7.

Jonathan D. Glater, "S.E.C. Adopts New Rules for Lawyers and Funds," *New York Times*, January 24, 2003, Section C, p. 1.

Jonathan D. Glater, "Lawyers Pressed to Give Up Ground on Client Secrets: A Confidentiality Issue, U.S. Leads Attack on Practice—Bar Association Seems Ready to Ease Its Code," *New York Times*, August 11, 2003, Section A, p. 1.

Jonathan D. Glater, "Bar Association's Guidelines on Client Secrets Are Eased," *New York Times*, August 12, 2003, Section C, p. 2.

Jonathan D. Glater, "Bar Association in a Shift on Disclosure," *New York Times*, August 13, 2003, Section C, p. 4.

Adam Liptak, "Lawyer Whose Disclosure of Confidence Brought Down a Judge Is Punished," *New York Times*, April 20, 2003, Section A, p. 14.

Akhil Reed Amar, "Foreword: Sixth Amendment First Principles," 84 *Georgetown Law Journal* 641, 644, 708–11 (1996).

Alan Hirsh, "The Moral Failure of Law Schools: The best minds of this generation are being ruined by the Socratic Method," *Law & Politics*, June 1998.

Linda Greenhouse, "Justices Hear Debate on Extending a Statute of Limitations," *New York Times*, April 1, 2003, Section A, p. 14.

Alan Riding, "Nazis' Human Cargo Now Haunts French Railway—Lawsuit Demands Company Repent," *New York Times*, March 20, 2003, Section A, p. 3.

Alan, Riding, "Suit Accusing French Railways of Holocaust Role Is Thrown Out," *New York Times*, May 15, 2003, Section A, p. 7.

Case Law

Morales v. Portuondo, 154 F. Supp. 2d 706 (S.D.N.Y. 2001).

Nix v. Whiteside, 475 U.S. 157, 171 (1986).

CHAPTER 8

Novels, Short Stories, and Films

Herman Melville, "Billy Budd, Sailor," in *Billy Budd And Other Stories* (New York: Penguin, 1986).

Erin Brockovich. Directed by Steven Soderbergh. Produced by Danny DeVito, Michael Shamberg, and Stacey Sher. 2 hr. 11 min. Universal/MCA. 2000.

Franz Kafka, *The Trial*, p. 174 (New York: Schocken, 1977).

Legally Blonde. Directed by Charles Herman-Wurmfeld. Produced by Marc Platt and David Nicksay. 1 hr. 34 min. MGM. 2001.

E. L. Doctorow, *The Book of Daniel*, p. 275 (New York: Plume 1996).

Herman Melville, "Billy Budd, Sailor," in *Billy Budd And Other Stories* (New York: Penguin, 1986).

Albert Camus, *The Stranger* (New York: Vintage Books, 1954).

William Shakespeare, *The Merchant of Venice* (New York: Penguin Books, 1970).

Articles

Nick Madigan, "Woman Who Killed Spouse with Car is Guilty of Murder," *New York Times*, February 14, 2003, Section A, p. 20.

CHAPTER 9

Case Law

Dennis v. United States, 183 F.2d 201, 226–27 (2nd Cir. 1950).

Schmidt v. United States, 177 F.2d 450, 451 (2nd Cir. 1949).

Lawrence v. Texas, 123. S. Ct. 2472 (2003).

Bowers v. Hardwick, 478 U.S. 186 (1986).

Planned Parenthood v. Casey, 505 U.S. 833 (1992).

Virginia v. Black, 123 S. Ct. 1536 (2003).

Republican Party of Minnesota v. White, 536 U.S. 765 (2002).

Spargo v. New York State Commission on Judicial Conduct, 244 F. Supp. 2d 72 (N.D.N.Y. 2003)

Articles

Thane Rosenbaum, ". . . But Morality Has Its Own Logic," *Forward,* December 21, 2001, p. 9.

Kenji Yoshino, "Can the Supreme Court Change Its Mind?" *New York Times,* December 5, 2002, Section A, p. 43.

Linda Greenhouse, "Justices, 6–3, Legalize Gay Sexual Conduct in Sweeping Reversal of Court's '86 Ruling," *New York Times,* June 27, 2003, Section A, p. 1.

Linda Greenhouse, "Justices Allow Bans on Cross Burnings that Are Intended as Threats," *New York Times,* April 8, 2003, Section A, p. 1.

Dahlia Lithwick, "Personal Truths and Legal Fictions," *New York Times,* December 17, 2002, Section A, p. 35.

Neil A. Lewis, "Judicial Nominee Distances Herself from Past Positions," *New York Times,* April 2, 2003, Section A, p. 15.

Patricia Cohen, "Judicial Reasoning Is All Too Human: Order in the Court? Yes, but Often Not in Judges' Minds," *New York Times,* June 30, 2001, Section B, p. 7.

Chris Guthrie and Jeffrey J. Rachlinski, "Inside the Judicial Mind," 86 *Cornell Law Review* 777, 780 (2001).

Sarah Boxer, "When Emotion Worms Its Way Into Law: Should a Disgusting Crime Have a Disgusting Punishment? Does Justice Have Room for Feelings of Shame or Spite?" *New York Times,* April 7, 2001, Section B, p. 7.

Dan M. Kahan, "The Anatomy of Disgust in Criminal Law," 96 *Michigan Law Review* 1621 (May 1998).

Alan Feuer, "A Judge Who Wears His Heart on His Robe," *New York Times*, December 19, 2000, Section B, p. 2.

Martha Minow, "The Hope for Healing: What Can Truth Commissions Do?" in *Truth v. Justice: The Morality of Truth Commissions*, p. 235, 247 (Robert I. Rotberg & Dennis Thompson, eds.) (New Jersey: Princeton University Press, 2000).

Adam Liptak, "Judges Mix with Politics," *New York Times*, February 22, 2003, Section B, p. 1.

James C. McKinley Jr., "U.S. Ruling Allows New York Judges to Take Part in Politics," *New York Times*, February 21, 2003, Section B, p. 1.

Linda Greenhouse, "Heartfelt Words from the Rehnquist Court," *New York Times*, July 6, 2003, Section 4, p. 3.

Novels, Films, and Plays

A Civil Action. Directed by Steven Zaillian. Produced by Robert Redford, Scott Rudin, and Rachel Pfeffer. 1 hr. 53 min. Touchstone Pictures. 1999.

William Shakespeare, *The Merchant of Venice* (New York: Penguin Books, 1970).

E. L. Doctorow, *The Book of Daniel*, p. 211 (New York: Plume, 1996).

Franz Kafka, *The Trial*, p. 117 (New York: Schocken, 1977).

The Verdict. Directed by Sidney Lumet. Produced by Richard D. Zanuck and David Brown. 2 hr. 9 min. Fox. 1982.

Books

Jerome Frank, *Law and the Modern Mind* (New York: Peter Smith Publishers, 1985).

CHAPTER 10

Articles and Transcripts

Bill Keller, "Who's Sorry Now?" *New York Times*, December 28, 2002, Section A, p. 19.

Howard W. French, "Korean Leader Quits His Party Over Scandal," *New York Times*, May 6, 2002, Section A, p. 5.

Jeffrey Toobin, "Coming to a Lawsuit," *Washington Post*, August 2, 1992, Book World, p.4.

Hiroshi Wagatsuma and Arthur Rosett, "The Implications of Apology: Law and Culture in Japan and the United States," 20 *Law & Policy Review* 461, 481 (1986).

"Effect of Commander Scott Waddle's Apology to Relatives of Japanese Victims of Crash Between USS Greeneville and Trawler." Host Linda Wertheimer and Robert Siegel. Report by Andy Bowers. *All Things Considered.* National Public Radio. WNYC, New York. March 9, 2001.

Nick Madigan, "Woman Who Killed Spouse With Car Is Guilty of Murder," *New York Times*, February 14, 2003, Section A, p. 20.

Steven Keeve, "Does Law Mean Never Having to Say You're Sorry?: Going to trial over a case is costly, frustrating—and can perhaps be avoided with a simple apology," *ABA Journal*, December 1999, p. 64 (85 *A.B.A.J.* 64).

Novels and Films

One Day in September. Directed by Kevin MacDonald. Produced by Arthur Cohn and John Battsek. 1 hr. 32 min. Sony Pictures Classics. 2000.

A Civil Action. Directed by Steven Zaillian. Produced by Robert Redford, Scott Rudin, and Rachel Pfeffer. 1 hr. 53 min. Touchstone Pictures. 1999.

Erin Brockovich. Directed by Steven Soderbergh. Produced by Danny DeVito, Michael Shamberg, and Stacey Sher. 2 hr. 11 min. Universal/MCA. 2000.

Regarding Henry. Directed by Mike Nichols. Produced by Scott Rudin and Mike Nichols. 1 hr. 47 min. Paramount. 1991.

CHAPTER 11

Articles

Hiroshi Wagatsuma and Arthur Rosett, "The Implications of Apology: Law and Culture in Japan and the United States," 20 *Law & Policy Review* 461 (1986).

Jonathan R. Cohen, "Advising Clients to Apologize," 72 *Southern California Law Review* 1009 (1998–99).

Jonathan R. Cohen, "Apology and Organizations: Exploring an Example from Medical Practice," 27 *Fordham Urban Law Journal* 1447, 1449 (June 2000).

Steven Keeve, "Does Law Mean Never Having to Say You're Sorry?: Going to trial over a case is costly, frustrating—and can perhaps be avoided with a simple apology," *ABA Journal*, December 1999, p. 64 (85 *A.B.A.J.* 64).

Rob Stein, "Teenage Girl in Botched Organ Transplant Dies," *Washington Post*, February 23, 2003.

Adam Liptak, "Not at All Remorseful, But Not Guilty Either," *New York Times*, November 3, 2002, Section 4, p. 4.

Robert D. McFadden and Susan Saulny, "13 Years Later, Official Reversal in Jogger Attack, A Probable Lone Rapist: Five Who Confessed Did Not Commit Attack in Central Park, Prosecutors Say," *New York Times*, December 6, 2002, Section A, p. 1.

Lee Taft, "Apology Subverted: The Commodification of Apology," 109 *Yale Law Journal* 1135, 1136 (March 2000).

Peter H. Rehm and Denise R. Beatty, "Legal Consequences of Apologizing," *Journal of Dispute Resolution*, 115 (1996).

Elizabeth Latif, "Apologetic Justice: Evaluating Apologies Tailored Toward Legal Solutions," 81 *Boston University Law Review* 289 (February 2001).

Bill Keller, "Who's Sorry Now?" *New York Times*, December 28, 2002, Section A, p. 19.

Howard W. French, "Korean Leader Quits His Party Over Scandal," *New York Times*, May 6, 2002, Section A, p. 5.

Books

Nicholas Tavuchis, *Mea Culpa: A Sociology of Apology and Reconciliation* (California: Stanford University Press, 1993).

Novels

Charles Dickens, *Bleak House*, p. 806–07 (New York: Bantam, 1992).

CHAPTER 1 2

Articles

Eric Schlosser, "A Grief Like No Other; the Parents of Murdered Children," *Atlantic Monthly*, September 1977, p. 37.

John Braithwaite, "Restorative Justice: Assessing Optimistic and Pessimistic Accounts," 25 *Crime and Justice* 1 (1999).

Serge Schmemann, "How to Face the Past, Then Close the Door," *New York Times*, April 8, 2001, Section 4, p. 1.

"Punishing a Terrorist by Showing Him His Victim's Humanity," *New York Times*, April 6, 2002, Section B, p. 9.

Sharon LaFraniere, "Courts Convicts 3 in 1994 Genocide Across Rwanda," *New York Times*, December 4, 2003, Section A, p. 1.

Books

Martha Minow, *Between Vengeance and Forgiveness: Facing History after Genocide and Mass Violence* (Boston: Beacon Press, 1998).

Telford Taylor, *The Anatomy of the Nuremberg Trials* (New York: Alfred A. Knopf, 1992).

Novels, Films, and Plays

William Shakespeare, *The Merchant of Venice*, Act IV, Scene 1 (New York: Penguin Books, 1970).

CHAPTER 1 3

Articles

Serge Schmemann, "How to Face the Past, Then Close the Door," *New York Times*, April 8, 2001, Section 4, p. 1.

Elizabeth Kiss, "Moral Ambition Within and Beyond Political Constraints," in *Truth v. Justice: The Morality of Truth Commissions*, p. 69, 72 (Robert I. Rotberg & Dennis Thompson, eds.) (New Jersey: Princeton University Press, 2000).

Michael Ignatieff, "Digging Up the Dead: Some people in South Africa wanted to know what happened under apartheid so badly that they were prepared to grant amnesty to the regime's worst culprits simply to learn the truth. Was it worth it?" *New Yorker*, November 10, 1977, p. 84, 93.

Robert I. Rotberg, "Truth Commissions and the Provision of Truth, Justice, and Reconciliation," in *Truth v. Justice: The Morality of Truth Commissions*, p. 3, 14 (Robert I. Rotberg & Dennis Thompson, eds.) (New Jersey: Princeton University Press, 2000).

Alex Boraine, "Truth and Reconciliation in South Africa: The Third Way," in *Truth v. Justice: The Morality of Truth Commissions*, p. 141, 147 (Robert I. Rotberg & Dennis Thompson, eds.) (New Jersey: Princeton University Press, 2000).

Suzanne Daley, "Apartheid Torturer Testifies as Evil Shows Its Banal Face," *New York Times*, November 9, 1997, Section A, p. 1.

Ginger Thompson, "South Africa to Pay $3,900 to Each Family of Apartheid Victims," *New York Times*, April 16, 2003, Section A, p. 7.

Dean E. Murphy, "Beyond Justice: The Eternal Struggle to Forgive," *New York Times*, May 26, 2002, Section 4, p. 1.

Nancy Ramsey, "Filming Rwandans' Efforts to Heal," *New York Times*, April 24, 2003, Section E, p. 1.

John Braithwaite, "Restorative Justice: Assessing Optimistic and Pessimistic Accounts," 25 *Crime and Justice* 1 (1999).

Paul Clark, "Restorative Justice and ADR: Opportunities and Challenges," 44 *The Advocate* 13 (November 2001) (Official Publication of the Idaho State Bar).

Russ Immarigeon, "Restorative Justice: Origins, Use, Impact and Resources," 6 *The Crime Victims Report* 5 (March/April 2002).

Elizabeth Latif, "Apologetic Justice: Evaluating Apologies Tailored Toward Legal Solutions," 81 *Boston University Law Review* 289, 293 (February 2001).

Alyssa H. Schenk, "Victim-Offender Mediation: The Road to Repairing Hate Crime Injustice," 17 *The Journal on Dispute Resolution* 185 (2001).

Deborah L. Levi, "The Role of Apology in Mediation," 72 *New York University Law Review* 1165 (1997).

Roslyn Myers, "Victims as Storytellers: The Importance of Victim Impact Testimony in Criminal Justice Proceedings," 5 *The Crime Victims Report* 85 (January/February 2002), 6 *The Crime Victims Report* 18 (May/June 2002), 6 *The Crime Victims Report* 33 (July/August 2002).

Andrea Kupfer Schneider, "The Intersection of Therapeutic Jurisprudence, Preventative Law, and Alternative Dispute Resolution," 5 *Psychology, Public Policy, and Law* 1084 (1999).

Carrie Menkel-Meadow, "And Now a Word About Secular Humanism, Spirituality, and the Practice of Justice and Conflict Resolution," 28 *Fordham Urban Law Journal* 1073, 1086 (2001).

David Wexler, "Therapeutic Jurisprudence: An Overview," 17 *Thomas M. Cooley Law Review* 125 (2000).

Michael L. Perlin, "The Law of Healing," 68 *University of Cincinnati Law Review* 407 (2000).

Peter Gabel, Thane Rosenbaum, and Nanette Schorr, "Plank on Law: Politics of Meaning Draft Platform," *Tikkun*, September/October 1996, Vol. 11, p. 31–33.

Books

Truth v. Justice: The Morality of Truth Commissions (Robert I. Rotberg & Dennis Thompson, eds.) (New Jersey: Princeton University Press, 2000).

Desmond Mpilo Tutu, *No Future Without Forgiveness* (New York: Doubleday, 2000).

Robert B. Coates, Boris Kalanj, Mark S. Umbreit, *Victim Meets Offender: The Impact of Restorative Justice and Mediation* (New York: Willow Tree Press, 2000).

CHAPTER 14

Articles

"The Good Samaritan." *Seinfeld.* Sony Television. New York. May 14, 1998.

Joshua Dressler, "Some Brief Thoughts (Mostly Negative) About 'Bad' Samaritan Laws," 40 *Santa Clara Law Review* 971 (2000)

Kathleen M. Ridolfi, "Law, Ethics, and the Good Samaritan: Should There Be a Duty to Rescue?" 40 *Santa Clara Law Review* 957 (2000).

Don Terry, "Mother Rages Against Indifference: Charges Sought Against Bystander in Rape and Murder of Girl," *New York Times,* August 24, 1998, Section A, p. 10.

Justin T. King, "Criminal Law: 'Am I My Brother's Keeper?' " Sherrice's Law: A Balance of American Notions of Duty and Liberty," 52 *Oklahoma Law Review* 613 (1999).

Marcia Ziegler, "Nonfeasance and the Duty to Assist: The American *Seinfeld* Syndrome," 104 *Dickinson Law Review* 525 (2000).

Tamar Lewin, "Legal Action After Killings at Schools Often Fails," *New York Times,* March 7, 2001, Section A, p. 14.

Ernest J. Weinrib, "The Case for a Duty to Rescue," 90 *Yale Law Journal* 247 (December 1980).

Case Law

Osterlind v. Hill, 160 N.E. 301, 302 (Supreme Judicial Court of Massachusetts 1928).

CHAPTER 15

Articles

Ernest J. Weinrib, "The Case for a Duty to Rescue," 90 *Yale Law Journal* 247 (December 1980).

Sharon LaFraniere, "Court Convicts 3 in 1994 Genocide Across Rwanda," December 4, 2003, Section A, p. 1.

Aaron Kirschenbaum, "The Bystander's Duty to Rescue in Jewish Law," 8 *The Journal of Religious Ethics* 204, 205 (Fall 1980).

Books

Robert P. George, *Making Men Moral: Civil Liberties and Public Morality* (New York: Oxford University Press 1995).

Films and Plays

The Accused. Directed by Jonathan Kaplan. Produced by Stanley R. Jaffe and Sherry Lansing. 1 hr. 50 min. Paramount. 1988.

Disney, *Beauty and the Beast*, Lunt-Fontainne Theatre, New York, New York.

CHAPTER 16

Articles

Thane Rosenbaum, "Lullabies for Butchers: Wilhelm Furtwängler Ought to Have Stopped the Music," *New York Sun*, September 8, 2003, p. 17.

Plays

William Shakespeare, *Othello* (New York: Penguin Books, 1970).

Case Law

Chaplinsky v. New Hampshire, 315 U.S. 568 (1942).

Virginia v. Black, 123 S. Ct. 1536 (2003).

Collin v. Smith, 578 F.2d 1197 (7th Cir. 1978).

Texas v. Johnson, 491 U.S. 397 (1989).

Fisher v. Carrousel Motor Hotel, Inc., 424 S.W.2d 627, 629 (Texas 1967).

Articles

Richard Delgado, "Words that Wound: A Tort Action for Racial Insults, Epithets, and Name Calling," in *Words That Wound: Critical Race Theory, Assaultive Speech, and the First Amendment*, p. 89 (Mari J. Matsuda, Charles R. Lawrence III, Richard Delgado, and Kimberle Williams Crenshaw, eds.) (Colorado: Westview Press, 1993).

Mari J. Matsuda, "Public Response to Racist Speech: Considering the Victim's Story," in *Words That Wound: Critical Race Theory, Assaultive Speech, and the First Amendment*, p. 17 (Mari J. Matsuda, Charles R. Lawrence III, Richard Delgado, and Kimberle Williams Crenshaw, eds.) (Colorado: Westview Press 1993).

Hiroshi Wagatsuma and Arthur Rosett, "The Implications of Apology: Law and Culture in Japan and the United States," 20 *Law & Policy Review* 461, 494 (1986).

Andrew Sullivan, "What's So Bad About Hate," *New York Times Magazine*, September 26, 1999, Section 6, p. 51, 104.

Nick Madigan, "Trial in Killing of Orthodontist Goes to Jury," *New York Times*, February 12, 2003, Section A, p. 32.

Nick Madigan, "Jury Gives 20-Year Term in Murder of Husband," *New York Times*, February 15, 2003, Section A, p. 15.

CHAPTER 17

Novels and Short Stories

Herman Melville, "Bartleby," in *Billy Budd and Other Stories* (New York: Penguin, 1986).

Books

Scott Turow, *One L: The Turbulent True Story of a First Year At Harvard Law School* (New York: Warner Books 1997).

John J. Osborn, *Paper Chase* (New York: Whitson Publishing Company 2003).

Cameron Stracher, *Double Billing: A Young Lawyer's Tale of Greed, Sex, Lies, and the Pursuit of a Swivel Chair* (New York: Perennial 1999).

Jerome Frank, *Courts on Trial: Myth and Reality in American Justice* (New Jersey: Princeton University Press, 1993).

Articles

David Leonhardt, "If Richer Isn't Happier, What Is?" *New York Times*, May 17, 2001, Section B, p. 9.

Alfi Kohn, "In Pursuit of Affluence, at a High Price," *New York Times*, February 24, 1999.

Susan Daicoff, "Lawyer, Know Thyself: A Review of Empirical Research on Attorney Attributes Bearing on Professionalism," 46 *American University Law Review* 1337, 1347, 1366 (1997).

Alan Hirsh, "The Moral Failure of Law Schools: The best minds of this generation are being ruined by the Socratic Method," *Law & Politics*, June 1998.

Carrie Menkel-Meadow, "The Trouble with the Adversarial System in a Postmodern, Multicultural World," 38 *William & Mary Law Review* 8 (1996–1997).

Andre Kupfer Schneider, "The Intersection of Therapeutic Jurisprudence, Preventative Law, and Alternative Dispute Resolution," 5 *Psychology, Public Policy, and Law* 1084 (1999).

CHAPTER 1 8

Novels and Films

Franz Kafka, *The Trial*, p. 121 (New York: Schocken, 1977).

Charles Dickens, *Bleak House*, p. 463 (New York: Bantam, 1992).

The Rainmaker. Directed by Francis Ford Coppola. Produced by Michael Douglas. 2 hr. 11 min. Paramount. 1997.

The Devil's Advocate. Directed by Taylor Hackford. Produced by Arnold Kopelson, Anne Kopelson, and Arnon Milchan. 2 hr. 24 min. Warner. 1997.

Changing Lanes. Directed by Roger Mitchell. Produced by Scott Rudin. 1 hr. 39 min. Touchstone Pictures. 2002.

Harper Lee, *To Kill a Mockingbird*, p. 30 (New York: Warner Books, 1982).

A Time to Kill. Directed by Joel Schumacher. Produced by Arnon Milchan, Michael Nathanson, Hunt Lowry, and John Grisham. 2 hr. 8 min. Warner. 1996.

Articles

Thane Rosenbaum, "The Writer's Story, and the Lawyer's," *New York Times Book Review*, August 20, 2000, p. 27.

Jennifer 8. Lee, "Dot-Com, Esq.: Legal Guidance, Lawyer Optional," *New York Times*, February 21, 2001, Section G, p. 1.

Robert J. Araujo, SJ, "The Lawyer's Duty to Promote the Common Good: The Virtuous Law Student and Teacher," 40 *South Texas Law Review* 83, 127 (1999).

Robert J. Araujo, SJ, "The Virtuous Lawyer: Paradigm and Possibility," 50 *Southern Methodist University Law Review* 433 (1997).

Laura Carrier, "Making Moral Theory Work for Law," 99 *Columbia Law Review* 1018 (1999).

Jeremy Waldron, "The Irrelevance of Moral Objectivity," in *Natural Law Theory: Contemporary Essays* (Robert P. George ed., Oxford: Clarendon Press 1992).

Neil MacCormick, "Natural Law and the Separation of Law and Morals," in *Natural Law Theory: Contemporary Essays* (Robert P. George ed., Oxford: Clarendon Press, 1992).

Adam Liptak, "Under Ashcroft, Judicial Power Flows Back to Washington," *New York Times*, February 16, 2003, Section 4, p. 5.

Dana Canedy, "After Conviction of Boy, Prosecutor Switches Sides: Lawyer Now Defends a Young Murder Suspect," *New York Times*, November 18, 2002, Section A, p. 14.

Jane E. Brody, "After a Death, Doctors Can Offer Families Healing Help," *New York Times*, May 15, 2001, Section F, p. 5.

Andrea Kupfer Schneider, "The Intersection of Therapeutic Jurisprudence, Preventative Law, and Alternative Dispute Resolution," 5 *Psychology, Public Policy, and Law* 1084 (1999).

Laura E. Little, "Adjudication and Emotion," 3 *Florida Coastal Law Journal* 205 (2002).

Carrie Menkel-Meadow, "And Now a Word About Secular Humanism, Spirituality, and the Practice of Justice and Conflict Resolution," 28 *Fordham Urban Law Journal* 1073, 1087 (2001).

Stephen, Labaton, "Judge Says Ruling on Microsoft Won't Come Quickly," *New York Times*, March 7, 2002, Section C, p. 6.

Robert A. Baruch Bush, "Mediation and ADR: Insights from the Jewish Tradition," 28 *Fordham Urban Law Journal* 1007 (2001)

Joseph Allegretti, "A Christian Perspective on Alternative Dispute Resolution," 28 *Fordham Urban Law Journal* 997 (2001).

Books

Richard H. Weisberg, *Poetics and Other Strategies of Law and Literature* (New York: Columbia University Press, 1992).

Richard A. Posner, *The Problematics of Moral and Legal Theory* (New York: Belknap Press 2002).

Richard A. Posner, *Overcoming Law* p. 381 (Cambridge: Harvard University Press, 1995).

Benjamin N. Cardozo, *The Nature of the Judicial Process* (Connecticut: Yale University Press, 1985).

Robert P. George, *Making Men Moral: Civil Liberties and Public Morality* (New York: Oxford University Press, 1995).

Case Law

Hynes v. New York Central Railroad Company, 131 N.E. 898, 899 (Court of Appeals of New York 1921).

CONCLUSION

Articles

Nina Siegel, "Moral Issues Gingerly Find a Place in Class," *New York Times,* March 15, 2000, Section B, p. 11.

Adam Liptak, "In 13 States, a United Push to Limit Fees of Lawyers: Trying to Cut Their Share of Settlements," *New York Times,* May 26, 2003, Section A, p. 10.

Plays

Eric Jensen and Jessica Blank, *The Exonerated,* The Culture Project, New York, 2003.

INDEX

CREDITS AND PERMISSIONS

Excerpts from the final episode of *Seinfeld* granted courtesy of
Castle Rock Entertainment.

The Sweet Hereafter by Russell Banks. Copyright © 1991 by Russell Banks. Reprinted by Permission of HarperCollins Publishers Inc.

To Kill a Mockingbird by Harper Lee. Copyright © 1960 by Harper Lee; renewed © 1988 by Harper Lee. Reprinted by Permission of HarperCollins Publishers Inc.

The Trial by Franz Kafka. Schocken Books. Copyright © 1964 by Alfred A. Knopf, Inc.

The Verdict © 1982 Twentieth Century Fox. Written by David Mamet. All Rights Reserved.

ABOUT THE AUTHOR

THANE ROSENBAUM is a novelist, essayist, and law professor. His novels include *The Golems of Gotham* (2002) (*San Francisco Chronicle* Top 100 book), *Second Hand Smoke* (1999), and the novel-in-stories, *Elijah Visible* (1996), which received the Edward Lewis Wallant Award in 1996 for the best book of Jewish-American fiction. His articles, reviews, and essays appear frequently in the *New York Times*, the *Los Angeles Times*, the *Wall Street Journal*, and the *Washington Post*, among other national publications. He teaches human rights, legal humanities, and law and literature at Fordham Law School. He lives in New York City with his daughter, Basia Tess.